REGULATING FRAUD ACROSS BORDERS

At a time when financial crime routinely crosses international boundaries, this book provides a novel understanding of its spread and criminalisation. It traces the international convergence of financial crime regulation with a uniquely comparative approach that examines key institutional and state actors including the European Union, the International Organization of Securities Commissions, as well as the United States, United Kingdom, Switzerland, France, Italy and Germany, all countries that harbour some of the most influential stock exchanges in the Western world.

The book describes and documents the phenomenon of internationalisation of securities frauds – such as insider trading and market manipulation – and the laws criminalising those acts, most notably those responding to recent dramatic transformations in securities markets, high frequency trading, and benchmark manipulation. At the European level, it shows the progressive uniformisation of laws culminating in the 2014 European Union Market Abuse Regulation.

The book argues that criminal prohibitions against internationalised market abuse must be understood as an economic and legal imperative to protect financial markets against activities that imperil its integrity, compromising the confidence of investors and thus affecting the economy as a whole. The book is supported by an extensive review of the most significant scholarship in each country.

Regulating Fraud Across Borders

Internationalised Criminal Law Protection of Capital Markets

Edgardo Rotman

•HART•
OXFORD • LONDON • NEW YORK • NEW DELHI • SYDNEY

HART PUBLISHING

Bloomsbury Publishing Plc

Kemp House, Chawley Park, Cumnor Hill, Oxford, OX2 9PH, UK

1385 Broadway, New York, NY 10018, USA

29 Earlsfort Terrace, Dublin 2, Ireland

HART PUBLISHING, the Hart/Stag logo, BLOOMSBURY and the Diana logo are trademarks of Bloomsbury Publishing Plc

First published in Great Britain 2021

A catalogue record for this book is available from the British Library.

Library of Congress Cataloging-in-Publication data

Names: Rotman, Edgardo, author.

Title: Regulating fraud across borders : internationalised criminal law protection of capital markets / Edgardo Rotman.

Description: Oxford, UK ; New York, NY : Hart Publishing, an imprint of Bloomsbury Publishing, 2021. | Includes bibliographical references and index.

Identifiers: LCCN 2020049939 (print) | LCCN 2020049940 (ebook) | ISBN 9781509943197 (hardback) | ISBN 9781509943234 (paperback) | ISBN 9781509943210 (pdf) | ISBN 9781509943203 (Epub)

Subjects: LCSH: Securities fraud. | Capital market—Law and legislation—Criminal provisions. | Insider trading in securities—Law and legislation—Criminal provisions. | Stock exchanges—Law and legislation—Criminal provisions. | Corporations—Corrupt practices.

Classification: LCC K1121 .R68 2020 (print) | LCC K1121 (ebook) | DDC 345/.0263—dc23

LC record available at https://lccn.loc.gov/2020049939

LC ebook record available at https://lccn.loc.gov/2020049940

ISBN: HB: 978-1-50994-319-7
ePDF: 978-1-50994-321-0
ePub: 978-1-50994-320-3

Typeset by Compuscript Ltd, Shannon

To my sister Viviana, for her unwavering encouragement,
help and advice, to my children Josefina, Margarita and Federico,
and to their mother Ines, for their loving care and concern,
and to my grandchildren Alex, Anna, Ian and Tom,
for their future promise.

ACKNOWLEDGEMENTS

In the many years I have been working on this book I was fortunate to receive assistance, advice and support from colleagues, students and staff at the University of Miami School of Law. I welcome the opportunity to acknowledge their help and remain grateful for their generosity.

Dean Patricia White's unswerving encouragement even after my retirement made this project possible.

Professors Caroline Bradley and Elliott Manning provided important insights and information. When I presented parts of the book at the local faculty seminar, Dean Patrick Gudridge and Professors Stephen J Schnably, Robert Rosen and David Abraham offered valuable feedback.

My warm thanks also to Carolyn Pickard for her expert suggestions and to Elisabeth Rabin, who ably carried out the necessary initial formatting for the publication of this manuscript.

Furthermore, I received different kinds of indispensable help from Barbara Cuadras, Ariel Gonzalez, Frank Olozaga, Bill Latham, Robin Schard, Pamela Lucken, Bianca Anderson, Farah Barquero, Helen Wohl, Mercy Hernandez-Ojeda, Mayra Martinez, Noel Nunez and Christian Rivas.

I had the privilege of conducting a large part of my research in the fabulous library of the Max-Planck Institute for Criminal Law in Freiburg, Germany. I am grateful to the Alexander von Humboldt Foundation for a generous fellowship that facilitated my stay in Germany. Among Institute colleagues that contributed to my research, I thank its former directors, Professor Doctors Albin Eser and Ulrich Sieber, Doctors Johanna Rinceanu, Benjamin Vogel, and Nandor Knust, Prof Dr Marc Engelhardt, and Elisabeth Martin, head of the library.

Several colleagues abroad offered valuable information. Among them Italian scholars Dr Benedetta Venturato and Professor Attilio Nisco, Professor Jean Pradel from France, Professor William Twining from the United Kingdom and the late Professor Klaus Tiedemann from Germany.

Thanks to the Law School's generous support, over the years I was able to recruit a group of talented research assistants, including some foreign ones with the special help of Carmen Perez-Llorca, Assistant Dean for International and Foreign Programs, among them Fiona Zhenying Li, Devon Frampton, Nancy Shalub, Danielle Benjamin, Alyssa Giordano, Simon Theis, Gerhard Althaus and Laura Rochdi.

Finally, I am grateful to Kate Whetter, my superb editor at Hart Publishing, for shepherding my manuscript with efficiency and care, and to Catherine Minahan for her skilful and thorough adaptation of the text to Hart Publishing style, as well as to four anonymous reviewers who provided helpful suggestions. Moreover, I thank Chris Harrison for his expert and meticulous copy-editing job.

CONTENTS

Introduction

This book traces and explains the dynamic convergence of a broad range of criminal laws protecting financial markets.

This remarkable process of internationalisation has been achieved in some countries such as the US and Switzerland through legislation and courts' decisions, while in EU Members States it was attained through major regional secondary legislation culminating in the 2014 European Union Market Abuse Regulation, complemented by the 2014 European Union Market Abuse Directive on criminal sanctions.

The starting point of this transformation is the phenomenon of globalisation. Globalisation in its present form is in fact the contemporary stage of an historically progressive linkage of the social world. This process began in archaic societies with the discovery of rudimentary tools that allowed the expansion of social systems and continued with myriad technical advances such as printing, railways, sailing vessels, steamships, telephones, jet planes and the internet. A consequential economic feature of this process has been the vast expansion of commercial and financial markets.

The beneficial economic and social aspects of globalisation, consisting in a greater international division of labour, a more efficient allocation of capital and increasing competition, productivity and average living standards should not blind us to its damaging effects.

The book concentrates on one negative outcome, the expansion of cross-border financial crimes such as insider trading and market manipulation. The global economic interdependence of countries worldwide demanded concerted action aimed at regulating and punishing these cross-national criminal activities. The internationalisation of financial crime thus triggered the internationalisation of crime control.

For example, laws criminalising insider trading proliferated during the 1990s. At the beginning of the decade only a few countries had outlawed such practices, while by the year 2000 the vast majority of nations had adopted its criminal prohibition. Meanwhile, market manipulation has dramatically expanded in the last few years as a result of high frequency trading and benchmark manipulation.

To trace the internationalisation of financial crimes and its regulation, this book provides a unique comparative analysis of the key institutional and state actors, namely the EU, the International Organization of Securities Commissions (IOSCO), the US, UK, Switzerland, France, Italy and Germany. Comparative law, conceived as an arsenal of possible solutions, is here applied in its two dimensions: synchronic or structural, as well as diachronic, that is, through time, a dimension by and large named 'legal history'. Moreover, comparative law is used critically to analyse the extraterritorial application of US law in Chapter 3. The analysis draws from my many years of researching and teaching comparative law, along with the examination of primary and secondary sources in their original language.

In sum, the central aim of this book is to describe the phenomenon of the internationalisation of market abuse and of the laws criminalising it. More fundamentally, the book argues that such regulatory internationalisation must be understood as an economic and legal imperative, indispensable for the protection of financial markets against activities that imperil its integrity, compromising the confidence of investors and thus affecting the economy as a whole.

1

The Internationalisation Process

I. The Concept of Legal Internationalisation

The globalisation of financial markets has resulted in an unprecedented expansion of financial crime and the progressive development and internationalisation of legislation to constrain it.

The overriding purpose of this book is to present, analyse and explain the different ways in which the laws criminalising securities frauds have internationalised.

Criminal law belonged traditionally to the hard core of the state's sovereignty and, thus, was recognised as national law par excellence.[1] The internationalisation of laws is a dynamic process that breaches a tradition of territorially enclosed legal systems.[2] Through this process certain areas of criminal law became internationalised in a broad sense.

The application of the broad dictionary meaning of the word 'internationalisation'[3] to the legal sphere encompasses not only the traditional strict, literal version of creation of public international law, but also other forms of transborder legal processes and interaction. These include non-traditional soft law mechanisms used by non-state actors to encourage and facilitate compliance, forms of international cooperation and extraterritorial jurisdiction, plus phenomena of harmonisation, convergence and private ordering designated by the elusive term 'transnational law'.[4]

This comprehensive approach avoids the risks identified by Bentham of 'putting the language in opposition to itself'.[5] The broadening of the concept

[1] I Anagnostopoulos, 'Vom nationalen Strafrecht zum Strafrecht der Nationen' in I Anagnostopoulos (ed), *Internationalisierung Des Strafrechts* (Baden-Baden, Nomos, 2003) 7.

[2] M Delmas-Marty, 'Introduction' in M Delmas-Marty and S Breyer (eds), *Regards Croisés sur l'Internationalisation du Droit: France_États-Unis* (Paris, Société de Législation Comparé, 2009) 15.

[3] The dictionary definition of the verb 'internationalise' reflects the breadth of the internationalisation process. *Webster International Dictionary* defines it as 'to make international in relations, effect, or scope'. Similarly, the *Oxford English Dictionary*, vol VII (Oxford, Clarendon Press, 1989) 1124, broadly defines the verb 'internationalise' as to 'render international in character or use'.

[4] See section IX.A.

[5] J Bentham, in *Traité de Législation Civile et Pénale*, vol I (Paris, E Dumont, 1820) 46 and 48, affirmed that 'the language of truth is uniform and simple and that the same ideas call for the same terms'.

of legal internationalisation does not exclude or ignore a narrower notion consisting in the formal creation of public international law. Internationalisation *stricto sensu* aims at regulating the relations between nation states, and it is governed by Article 38 of the Statute of the International Court of Justice.[6] This traditional form of internationalisation is achieved in the field of business-related criminal law by the use of treaties or conventions[7] either directly or indirectly: (a) directly, through suppression conventions,[8] as for example, in the case of bribery of foreign public officials; (b) indirectly, through the creation of the EU as a supranational organisation that, in turn, internationalises certain business criminal law-related areas employing regulations and directives[9] as in the case of market abuse.[10]

Customary law as a source of internationalisation, on the contrary, is reserved for core international crimes such as genocide, war crimes and crimes against humanity, and currently has no role in the area of business crimes. This does not preclude, however, that when business crimes attain catastrophic proportions, they may, in the future, be included among crimes under customary international law.[11]

[6] Art 38 of the Statute of the International Court of Justice enumerates the sources of international law, prescribing that:

1. The Court, whose function is to decide in accordance with international law such disputes as are submitted to it, shall apply
   a. international conventions, whether general or particular, establishing rules expressly recognized by the contesting states;
   b. international custom, as evidence of a general practice accepted as law;
   c. the general principles of law recognized by civilized nations;
   d. subject to the provisions of Article 59, judicial decisions and the teachings of the most highly qualified publicists of the various nations, as subsidiary means for the determination of rules of law.
2. This provision shall not prejudice the power of the Court to decide a case *ex aequo et bono*, if the parties agree thereto.

[7] According to Art 2.1(a) of the Vienna Convention on the Law of Treaties, a 'treaty' means an international agreement concluded between states in written form and governed by international law, whether embodied in a single instrument or in two or more related instruments and whatever its particular designation. R Wallace and O Martin-Ortega, in *International Law* (London, Sweet & Maxwell, 2009) 265, point out that '"treaty" is a generic term used to embrace convention, agreement, arrangement, protocol, and exchange of notes'.

[8] 'Suppression conventions' are multilateral treaties requiring states to criminalise certain conducts of international concern. See section VI.

[9] Regulations are legislative acts of the EU that become directly and immediately enforceable in all Member States simultaneously, while directives are also legislative acts obligatory for the Member States with respect to result but allowing them to choose the means to achieve it. See section VII.

[10] Regulation EU No 596/2014 of the European Parliament and of the Council of 16 April 2014 on market abuse (Market Abuse Regulation (MAR)) and Directive 2014/57/EU of the European Parliament and of the Council of 16 April 2014 on criminal sanctions for market abuse (Market Abuse Directive (MAD II)).

[11] Y Radi, 'Du Dilemme du Prisonnier au Jeu de l'Intégration: l'Internationalisation de l'Incrimination Pénale de Corruption Active Transnationale' in D Dormoy (ed), *La corruption et le droit international* (Brussels, Bruylant, 2010) 169.

Michel Massé emphasises the dynamic nature of internationalisation in the legal field, affirming that it is essentially a 'movement' leading to different results;[12] while Alberto di Martino underscores the breadth of such process by indicating that it encompasses a 'multiform constellation of phenomena' involving more than one country[13] – a multiplicity that may attain different degrees of intensity.[14]

This broad conceptualisation underpins the analysis of the following forms of internationalisation of the law criminalising securities frauds: extraterritorial application of national law; international cooperation, mutual recognition of judicial decisions; diffusion of the American legal model; EU regulations and directives; suppression treaties and conventions; legal harmonisation; and other concerted transnational legal processes. The forms of internationalisation that I enumerate in sections II to IX of this chapter are sometimes juxtaposed to each other so that some forms may refer to an earlier stage of internationalisation covering less areas than the all-encompassing 2014 Market Abuse Regulation and Market Abuse Directive on criminal sanctions that I cover in section VII.

II. Extraterritorial Application of National Law

The most rudimentary form of criminal law internationalisation is the unilateral application of domestic law beyond its national territory. The frequent use in recent times of this form of internationalisation by powerful nations has led some scholars to dub it as 'hegemonic'[15] and 'imperialistic'.[16]

The territorial nature of criminal law has deep roots in the common law. However, the extraterritorial application of domestic law has not always been excluded. For example, in *Treacy v DPP*, Lord Diplock expressed that there is no reason why persons who have committed acts outside England, which caused harms to persons within England, should not be tried in English courts.[17] In the US, the notion of extraterritoriality experienced dramatic changes since its early formulation in the 1824 *Appollon* case.[18] According to this decision, a nation is

[12] M Massé, 'Des Figures Asymétriques de l'Internationalisation du Droit Pénal', *Revue de Science Criminelle et de Droit Pénal Comparé* (October/December 2006) 755; Mireille Delmas-Marty also describes internationalisation as a movement. M Delmas-Marty, *Les Forces Imaginantes du Droit*, vol 2: *Le Pluralisme Ordonné* (Paris, Seuil, 2006) 255.

[13] A di Martino, *La Frontiera e il Diritto Penale: Natura e Contesto delle Norme di 'Diritto Penale Transnazionale'* (Turin, G Giappichelli Editore, 2006) 5.

[14] V Malabat, 'Les Procédés de l'Internationalisation du Droit Pénal', *Revue Droit Penal* (LexisNexis, 2006) 23.

[15] M Delmas-Marty, 'Aplanir le terrain de jeu' in 'Les Figures de l'Internationalisation en Droit Pénal des Affaires' (2005) 4 *Revue de Science Criminelle et de Droit Pénal Comparé* 735, 737.

[16] Massé, 'Des Figures Asymétriques' (n 12) 755, 759; P Roegele, *Deutscher Strafrechtsimperialismus:ein Beitrag zu den Völkerrechtlichen Grenzen Extraterritorialer Strafgewahltausdehnung* (Hamburg, Verlag Dr Kovač, 2014).

[17] Per Lord Morris of Borth-y Gest in *Treacy v DPP* [1971] AC 537, 552–53.

[18] *The Appollon*, 22 US 9 Wheat 362 (1824).

entirely precluded from extending its laws beyond its own borders, 'except so far as regards its own citizens'.[19]

In the present era of globalisation, the exercise of extraterritorial jurisdiction has been deemed inevitable, given that 'the expansion of commercial and financial interstate links has increased the vulnerability of States to adverse domestic effects of foreign activities'.[20] In the field of securities law, the extraterritorial reach of national law may become necessary when some states set low standards to attract investors, refuse to criminalise certain fraudulent activities such as insider trading, or avoid stringent corporate governance regulations.[21]

Several factors, such as the globalisation of financial markets, advances in communications and transportation technologies, decreasing relevance of national borders, emergence of computer networks, reduced state authority, increasing cyber finance and offshore banking, and high demand for American securities abroad and vice versa, have increased the potential for transnational criminal securities fraud.

The extraterritorial application of national laws constitutes an immediate response to such challenges. The international legal limits to extraterritorial jurisdiction can be inferred from the unofficial 1935 Harvard Research Draft Convention on Jurisdiction with Respect to Crime.[22] This Draft Convention, based on an extensive survey of state practice, identifies five bases of jurisdiction over persons, natural or legal, in international law: (1) *territorial jurisdiction* over offences completed in the territory of the claimant country (objective territoriality) or over offences commencing in its territory (subjective territoriality); (2) *nationality jurisdiction* permitting a state to exercise jurisdiction over offences committed by its nationals; (3) *universal jurisdiction* depending only on the abhorrent nature of the offence independently both from the territory where it was committed and of the nationality of the offender; (4) *protective jurisdiction* over offences producing deleterious effects on the welfare or security of the claimant state or, according with the more recent *effects doctrine* over any matters producing effects in their territory; (5) *passive personality jurisdiction*, based on the nationality of the victim of the criminal offence.[23]

In the field of securities fraud, the intensification of international transactions, the globalisation of the market economy, and the need to maintain a level playing field in the global market have created the need to apply extraterritorially laws criminalising insider trading and market manipulation.

[19] ibid, 370. This exception was confirmed by Joseph Story, in *Commentaries on the Conflict of Laws: Foreign and Domestic, in Regards to Contracts, Rights, and Remedies* (1834) 22 (expressly stating that every nation has a right to bind its own citizens by its own laws in every place beyond its boundaries).

[20] See C Ryngaert, *Jurisdiction in International Law* (New York, Oxford University Press, 2008) 187.

[21] ibid.

[22] 'Draft Convention on Jurisdiction with Respect to Crime' (1935) 29 *American Journal of International Law* 439.

[23] ibid.

III. International Cooperation

International cooperation is a first stage in the process of progressive internationalisation of domestic criminal law systems. Through cooperation autonomous criminal justice systems cease to remain isolated within their borders[24] communicating with each other to obtain evidence or to make law enforcement possible. In addition to the traditional forms of judicial cooperation through extradition treaties and letters rogatory, there are also informal ways of cooperation such as mutual legal assistance treaties (MLATs) and law enforcement access to electronic evidence held in other countries.[25]

Alberto di Martino has pointed out the existence of an inverse proportion between extraterritorial expansion of criminal statutes and international cooperation: 'the greater the nationalistic pretences are, the more the space for international cooperation is reduced and vice versa'.[26] However, as di Martino also observes, this seemingly logical conclusion does not always correlate with the reality of present international relations in the field of criminal law.[27] Often an effective international cooperation demands agreements through which both parties have to extend their national jurisdiction to offences committed abroad in a way that extraterritorial application of national law becomes a condition for such international cooperation.[28]

Pierre Marie Dupuy has emphasised the interdependence amongst states as a fundamental characteristic of the international community at the dawn of the twenty-first century. He ascertains that more and more states are neighbours to the extent that what happens in the territory of each of these countries affects the others, resulting in universal interdependence at the political, strategic, economic and environmental levels.[29] Because of this interdependence, states are now constrained not only to coexist but also to cooperate. This cooperation encompasses many fields such as rationalising economic exchanges, favouring growth, fighting against epidemics, international terrorism, and environmental threats.[30] For the same reasons international cooperation has become indispensable in the area of business-related criminal law. An example of such cooperation and resulting decrease in autonomous national regulation is the mutual legal assistance and extradition components of the OECD Convention Against Corruption. The strict dual criminality requirement[31] is deemed satisfied if the offence is

[24] Massé, 'Des Figures Asymétriques de l'Internationalisation du Droit Pénal' (n 12) 755, 756.

[25] See B Zagaris, 'United States Treaties on Mutual Assistance in Criminal Matters' in M Cherif Bassiouni (ed), *International Criminal Law*, 3rd edn (Leiden, Brill, 2008) 385.

[26] di Martino, *La Frontiera e il Diritto Penale* (n 13) 45.

[27] ibid.

[28] ibid.

[29] PM Dupuy, *Droit International Public*, 6th edn (Paris, Dalloz, 2002) 2.

[30] ibid.

[31] Dual criminality is a requirement for extradition, meaning that the crime charged in the requested state should also be a crime in the requesting state. See M Cherif Bassiouni, *International Extradition: United States Law and Practice* (New York, Oxford University Press, 2007) 949.

covered by the Convention. Furthermore, the Convention can be the basis for extradition between countries lacking extradition treaties.[32]

In the field of securities frauds, following the general characteristics of international financial regulation,[33] cross-border cooperation is governed informally through soft law and transnational regulatory networks such as the International Organization of Securities Commissions (IOSCO). Information-sharing and enforcement cooperation is often in the form of memoranda of understanding (MOUs).[34] In 2002 IOSCO formulated a Multilateral Memorandum of Understanding Concerning Consultation and Cooperation and the Exchange of Information (MMoU), considered by IOSCO as a 'key weapon in the arsenal of securities commissions to tackle securities fraud which increasingly is no longer confined to jurisdictional boundaries'.[35]

IV. Mutual Recognition

Mutual recognition of judicial decisions is a new form of international cooperation specific to EU law that facilitates and accelerates traditional cooperation in criminal matters, preventing criminal offenders from attaining impunity by crossing national borders. This form of cooperation is possible even when the criminal laws of the Member States are dissimilar. Mutual recognition can, therefore, function without considerable harmonisation of the Member States' criminal law.[36] Criminal law was one of the last bastions of national resistance against the EU's constant movement towards rapprochement and collaborative growth.[37] This resistance has been explained by the particular intensity and intrusiveness of criminal sanctions and their tight connection with popular values and representations, as well as by the perception of criminal law as an expression of state sovereignty.[38] However, transborder criminality, uncontrolled migration, and forum shopping led Member States to undertake a long process of harmonisation while intensifying international cooperation through mutual recognition of judicial decisions.

[32] H Lowell Brown, 'Extraterritorial Jurisdiction Under the 1998 Amendments to the Foreign Corrupt Practices Act: Does the Government's Reach Now Exceed its Grasp?' in (2000) 26 *North Carolina Journal of International Law & Commercial Regulation* 239, 282.

[33] C Brummer, 'Why Soft Law Dominates International Finance and not Trade' (2010) 13 *Journal of International Economic Law* 623.

[34] ibid, 630.

[35] J Austin, 'IOSCO's Multilateral Memorandum of Understanding Concerning Consultation and Cooperation and the Exchange of Information-a Model for International Regulatory Convergence' (2012) 23(4) *Criminal Law Forum* 393.

[36] A Suominen, *The Principle of Mutual Recognition in Cooperation in Criminal Matters: A Study of the Principle in Four Framework Decisions in the Implementation Legislation in the Nordic Member States* (Cambridge, Intersentia, 2011) 4.

[37] MA Zöller, 'Das Prinzip des Gegenzeitigen Annerkennung in der Europäischen Union' in A Sinn, Hsiao-Wen Wang, Jiuan-Yih Wu and M Zöller (eds), *Strafrecht ohne Grenzen: 3. Deutsch-Taiwanesisches Strafrechts Forum, Kaohsiung/Tainan/Taipeh (2013)* (Heidelberg, CF Müller, 2015) 15.

[38] ibid.

Mutual recognition began functioning in criminal matters through framework decisions.[39] The idea was introduced when the Treaty of Amsterdam entered into force in 1999. This treaty set the aim of developing the Union as an 'Area of Freedom, Security and Justice' together with the possibility of adopting binding EU legislation harmonising Member States' criminal justice legislation.[40] At the European Council meeting at Tampere, Finland, on 16 and 17 October 1999, mutual, direct and automatic recognition of a Member State's decisions in the area of criminal law was proclaimed as the cornerstone of judicial cooperation in civil and criminal matters within the EU.[41] In line with the Tampere conclusions, the European Commission suggested that mutual recognition did not preclude the efforts of rapprochement and harmonisation and that both should work in unison while maintaining or improving the present standards regarding the treatment of suspects and the rights of the defence.[42]

After the entry into force of the Treaty of Lisbon, the provisions related to police and judicial cooperation were transferred from the EU Treaty to the Treaty on the Functioning of the EU, further increasing the significance of mutual recognition.[43] Aiming at increasing the effectiveness of judicial cooperation in criminal matters, the principle of judicial recognition is now incorporated into the Treaty on the Functioning of the European Union Article 82, Section 1 in accordance with the Treaty of Lisbon. This provision establishes that 'the judicial cooperation in criminal matters in the Union is founded on the principle of mutual recognition of judicial judgments and decisions'.[44] According to this principle, lawfully issued judicial decisions of an EU Member State, as for example a judgment, an arrest warrant or a seizure warrant, must also be directly and automatically recognised as such in each other EU Member State with the same validity and enforceability.[45]

[39] Framework decisions, created by the Amsterdam Treaty, were a type of legislative act of the EU used exclusively within the EU's jurisdiction in criminal justice matters. They were similar to directives because they required Member States to achieve particular results without dictating the means of achieving that result. However, framework decisions had no direct effect and they were only subject to the optional jurisdiction of the European Court of Justice. The Lisbon Treaty abolished them and today the EU can enact criminal justice-related new regulations and directives through the ordinary legislative procedure.

[40] W van Ballegooij, *The Nature of Mutual Recognition In European Law* (Cambridge, Intersentia, 2015) 121.

[41] Zöller, 'Das Prinzip des gegenzeitigen Annerkennung' (n 37) 19.

[42] Ballegooij, *The Nature of Mutual Recognition* (n 40) 128.

[43] Consolidated Version of the Treaty on the Functioning of the European Union [2012] OJ C326/47. In Title V, Area of Freedom, Security and Justice, Art 67(3) demands that 'the Union shall endeavour a high level of security through measures to prevent and combat racism and xenophobia and through measures for coordination and cooperation between police and judicial authorities, and other competent authorities, as well as through the mutual recognition of judgments in criminal matters and, if necessary, through the approximation of criminal laws'.

[44] Zöller, 'Das Prinzip des gegenzeitigen Annerkennung' (n 37) 14.

[45] ibid, 11.

The use of mutual recognition, in the same way as the 1989 Insider Dealing Directive, represent stages in the harmonisation process of EU securities regulation, aimed first at completing the internal market and opening the European market for investments, and later intensifying the protection of the financial markets with the 2003 Market Abuse Directive. In line with a policy of increasingly introducing protective minimum criminal law standards, this process culminates with the 2014 MAR and MAD II, dealt with at the end of section VII.

V. The Diffusion of the American Legal Model

Addressing the hypothesis of the Americanisation of French criminal law, Jean Cedras distinguishes between the active exercising of influence and its actual reception. He points out that, supported by a neo-liberal discourse and a superior logistic, the global influence of American criminal law and especially of its criminal procedure is undeniable. The reception of this influence, however, has only just reached French legal thinking, but its impact on positive law remains unverified.[46]

Responding to this challenge, Adrian Nieto Martin takes upon himself the task of verifying the impact of Americanisation in the field of the positive law governing corporate crime in Europe.[47] After focusing on the vast influence of US law in the field of competition law, he addresses its influence in the area of securities law. He notices that while the Sherman Act model began to establish itself from the mid-1950s onwards, the American model on securities law started to exercise its influence in the late 1980s beginning by pressuring Switzerland to introduce the crime of insider trading in its legislation[48] and later by contributing to the shaping of the European Convention on insider trading and Directive on market abuse.[49]

Furthermore, Nieto Martin underscores that 'the Americanization of corporate crime is as much the consequence of pressure, as it is of the conviction that these types of norms are both necessary and useful for the market'.[50] Nieto Martin also points out that Americanisation is not only limited to the adoption of legal

[46] J Cedras, 'L'Hypothèse de l'américanisation du droit pénal français' in *L'Américanisation du Droit*, vol 45 (Paris, Dalloz, 2001) 149.

[47] A Nieto Martin, 'Americanisation or Europeanisation of Corporate Crime' in M Delmas-Marty, M Pieth and U Sieber (eds), *Les Chemins de l'Harmonisation Pénale/Harmonizing Criminal Law* (Paris, Société de législation comparée, 2008) 327.

[48] See ch 4, section III.

[49] Council of Europe, Convention on Insider Trading, Strasbourg, 20/04/1989 ETS No 130, and Directive 2003/6/EC of the European Parliament and of the Council of 28 January 2003 on insider dealing and market manipulation (MAD), replaced more recently by MAR and MAD II.

[50] Nieto Martin, 'Americanisation or Europeanisation of Corporate Crime' (n 47) 336.

rules, but also includes American crime policy strategies such as whistleblowing and gatekeeper liability.[51]

VI. Suppression Treaties and Conventions

Suppression treaties or conventions are 'those treaties, usually multilateral, which are concluded between states in order to coordinate crime suppression efforts between them'.[52] This type of international agreement obligates its parties to criminalise certain behaviours of international concern. Often suppression conventions contain a provision mandating its parties either to exercise territorial jurisdiction over perpetrators found within their borders, or to extradite these offenders to other member countries willing to prosecute them (*aut dedere aut prosequi*).[53] There are at least 267 multilateral suppression treaties requiring the criminalisation of conduct considered offensive to the interests of the international community.[54] Their language varies considerably, however. This can range from a statement by which the parties simply agree to cooperate in suppressing the conduct in question, to a more definite obligation to subject such conduct to criminal sanctions and to prosecute and punish the offenders.[55]

As pointed out in section III, in the case of securities fraud, international cooperation takes place through transnational regulatory networks rather than with hard law treaties. In this respect the IOSCO is a global network of securities regulators formed in 1983 from an Inter-American regional organisation expanding it beyond the Americas.[56] Based in Madrid, IOSCO cooperates with the G-20 and the Financial Stability Board (FSB) with members covering 95 per cent of world securities markets in over 110 jurisdictions.[57]

VII. Internationalisation through EU Directives and Regulations

The internationalisation of law becomes more complex when treaties governed by classic international law create a supranational organisation capable, in turn, of

[51] ibid, 340 ff.

[52] RJ Currie, *International & Transnational Criminal* Law (Toronto, Irwin Law Inc, 2010) 305.

[53] M Cherif Bassiouni and EM Wise, *Aut Dedere aut Judicare: The Duty to Extradite or Prosecute in International Law* (Leiden, Martinus Nijhoff, 1995).

[54] ES Pogdor, RS Clark and LN Dervan, *International Criminal Law* (Durham, NC, Carolina Academic Press, 2016) 42.

[55] ibid, 44.

[56] J Austin, 'The Power and Influence of IOSCO in Regulating and Enforcing Securities Regulations' (2015) 15 *Asper Review of International Business & Trade Law* 1, 3.

[57] T Papadopulos, 'International Organization of Securities Commissions (IOSCO)' in R Wolfrum (ed), *Max Planck Encyclopedia of Public International Law* (New York, Oxford University Press, 2015) (article last updated January 2019).

generating forms of legal internationalisation. This is the case of the EU endowed with the power to issue self-executing regulations directly applicable to Member States, as well as directives setting obligatory goals attainable by the Member States through a process of harmonisation of their respective legislations.[58]

These directives are issued by the Council of the European Union establishing policies that are left to Member States to adapt to their own legal system.[59] Regulations, on the other hand, are binding legislative acts that must be applied in their entirety by all the EU Member States. Both directives and regulations are subject to legislative procedures initiated by the European Commission and continued by the Parliament and the Council of the EU.

Historically, since its inception through the 1953 Treaty of Rome, the European Economic Community had no jurisdiction in the area of criminal law. The 1993 Treaty of Maastricht (Treaty on European Union) structured the EU in three pillars, the third of which, called 'Justice and Home Affairs', was devoted to police and judicial cooperation in criminal matters. Under the 1999 Amsterdam Treaty, the Member States entrusted the European Parliament to legislate in several specific fields, including criminal matters.[60] The 2009 Lisbon Treaty[61] amended both the Maastricht Treaty and the 1957 Treaty of Rome. The latter was renamed the Treaty on the Functioning of the European Union (TFEU).[62] Article 83(1), TFEU allows the European Parliament and the Council to adopt directives establishing 'minimum rules concerning the definition of criminal offences and sanctions in the areas of particularly serious crimes with a cross-border dimension resulting from the nature or impact of such offences or from a special need to combat them on a common basis'.

After enumerating a number of 'Euro crimes', as for example terrorism, corruption, and various forms of human trafficking, the TFEU empowers the Council, on the basis of new developments in crime, to adopt a decision identifying other criminal areas that meet the criteria specified in the paragraph. The Council must act unanimously after obtaining the consent of the European Parliament. Moreover, Article 83(2), TFEU allows the European Parliament and the Council, at a proposal from the Commission, to establish minimum rules with regard to the definition of criminal offences and sanctions. The approximation between criminal laws and regulations of the Member States have to prove essential to ensure the effective implementation of a Union policy in an area which has been subject to a harmonisation measure. Article 83(2), TFEU constitutes the legal basis for the future Directive on criminal sanctions for Market Abuse.

[58] RH Folsom, *Principles of European Union Law*, 2nd edn (The Concise Hornbook Series, Saint Paul, MN, West Academic Press, 2009) 34.

[59] ibid.

[60] This Treaty created framework decisions as a form of legislative act (see n 39).

[61] Treaty of Lisbon Amending the Treaty on European Union and the Treaty establishing the European communities (hereinafter 'Treaty of Lisbon') [2007] OJ C306/01, Art 69 B(2).

[62] Consolidated Version of the Treaty on the Functioning of the European Union (n 43).

Previously, the 1989 Insider Trading Directive, prohibiting for the first time insider trading within the EU, was one of the early measures towards the harmonisation of European Union securities regulation.[63] In 2003, the Market Abuse Directive (MAD) 2003/6/EC addressed insider dealing and market manipulation practices requiring Member States to adopt the necessary administrative measures and sanctions to prevent these behaviours. Dissatisfaction with the results led to the Commission communication on 'Reinforcing sanctioning regimes in the financial services sector',[64] leading ultimately to the 2014 Directive on Criminal Sanctions for Market Abuse.[65] First, the Directive 2003/6/EC of the European Parliament and of the Council was repealed by the Regulation (EU) No 596/2014 of the European Parliament and of the Council of 16 April 2014 on market abuse[66] regulation. Subsequently, the Directive on criminal sanctions for market abuse 2014/57/EU entered into force on 3 July 2014 (MAD II).[67]

VIII. Harmonisation

Harmonisation of criminal law provisions stays at the vanguard of present internationalisation efforts and is the subject of increasing scholarly focus. Mark Pieth points out that the evolution of harmonisation cannot be described in terms of legal categories alone without taking into account the influence of complex political and economic developments, as, for example, the opening of new markets after the end of the Cold War.[68]

Furthermore, Pieth identifies new players working toward international harmonisation, such as inter-governmental organisations, non-governmental organisations, the private sector and the civil society. International organisations are supplemented and coordinated by task force-type structures, usually made up of other international organisations, states and occasionally members of the private sector or of the civil society.[69] Pieth also underscores the more dynamic role of the new non-state actors with the use of soft law,[70] peer pressure and hybrid

[63] Council Directive 89/592 (EC) [1989] OJ L334/30.

[64] *Communication of the Commission on Reinforcing Sanctioning Regimes in the Financial Services Sector*, COM (2010) 716 final (8 December 2010).

[65] MAD II.

[66] The Regulation (EU) No 596/2014 of the European Parliament and of the Council on market abuse (MAR) constitutes the culmination of this type of regional internationalisation. According to Recital (7) of the Regulation, 'market abuse is a concept that encompasses unlawful behaviour in the financial markets and, for the purposes of the Regulation, it should be understood as consisting of insider dealing, unlawful disclosure of inside information and market manipulation'.

[67] Directive on criminal sanctions for market abuse (n 65).

[68] M Pieth, 'The Agents of Change' in Delmas-Marty, Pieth and Sieber (eds), *Les Chemins de l'Harmonisation Pénale* (n 47) 369.

[69] ibid, 372–73.

[70] See JE Gersen and EA Posner, 'Soft Law', *University of Chicago Public Law and Legal Theory Working Paper Series* (2008) available at ssrn.com/abstracts=1113537.

public-private initiatives,[71] while recognising their vulnerability where legitimacy is concerned. Task forces are able to bind their constituency through political peer pressure, tending to use soft law instead of conventions.[72] Pieth raises the question of the democratic legitimacy of this action by non-state actors because it places national legislators in the situation of a fait accompli and subjects dissenting states to political pressure to go along with the majority interest.

The three main partners in regulating, implementing, and monitoring of the harmonisation process are the government and/or international organisations, the private sector and the civil society.[73] The private sector is composed by multinational enterprises as well as by medium and small-sized enterprises frequently pursuing different goals. The civil society as an agent of harmonisation includes the media, academia, NGOs, trade unions and political parties.

Ulrich Sieber thoroughly analyses the forces behind the harmonisation of criminal law in general and explores the varying degrees and speeds with which it was undertaken in different areas. He also analyses the interrelationship between the various forces that either support or hinder harmonisation,[74] pointing to the difficulties of harmonising in a sovereignty-centred criminal law where each country has different historical, cultural and economic characteristics that make criminal law harmonisation problematic.

Even though nation states resist harmonisation and try to preserve their sovereignty, they are willing to relinquish autonomous national regulation when such harmonisation 'facilitates the enforceability of law, increasing security and serving other national interests'.[75] Nation states tend to embrace harmonisation in an area such as business crimes where economic globalisation makes it indispensable for effective criminal prosecutions. Moreover, the process of harmonisation has been generated by other factors such as the international exchange of scientific knowledge, the growing interconnectedness of national economies, the global scope of today's media and the high degree of political cooperation among interdependent states.[76]

In the area of business-related criminal law, harmonisation has been particularly intensive at the EU level because of the common economic interest of each Member State. The EU's harmonised criminal law protects the financial interests of the EU, as well as other economic interests through provisions on fraud, corruption and prohibition of insider trading.

Sieber includes among the significant forces that drive the harmonisation of criminal law the influence of non-state actors in the design of crime policies.[77]

[71] M Delmas Marty, 'Introduction: Objectifs et Méthodes' in Delmas-Marty, Pieth and Sieber (eds), *Les Chemins de l'Harmonisation Pénale* (n 47) 29.

[72] Pieth, 'The Agents of Change' (n 68) 373.

[73] ibid, 374.

[74] U Sieber, 'The Forces Behind the Harmonization of Criminal Law' in Delmas-Marty, Pieth and Sieber (eds), *Les Chemins de l'Harmonisation Pénale* (n 47) 386.

[75] ibid, 396.

[76] ibid, 387.

[77] ibid, 387.

Further, he points out new and effective instruments and methods of criminal law harmonisation. Some are of 'soft law' nature such as the OECD recommendations, while others are decidedly binding such as the Security Council Resolutions. As explained in section III, financial 'soft law' dominates financial regulations and IOSCO is devoted to establishing harmonised international standards for the regulation of securities issuances and trading.[78]

IX. Transnationalisation as a Subcategory of Legal Internationalisation *Lato Sensu*

A. Transnational Law in General

The comprehensive notion of internationalisation announced in section I includes transnational law as one of its forms of manifestation. 'Transnational law' is a new term used by scholars to indicate 'new legal relations, influences, controls, regimes, doctrines, and systems that are not those of nation-state (municipal) law, but they are not fully grasped by extended definitions of the scope of international law'.[79] The expression 'transnational law' was first used in a private law context in the 1930s. In 1931, Max Gutzwiller[80] spoke of 'transnational norms' with reference to norms of private international law[81] accepted beyond borders. Similarly, in 1934, the Austrian professor Gustav Walker[82] used the expression 'transnational law' with reference to rules of an international common private law and in 1945, in Germany, Ernst Rabel spoke of 'transnational rules' referring to 'certain rules of private international law of almost universal force'.[83]

The more influential definition came from Philip C Jessup in his book *Transnational Law*, reproducing the Storrs lectures that he delivered in 1956 at the Yale Law School. As opposed to previous definitions, he defined transnational law very broadly as 'laws that transcend national frontiers'.[84] He believed that the term 'international' was too narrow because it only covered relations between national states and ignored private actors such as multinational corporations and non-governmental organisations which had an important role in matters of transborder nature. Jessup included in his broad conception of transnational law

[78] RS Karmel, 'IOSCO's Response to the Financial Crisis' in *Brooklyn Law School Legal Studies No 268*, available at ssrn.com/abstract=2025115, 50.

[79] R Cotterrell, 'What is Transnational Law?' (2012) 37(2) *Law & Social Inquiry* 500, 501.

[80] M Gutzwiller, 'Das Internationalprivatrecht der durch die Friedensverträge eingesetzen Gemischten Schiedsgerichtshöfe' in *Internationales Jahrbuch für Schiedsgerichtswesen in Zivil und Handelssachen* (Berlin, Carl Heymanns Verlag, 1931) 123, 128.

[81] Civil law system's equivalent of what the common law denominates 'conflict of laws'.

[82] G Walker, *Internationales Privatrecht* (Vienna, Österreichische Staatsdrukerei, 1934) 13.

[83] E Rabel, *The Conflict of Laws: A Comparative Study* (Chicago, IL, Callaghan & Company, 1945) 39.

[84] PC Jessup, *Transnational Law* (New Haven, CT, Yale University Press, 1956) 2.

both public and private international law together with other rules that did not fit into any of these categories.[85]

Following Jessup's conception, Christian Tietje referred, as early as 2006, to a transnational business-related law (*transnationalen Wirtschaftsrecht*) as a network of legal norms and legal subjects involved in the execution of cross-border transactions of both private and public nature.[86]

Later definitions of transnational law have narrowed this notion considerably. For example, Lars Klöhn rejected Jessup's definition of transnational law as too general because it embraces every legal rule, regardless of its nature, as long as it addresses cross-border activity. For Lars Klöhn, excessive generality leaves Jessup's formulation with 'almost no definitional power'.[87] Klöhn proposes to define transnational law as a fourth category of law beyond the triad of national, international and supranational law. He considers that transnational law 'refers to any legal rule which evolves beyond the state as such because of private ordering, social convenience, and non-legal convention'.[88]

Halliday and Shaffer speak of transnational legal orders not only in the obvious loose sense of law applying to two or more countries, but also in the sense of transnational legal orders disassociated from the law of the nation state.[89] They explain that modern economic and cultural globalisation blurred the basic coordinates of traditional international law and as a reaction scholars have tried to make sense of legal processes between nation states that do not necessarily involve traditional international law.[90] Another way to articulate a comprehensive view of the internationalisation movement is to speak of 'transnational legal processes'.[91] On the basis of four comparative empirical studies, Shaffer underscores the importance of these transnational legal processes, which may overtime become transnational legal orders created by treaties, nonbinding standards, model codes, and different forms of institutional monitoring and dispute settlements.[92]

In this context, transnational legal orders have been defined as a 'collection of formalized legal norms and associated organizations and actors that

[85] ibid, 106.

[86] C Tietje, 'Transnationalisierung der Wirtschaftsstrafrechts' in G-P Callies (ed), *Transnatinales Recht* (Heidelberg, Mohr Siebeck, 2014). In this contribution he cites his article for the 50th Anniversary of Philip C Jessup's *Transnational Law* at 240.

[87] L Klöhn, Transnational Financial Markets Regulation – a Conference, 15 July 2010, available at ssrn.com/abstract=1640459.

[88] ibid.

[89] TC Halliday and G Shaffer, 'Transnational Legal Orders' in TC Halliday and G Shaffer (eds), *Transnational Legal Orders* (Cambridge, Cambridge University Press, 2015) 3, 7–21.

[90] ibid, 4; see also W Twining, *Globalisation and Legal Theory* (London, Edinburgh and Dublin, Butterworth, 2000) 50 ff.

[91] G Shaffer, 'Transnational Legal Process and State Change' (2012) 37 *Law & Social Inquiry* 229, 235; H Hongju Koh, 'Opening Remarks: Transnational Legal Process Illuminated,' in M Likosky (ed), *Transnational Legal Processes: Globalization and Power Disparities*, (London, Butterworths Tolley, 2002), 327–332.

[92] Shaffer, 'Transnational Legal Process and State Change' (n 91) 236.

authoritatively order the understanding and practice of law across national jurisdictions'.[93] In this respect, IOSCO created new international principles for securities regulations in 1998[94] and the Organization for Economic Cooperation and Development carried out a similar function in the field of international corruption, especially through the Convention on Combating Bribery of Foreign Public Officials in International Business Transactions, which entered into force in 1999.

Lars Viellnechter points out that the notion of transnational law is inconsistently applied as a result of four basically different points of reference for interpreting the transnationality of law.[95] The first reference point is the *object* of the law; that is, the transborder circumstances regulated by the law, or as Jessup put it, 'all actions or events that transcend national borders'.[96] The second point of reference is the *effects* of the law; that is, the transnational effects of a domestic law endowed with extraterritorial power. The third point of reference, the *content* of the law, refers to situations of convergence of various legal systems on certain norms or areas of the law. Transnational law would result either from legal rules or principles common to a number of legal systems or from a hybrid combination of legal rules belonging to each legal system. The fourth reference point is the *authorship* of the law, referring to non-state actors, international organisations or 'communities of interest that cut across nation-state boundaries',[97] or transnational communities.[98] Viellechner proposes to avoid the discrepancies between the four reference points by reconstructing transnational law conceptually, lumping those reference points together evenly in one definition. He therefore proposes that transnational law should be understood as a law that: (1) is addressing transborder circumstances not necessarily global; (2) is regulating individual relations as well as those matters of general interest, usually limited to a single area; and (3) does so predominantly but not exclusively through non-state actors.[99]

According to Gregory Shaffer the concept of transnational law has been developed to 'address legal norms that do not clearly fall within traditional concepts of national or international law but are not necessarily global in nature'.[100] He also observes that the expression 'transnational law' is increasingly used without specifying its meaning.[101] For this purpose, he distinguishes between two categories of concepts on the basis of whether they focus on the transnational activities or situations addressed by the law, or rather on the sources of the law that operate

[93] Halliday and Shaffer, 'Transnational Legal Orders' (n 89) 11.

[94] E Helleiner, 'Regulating the Regulators: The Emergence and Limits of the Transnational Financial Legal Order' in Halliday and Shaffer (eds), *Transnational Legal Orders* (n 89) 238.

[95] L Viellechner, *Transnationalisierung Des Rechts* (Weilerswist, Velbrück Wissenschaft, 2013) 165.

[96] Jessup, *Transnational Law* (n 84) 2.

[97] HJ Berman, *Law and Revolution: The Formation of the Western Legal Tradition* (Cambridge, MA, and London, Harvard University Press, 1983) 476.

[98] Cotterrell, 'What is Transnational Law?' (n 79) 501.

[99] Viellechner, *Transnationalisierung Des Rechts* (n 95) 180.

[100] Shaffer, 'Transnational Legal Process and State Change' (n 91) 232.

[101] ibid, 233.

across borders. Adopting the latter perspective, he defines transnational law as 'law in which transnational actors, be they institutions or networks of public or private actors, play a role in constructing and diffusing legal norms, even if the legal norm is taken in great part from a national legal model, including those of a powerful state such as the United States'.[102]

B. Transnational Criminal Law

Turning to the specific field of transnational criminal law, some scholars apply the concepts of transnational criminal and international criminal law as synonyms.[103] Others, as Neil Boister, use the term 'transnational criminal law' referring to the law resulting from suppression conventions. Through these mostly multilateral treaties, countries obligate themselves to criminalise certain behaviours that raise international concern. Transnational law, as Boister puts it, consists in 'the indirect suppression by international law through domestic penal law of criminal activities that have actual or potential trans-boundary effects'.[104] The introduction of the term 'transnational' is to better correlate this type of law with the term 'transnational crime' often used by criminologists, criminal justice officials and policymakers.[105] On the other hand, Boister reserves the term 'international criminal law' for the core crimes that shock the consciousness of humanity to the degree of being criminalised as a matter of customary international law. Still others identify as transnational criminal law the rules about territorial scope of validity of national criminal law, or the provisions about international cooperation in criminal matters.

Florian Jeβberger, in his 2011 book about the transnational scope of validity of German criminal law, proposed to combine the rules on the transnational scope of validity of criminal law with the rules about international cooperation in criminal matters under the umbrella term of transnational criminal law.[106] In 2014, Jeβberger affirmed that common to the different conceptions of transnational criminal law is the aim to make conceptually visible the criminal law regulation of transborder events and/or the transborder events relevant to criminal law. He also points out that unlike the latest developments of the notion of transnational law in other fields, the conceptualisation of 'transnational criminal law' does not

[102] ibid, 235.

[103] F Jeβberger, 'Transnationales Srafrecht, Internationales Strafrecht, Transnationale Rechtsgeltung und Orientierung' in G-P Calliess (ed), *Transnationalen Recht: Stand und Perspektiven* (Tübingen, Mohr Siebeck, 2014) 528.

[104] N Boister, 'Transnational Criminal Law?' (2003) 14(5) *European Journal of International Law* 953, 955.

[105] ibid, 955, 956.

[106] F Jeβberger, *Der Transnationalen Geltungsbereich des Deutschen Strafrechts* (Tübingen, Mohr Siebeck, 2011). This conceptualisation of transnational criminal law is cited retrospectively by the same Jeβberger in his contribution 'Transnationales Srafrecht' (n 103) 528.

include regulation through non-state actors, and that, therefore, transnational criminal law does not correlate with transnational law in general.[107] He attributes this lack of correspondence between the conceptual development of transnational law in other areas and transnational criminal law to the fact that criminal law scholars have only begun their theoretical inquiry in a comparatively recent time, or, rather, to the fact that the theoretical developments at the beginning of the twentieth century[108] had remained buried for many decades. Hence, he is not surprised about the present absence of efforts towards building a model conceptual framework regarding the transnational dimension of criminal law. Today both the scholarly perception of the subject matter and its systematic organisation are at its beginnings.

On the other hand, Ingeborg Zerbes[109] points out the paradoxical nature of the notion of 'transnational' criminal law given that criminal law is by definition national law and criminal punishment has been traditionally monopolised by the national state. She observes, however, that a number of instruments, methods and mechanisms of modern business-related criminal law are increasingly shaped by the co-participation of non-state actors.[110] For example, compliance mechanisms, internal investigations and disgorgement sanctions elude the exclusive influence of the state and develop beyond its sovereign power and territorial borders.[111] These new instruments can be found at three levels: (a) substantive criminal law; (b) criminal procedure; and (c) criminal sanctions.

At the substantive criminal law level, compliance measures undertaken by the enterprise may determine the extent of its criminal responsibility.[112]

At the procedural criminal law level, enterprises involved in complex business-related criminal cases, may undertake internal investigations hiring specialised lawyers, thus displacing searches carried out by official authorities. Moreover, in large business-related criminal law cases, bargaining and deal making often displace classic judicial decision-making.[113] At the level of criminal sanctions, given the very high profits derived from business crimes, disgorgement of ill-gotten profits has supplemented a limited sanctioning system for this type of offence. Consequently, disgorgements have become an essential aspect of international negotiations and prosecutorial agreements. Independently, new measures have gained acceptance, such as the appointment of non-official monitors.

[107] Jeβberger, 'Transnationales Strafrecht' (n 103) 528 and 529.

[108] See nn 80, 82 and 83.

[109] I Zerbes, 'Transnationales Korruptionsstrafrecht: Gestaltungsmacht privater Akteure hinter staatlichem Regelungsanspruch' in Calliess (ed), *Transnationalen Recht* (n 103) 541.

[110] ibid, 541.

[111] See Delmas-Marty, 'Aplanir le terrain de jeu' (n 15) 735, where she argues that codes of conduct and other forms of self-regulation are part of the way non-state actors work to limit the impact of state's criminal law.

[112] See Zerbes, 'Transnationales Korruptionsstrafrecht' (n 109) 541.

[113] ibid, 542.

Unlike Jesβberger, Zerbes' observations imply a certain correspondence between transnational criminal law and other areas of transnational law.[114] According to Zerbes, transnational criminal law does include, to a certain extent, regulation through non-state actors[115] and, therefore, it does correlate with transnational law in general.

C. 'Transnationalisation'

In recent years, several scholars have preferred to use the term 'transnationalisation' rather than 'internationalisation'. Transnationalisation conceived as the process leading to the formation of transnational law is indeed one of the forms of internationalisation in the broad sense, as characterised in section I.[116] Moreover, in the context of transnational criminal law[117] the use of the neologism 'transnationalisation' would denote the process of concerted criminalisation of certain behaviours of international concern accomplished through suppression conventions,[118] or designate the process leading to the formation of the body of rules governing both the transnational scope of validity of national criminal law and international cooperation in criminal matters,[119] including the new instruments and regulations created by non-state actors underscored by Zerbes.[120]

There is, however, a caveat in the use of the word transnationalisation – its association with the demonstrated equivocality of the expression 'transnational law'.[121] The notion of transnational law has a number of meanings that makes it elusive and ambiguous. As Cotterrell ascertains, the new term 'transnational law' is 'widely invoked but never defined with much precision'.[122] After a comprehensive overview of German research and perspectives on the notion of 'transnational law' both in general and in specific branches of the law, Gralf-Peter Callies and Andreas Maurer conclude that it remains a fuzzy concept even after 15 years of

[114] ibid.

[115] ibid. Further, the entities subject to the criminal sanctions are also non-state actors, and some of them are multinational entities, such as multinational banks. See LD Dervan, 'Evaluating Corporate Criminal Liability: the DOJ's Internal Mutual Culpability Standard for Corporate Criminal Liability' (2011) 41 *Stetson Law Review* 7; K Tiedemann (ed), *Multinationalen Unternehmen und Strafrecht: Beiträge zum Problem der Kriminalität ins grenzübershreitenden Geschäftsverkehr* (Cologne, Berlin, Bonn and Munich, Carl Heymanns Verlag, 1979).

[116] In section I, the term 'internationalisation' is used in its broad dictionary meaning. It encompasses traditional international law formation and new forms of internationalisation, including self-regulation and the action of non-state actors.

[117] To adapt the legal terminology to the criminological notion of transnational crimes, see N Boister, 'Transnational Criminal Law'? (2003) 14(5) *European Journal of International Law* 953, 954.

[118] See section VI.

[119] This is how Jeβberger conceives transnational criminal law. See Jeβberger, *Der Transnationalen Geltungsbereich des Deutschen Strafrechts* (n 106).

[120] Zerbes, 'Transnationales Korruptionsstrafrecht' (n 109) 541.

[121] See section IX.A.

[122] Cotterrell, 'What is Transnational Law?' (n 79) 501.

doctrinal developments.[123] Furthermore, Callies and Maurer consider that this fuzziness is a natural consequence of the removal of transnational law from the national state without any alternative point of reference. As a result, legal scholars find themselves at a time of upheaval comparable to the codification movement of the nineteenth century.[124]

X. Economic Underpinnings

A. The Globalisation of Financial Markets

The globalisation of financial markets is the economic motor that triggered the internationalisation of securities frauds; therefore, it is necessary to begin with an inquiry into the notion of globalisation.

Globalisation touches upon virtually every domain of human life: economy, politics, culture, law, public health, science and ecology. Numerous theories revolve around the notion of globalisation and its multiple meanings. Faced with such a complex constellation of theoretical and semantic propositions, one must emphasise that globalisation is not merely an idea but, first and foremost, a fact.[125]

Roland Robertson best characterised globalisation as a 'compression of the world' as exemplified by prodigious developments in the technology of transportation, communication and information transmission.[126] Viewed in a historical context, our present globalisation is only a stage in the progressive linkage of humanity. This process began in archaic societies with the discovery of rudimentary tools that allowed the gradual enlargement of social systems and continued through numerous technological advances such as printing, railways, sailing vessels, steamships, telephones, jet planes and the internet.[127] In sum, the process of globalisation is characterised by the broadening of worldwide communication, interaction and organisation.[128]

[123] G-P Callies and A Maurer, 'Transnationales Recht-eine Einleitung' in Calliess (ed), *Transnationalen Recht* (n 103) 36.

[124] ibid.

[125] E Rotman, 'The Globalization of Criminal Violence' (2000) 10(1) *Cornell Journal of Law and Public Policy* 2.

[126] R Robertson, *Globalization: Social Theory and Global Culture* (Thousand Oaks, CA, Sage Publications, 1992) 8; B Schünemann, 'Das Strafrecht im Zeichen der Globaliesierung,' in *Goltdammer's Archive für Strafrecht*, 5/2003, 299, notes that although he does not know another word in the history of humankind having such a triumphant and overwhelming trajectory as 'globalisation', the concept is still far from being precise. He assigns to the notion of globalisation all that is beyond the control of the national states.

[127] See JD Sachs, 'Globalization and the Rule of Law', *Yale Law School Occasional Papers*, Second Series, Number 4, 1998; Twining, *Globalisation and Legal Theory* (n 90) 7.

[128] U Sieber, 'Grenzen des Strafrechts' (2007) 119 *Zeitschrift für das gesamte Strafrechtswissenschaft* 4.

To understand the legal responses to this phenomenon, one should pay attention to William Twinning's warnings regarding superficial and exaggerated generalisations,[129] bearing in mind that there are intermediate levels between the very local and the global.

The beneficial aspects of globalisation are increasing international division of labour, more efficient allocation of capital, growing competition and productivity, and a rise of average living standards.[130] But not all the effects of globalisation are benign. Unbridled greed may find new criminal opportunities in a globalised economy. The following factors have enabled criminal undertakings to create flexible, global networks, and thus evade state regulations and cumbersome international law enforcement: advances in communication and transportation technology; openness of borders; computer networks that make such borders irrelevant; reduced state authority; cyber finances; and offshore banking.

The degree of globalisation of financial markets has been underscored by a group of 42 law professors under the heading 'The Fluid, International Character of Modern Financial Markets'.[131] They pointed out that 'markets are moving to a point where the "site" of a trade is happenstance', emphasising the necessity to focus on the international character of modern financial markets to establish the adequate jurisdiction for transnational securities frauds.[132]

Technological progress and the internet allow investors to access capital markets around the world and trade globally at a breath-taking speed increasing the opportunities of cross-border fraud dramatically. Sieber analyses how advances in communication and transportation[133] have made possible the development of transborder crimes that can be committed in a matter of seconds.[134] He also examines the effects of new European policies that transformed the European space through free traffic of persons, goods and services, and have led to border-free opportunities to commit transnational crimes.[135]

The globaliation and interconnection of financial markets make the protection of local law insufficient. The seriousness of certain financial frauds affects the integrity of financial markets to the point of compromising the health of the national economy as a whole, thus warranting the operation of criminal law not only domestically but also transnationally.[136]

[129] W Twining, *General Jurisprudence: Understanding Law from a Global Perspective* (Cambridge, Cambridge University Press, 2009) 15.

[130] Rotman, 'The Globalization of Criminal Violence' (n 125) 42.

[131] Bartlett et al, Communication to the SEC, File No 4-617, Release No 34-63174, Study on Extraterritorial Private Rights of Action, 7 (2011).

[132] ibid.

[133] Sieber, 'Grenzen des Strafrechts' (n 128) 4.

[134] ibid, 7.

[135] ibid, 6.

[136] CG Jara Diez, *La Proteccion Penal Transnacional De Los Mercados Financieros* (Madrid, Marcial Pons, 2014) 24–25.

B. Relationship between the Economy and Business-Related Criminality

Sieber illustrates the general influence of the economy on business-related criminality by emphasising market globalisation as an economic source of transnational commission of business crimes.[137] Furthermore, Adrian Nieto Martín demonstrates the influence of the economy on white-collar criminality by providing a succinct account of how business-related criminal law has tracked successive economic models throughout history.[138]

Nieto Martin recalls how in Europe during the low Middle Ages, the flowering of commerce gave pre-eminence to bankruptcy crimes. Business failures became criminal when the merchants' behaviour was in acute contradiction with accepted commercial practices. After the French Revolution, beginning with the Napoleonic Criminal Code at the height of economic liberalism, schemes to alter the natural formation of prices became the prototype of business-related crimes. At the end of the nineteenth century, the development of big corporations and the related financial scandals[139] led to detailed legislation criminalising violations of rules that govern the functioning of those corporations. Turning to state intervention in the economy as a predominant trait of the twentieth-century economic model, Nieto Martin considers that the paradigmatic crimes were tax crimes and serious violations of the rules protecting workers and consumers.[140] This state interventionist model originated subsidy and social security-related frauds in the 1970s.

In an article published in 1977, I explained the relationship of various forms of business criminality with the main traits of the economic realities at the time. I characterised that economic situation by its general trend towards accelerated growth resulting from the massive increase of production through a more and more complicated technology.[141] This massive production created the need to protect consumers against low-quality or dangerous products, especially when they were introduced into the market through deceitful advertising. Moreover, the diversification and massification of production reflected the growing role of large enterprises. These phenomena led corporations to extend their activities across borders in the form of multinational corporations generating or facilitating new forms of transnational criminality. The end of the twentieth century witnessed the criminalisation of forms of corruption and fraud through the enactment of

[137] Sieber, 'Grenzen des Strafrechts' (n 128) 6–7.

[138] A Nieto Martín, '*Regulatory Capitalism* y Cumplimiento Normativo' in A Zapatero and A Nieto Martin (eds), *El Derecho Penal Económico en la Era Compliance* (Valencia, Tirant Lo Blanch, 2013) 11.

[139] E Rotman, 'La Criminalidad Financiera en el Siglo XIX' *Revista de Derecho Penal y Criminolgia* (April–June 1969) 228, 229.

[140] Nieto Martín, '*Regulatory Capitalism* y Cumplimiento Normativo' (n 138) 11.

[141] E Rotman, 'Natur und Umfang der Wirtschaftsstraftaten in ihrer Abhängigkeit von einigen Grundzügen des heutigen Wirtschaftslebens' *Kriminalistik* (May 1977) 213.

the Foreign Corrupt Practices Act and the beginnings of the US Supreme Court insider trading's jurisprudence.

In the twenty-first century, compliance becomes a critical control strategy to address deviant corporate behaviour. Nieto Martín characterises the new economic model as regulatory capitalism in which the need to regulate collides with the simultaneous trend towards privatisation.[142] The twenty-first century also raises the question of guaranteeing the effectiveness of business-related controls when the subjects of these regulations are global enterprises that carry out their activities in many states and when the power of these corporate subjects surpasses state power. In response, various strategies have been developed: compliance, soft law and forms of private enforcement parallel to the public one. Nieto Martín concludes his synthetic historical analysis pointing out the main characteristics of today's European business-related criminal law: creation of blanket criminal law provisions that incorporate by reference the rules and administrative regulations existing in other sectors of the legal system[143] and creation of crimes that do not require actual harm but a mere danger to a protected legal interest.[144] These general features of contemporary business related criminal law will be analysed in future chapters specifically addressing the internationalisation of securities frauds.

XI. Social and Psychological Underpinnings: White-Collar Criminality in the Context of a Globalised Economy

Securities frauds have spread across a globalised economy creating the need for an international response. To meet this challenge, it is helpful to inquire into the criminological and sociological features underlying the conduct of potential infringers of the new internationalised provisions. Securities fraud fits within the general sociological category of white-collar crime and shares historical and criminological characteristics.[145] As David O Friedrichs underscored, to reach a richer

[142] Nieto Martín, '*Regulatory Capitalism* y Cumplimiento Normativo' (n 138) 13.

[143] The notion of blanket criminal norms is basically a legislative drafting technique that entails the incorporation by reference of a norm existing elsewhere in the legal system to complete a criminal provision. In later developments this doctrine included the incorporation by reference of norms existing within the same statute. The subject of blanket criminal norms is developed in detail in ch 3, section V.B, specifically in the text corresponding to nn 140 to 145.

[144] H-H Jescheck and T Weigend, *Lehrbuch des Strafrechts: Allgemeiner Teil* (Berlin, Duncker & Humblot, 1996) 264, explain that in the crimes of abstract danger the punishment is based on the general dangerousness of the act, situations that, as Jose Hurtado Pozo points out, may include responses to the modern need to protect certain social interests such as those embodied in the stock market (J Hurtado Pozo, *Manual de Derecho Penal: Parte General* (Lima, Editora Jurídica Grijley, 2005) 785.

[145] Edwin Sutherland coined the phrase in 'White-Collar Criminality' (1940) 5 *American Sociological Review* 1. He defined white-collar crime as 'a crime committed by a person of respectability and high social status in the course of his occupation' in *White-Collar Crime: The Uncut Version* (New Haven, CT, Yale University Press, 1983) 7. This first definition was followed by many others, see also S Green,

and deeper knowledge of white-collar crime, scholars will increasingly have to understand it in terms of globalisation.[146] Similarly, Peter Grabosky points out that crime follows opportunity and that globalisation created an abundance of opportunities. White-collar crime is, thus, associated with technological developments, with the increase of the number of accessible targets resulting from the proliferation and widespread distribution of professional and organisational life, and with the unprecedented abundance of consumer goods and services exchanged across international frontiers.[147]

The extremely damaging consequences of white-collar crime are multiplied in the context of a globalised economy mainly founded on public savings channelled through corporations. The illegal appropriation of other people's money through convoluted accounting frauds in massive quantities disrupted internationalised financial markets, created upheaval in the economic life of nations, and destabilised political and institutional regimes. Equally damaging side-effects include the destruction of public trust, depressed social morale, disorganisation, and a series of indirect consequences to the health and well-being of the population. Moreover, white-collar crimes distort markets and competition; breed cynicism among citizens; undermine the rule of law; damage government legitimacy and corrode the integrity of the private sector.[148]

Furthermore, what Sharon Eicher points out with reference to corruption[149] is also applicable to frauds in the sense that they too worsen inequality, hinder economic development, destroy the level playing field among market participants and distort market outcomes.

When corporations play a structural role in the economy, white-collar crimes gravely affect collective wealth by damaging private finances on a large scale, thus eliminating important sources of production. Because of the magnitude of the damage, infringements contemplated in national legislations as simple property crimes not only harm their numerous victims but also affect the economy as a whole. But the most damaging effect of business crimes is that they create distrust toward the system and its healthy components.[150] Large-scale financial

'The Concept of White Collar Crime in Law and Legal Theory' (2004) 8 *Buffalo Criminal Law Review* 101, 104. White-collar crimes are also called indistinctly, business, economic and financial crimes.

[146] DO Friedrichs, 'White-Collar Crime in a Postmodern, Globalized World' in HN Pontell and G Geis (eds), *International Handbook on White Collar And Corporate Crime* (Boston, MA, Springer Verlag, 2007) 176.

[147] P Grabosky, 'Globalization and White-Collar Crime' in S Simpson and D Weisburd (eds), *The Criminology of White-Collar Crime* (New York, Springer, 2009) 131 ff.

[148] B Heinemann, Jr and F Heimann, 'The Long War against Corruption' *Foreign Affairs* (May/June 2006), cited by S Eicher, 'Introduction: What Corruption is and Why it Matters' in S Eicher (ed), *Corruption in International Business: The Challenge of Cultural and Legal Diversity* (Burlington, VT, Gower, 2009) 12.

[149] Eicher, *Corruption in International Business* (n 148) 12 and 13.

[150] E Sutherland, *White Collar Crime* (New York, Holt, Reinhardt & Winston, 1949) 13 underscores that the most important damage resulting from white-collar crime is the one caused in social relations by destroying trust, depressing social morale and producing disorganisation.

crimes can shake the confidence of global markets.[151] The very magnitude of their damage is measured 'by its injury to public trust, the vital sapping of the economy'.[152]

Securities frauds were associated with these financial cataclysms since the times of the South Sea Bubble.[153] A considerable number of people were ruined by the collapse of the South Sea Company's shares, and the national economy was greatly reduced as a result. The founders of the scheme engaged in insider trading, using their advance knowledge of when national debt was to be consolidated to make large profits from purchasing debt in advance. Huge bribes were given to politicians to support the Acts of Parliament necessary for the scheme.[154] Company money was used to deal in its own shares. Selected individuals purchasing shares were given loans backed by those same shares to spend on purchasing more shares. The expectation of vast wealth from trade with South America was used to encourage the public to purchase shares, despite the limited likelihood this would ever happen. The only significant trade that did take place was in slaves, but the company failed to manage this profitably.[155]

Catastrophic financial crimes have led to legislation aimed at the refinement of corporate governance and its reinforcement with reinvigorated criminal sanctions. The internationalisation of the new corporate governance is an important ingredient of modern anti-fraud policies.

However deleterious, financial crimes have traditionally been disregarded, dismissed, underestimated or viewed as professional risk-taking, and their penalties tended not to be stigmatising. They historically received less punishment than the ones reserved for the crimes committed by the 'dangerous classes',[156] be it against persons or property. The motivation of business criminals is influenced by a society galvanised by the guiding idea of overriding economic progress.[157] In 1901, Laschi wrote that an 'undefined feeling of complicity lead the public

[151] Grabosky, 'Globalization and White-Collar Crime' (n 147) 133 ff.

[152] E Rotman, *Los Fraudes al Comercio y a la Industria* (Buenos Aires, Abeledo-Perrot, 1974) 30.

[153] The South Sea Company was founded in 1711 as a joint-stock company (corporation with transferable shares) to relieve the government of its burdensome unsecured public debt. The £9 million worth of unfounded government securities were to be exchanged compulsorily for shares at par of the South Sea Company. By an Act of Parliament this company obtained the monopoly of England's trade with Spanish colonies in the West Indies and South America. In addition to this monopoly, the company was guaranteed by state an annual payment from the Exchequer of 6% on the debt taken over. See J Carswell, *The South Sea Bubble* (Stanford, CA, Stanford University Press, 1960) 54.

[154] R Dale, *The First Crash: Lessons From The South Sea Bubble* (Princeton, NJ, Princeton University Press, 2004) 149–52.

[155] ibid, 49.

[156] Sociologists and criminologists took this expression from CL Brace, *The Dangerous Classes of New York* (New York, Wynkoop & Hallenbeck, 1872).

[157] Rotman, 'La Criminalidad Financiera en el Siglo XIX' (n 139) 231.

opinion to admire, approve, and absolve the great financial adventurers'.[158] Similarly, Marc Ancel affirmed that public opinion 'tolerates economic crimes and tends to admire the perpetrators. Even the victim seems to encourage and even provoke the offense.'[159] Such responses are captured by the comment made by a fraudster to Lombroso, 'the world of business fever that pushes us to deceive, also pushes our victims to be deceived'.[160] Robert K Merton explains how the 'reluctant admiration expressed frequently in private and not seldom publicly, of these "shrewd, smart, and successful" men is a product of a cultural structure in which the sacrosanct goal virtually consecrates the means'.[161]

In 1975, Michel Foucault viewed the criminal justice system as a mechanism devised not to eliminate crimes but to manage them in a socially differential way by emphasising the crimes of the poor and concealing the illegalities of the powerful.[162] Delmas-Marty suggests that Foucault's vision was reinforced by economic and financial globalisation in which the criminal risk 'becomes part of the totality of business risks, morally tolerated and without bringing about the stigmatization that characterized common criminality'.[163] She considers that the long-standing tolerance towards white-collar criminals is buttressed today by codes of conduct, peer evaluations and other forms of self-regulation, because these allow business-related misdeeds to remain contained within the bounds of the business community and resolved by its own players.[164]

This situation significantly changed, however, when in response to globalisation, the world market recycled criminal law as an instrument to address dangerous imbalances among countries that compete in the world market. In contrast with the traditional attitude that dismissed business-related crimes, world trade now requires the use of criminal law to guarantee equality among competitors. Delmas-Marty contends that even though the differential management of illegalities exposed by Foucault still might be true at the national level, the world

[158] R Laschi, *Le crime financier dans la sociologie criminelle l'histoire et le droit* (Paris, Masson et Cie. Éditeurs, 1901) 107. In this respect, La Bruyère said, 'if the financier fails, the nobleman says about him – he is a bourgeois, a nobody, a shameless person – but if he is successful, they offer him the hand of their daughters': J de la Bruyère, *Les Caractères* (Paris, Ed Garnier, 1960) 160.

[159] Marc Ancel, Preface to Enrique Aftalion, *Derecho Penal Economico* Buenos Aires: Abeledo-Perrot (1959) 11.

[160] Laschi, *Le crime financier* (n 158) 113. D Mills and R Weisberg, 'Corrupting the Harm Requirement in White Collar Crime' (2008) 60 *Stanford Law Review* 1345, 1375, point out that the victim of corporate crime can be seen as a cohort of the perpetrator who ended up on the wrong end of the deal.

[161] RK Merton, *Social Theory and Social Structure* (New York, The Free Press, 1968) 196.

[162] M Foucault, *Discipline and Punish: The Birth of the Prison* (New York, Vintage Books, 1979) 89.

[163] Delmas-Marty, 'Aplanir le terrain de jeu' (n 15) 735.

[164] ibid. Compare, however, with Sieber, who points out that soft-law mechanisms for harmonising law led to a higher degree of harmonisation, and favour implementation and enforcement devices: Sieber, 'The Forces Behind the Harmonization of Criminal Law' (n 74) 408.

market requires the criminalisation of certain behaviours in order to level the playing field among market participants.[165] This phenomenon is visible through the numerous countries that compete today in the prosecution or otherwise targeting of corporations and individuals involved in foreign corrupt practices and in the astronomical financial penalties[166] and disgorgement amounts exacted from the perpetrators.

[165] Delmas-Marty, 'Aplanir le terrain de jeu' (n 15) 735.

[166] These penalties have been considered insufficient, however. DD Stevenson and NJ Wagoner, 'FCPA Sanctions: Too Big to Debar?' (2011) 80 *Fordham Law Review* 775, 820, express that 'despite the magnitude of recent fines and penalties for FCPA violations, these sanctions represent a tiny fraction of the potential revenue available from lucrative government contracts'. T Krever, 'Curbing Corruption: the Efficacy of the Foreign Corrupt Practices Act' (2007) 33 *North Carolina Journal of International Law and Commercial Regulation* 83, 102, points out that 'when the largest penalty ever imposed for foreign bribery is only 28.5 million dollars, large corporations may still consider bribery a prudent business practice and fines a worthwhile risk'. M Kohler, 'The Façade of FCPA Enforcement' (2010) 41 *Georgetown Journal of International Law* 907, indicates that the FCPA simply means what the DOJ and SEC say it means and that '"FCPA law" largely develops through privately-negotiated agreements, subject to little or no judicial scrutiny'.

2

The Internationalisation of Securities Fraud-Related Criminal Law in General

I. Introduction

The internationalisation of securities markets spurred a considerable increase in the frequency and magnitude of securities frauds. As a response to this challenge, the criminal law protection of securities markets also internationalised.

Before addressing the process of legal internationalisation, this chapter will begin by examining the internationalisation of securities' markets as a social, economic and technological phenomenon. Since the 1980s, national borders became increasingly permeable to capital flows as national restrictions were gradually relaxed. Considerably more investors gained access to foreign securities and more issuers could raise equity capital in the major stock markets in the US and Europe.[1] Indicators of such internationalisation, according to Faure and Leger, are cross listing of securities,[2] cross country hedging[3] and portfolio diversification, open national stock markets and 'passing the book'.[4]

Stock markets have substantially changed since the end of the twentieth century. Janet Austin indicates that competition between markets increased the volume and variety of trading to the point that securities markets today bear little resemblance to the stock exchanges that operated up until the 1970s and 1980s

[1] MG Faure and C Leger, 'The Directive on Criminal Sanctions for Market Abuse: A Move Towards Harmonizing Insider Trading Criminal Law' (2015) 9 *Brooklyn Journal of Corporate, Financial & Commercial Law* 387, 412.

[2] According to Faure and Leger (ibid, fn 133), 'Cross-listing means that a company incorporated in one country lists its securities on an exchange in another country.'

[3] According to the American website Investopedia.com, 'cross hedging is when one hedges a position by investing in two positively correlated securities or securities that have similar price movements. The investor takes opposing positions in each investment in an attempt to reduce the risk of holding just one of the securities.'

[4] According to the internet-based CR Harvey's *Hyper textual Financial Glossary* (2011): Cross-national portfolio investment is 'the degree to which investors of a country buy securities listed in another country'. 'Passing the book' is 'the process of transferring responsibility for a brokerage firm's trading account from one office to another around the world in order to benefit from trading 24 hours a day'.

mostly within an environment defined by national borders.[5] Likewise, Eric Chafee points out that 'in recent years the world's capital markets have experienced a dramatic transformation as they have shifted from being national or regional in nature to being global',[6] and that the emergence of global capital markets has eroded the influence of the US on other nations' capital markets and systems of securities regulations.[7] After the 1970s, institutions became the main investors, growing in size and number at a breath-taking pace. Government provisions for retirement declined, pressing individuals to provide for their own retirement, frequently through mutual funds.[8] Their competition led to the abandonment of old, anti-competitive practices of traditional exchanges such as fixed commissions and restrictive membership requirements with the consequent reduction of brokerage fees.[9] Moreover, dramatic progress in communication and trading technology, including the movement from trading floors to screen trading systems, allowed the expansion of electronic trading.[10] Corporations were no longer bound to issue or list their securities on exchanges to which they were geographically connected, but they were able instead to look for capital or to trade in any part of the world.[11]

The need to protect the efficiency as well as the integrity of financial markets demanded the use of criminal sanctions for the most serious violations. Austin points out that protecting market integrity encompasses, at a minimum, the elimination of dishonest practices such as market manipulation and insider trading.[12] Market integrity is crucial for the promotion of investment, which is, in turn, 'important for the economic development of a country'.[13]

[5] J Austin, 'Protecting Market Integrity in an Era of Fragmentation and Cross-Border Trading' (2014) 46:1 *Ottawa Law Review* 25, 30.

[6] EC Chafee, 'Finishing the Race to the Bottom: an Argument for the Harmonization and Centralization of International Securities Law' (2012) 40 *Seton Hall Law Review* 1581, 1586.

[7] ibid, 1587.

[8] Austin, 'Protecting Market Integrity' (n 5) 30.

[9] ibid, 31. See also MB Fox, LR Glosten and GV Rauterberg, 'The New Stock Market: Sense and Nonsense' (2015) 65(2) *Duke Law Journal* 1, who point out that 'how the stocks are traded in the United States has been totally transformed. Gone are the dealers on NASDAQ and the specialists at the NYSE. Instead, a company stock can be traded today on up to sixty competing venues where a computer matches incoming orders. A majority of quotes are now posted by high frequency traders (HFT) making them the preponderant source of liquidity in the new market.'

[10] Austin, 'Protecting Market Integrity' (n 5) 31. See also JF Lermettre, 'Quel Futur pour l'Industrie Boursière?: Analyse d'un Processus de Transformation' *Innovations* 2009/2 No 30, 157, who indicates that after the end of the 1980s organised financial markets were affected by three phenomena: first they saw their activity and volume grow; next, the main American and European stock markets undertook a process of concentration; and, third, 'new actors appeared with the creation of electronic markets by banking consortiums and big market operators'.

[11] Austin, 'Protecting Market Integrity' (n 5) 31.

[12] ibid, 28.

[13] ibid.

The internationalisation of securities fraud-related criminal law takes place through different forms: extraterritorial application of national law[14] diffusion of the American legal model;[15] EU directives and regulations;[16] legislative convergence; as well as informal international cooperation of securities supervisory national authorities within the heart of the International Organization of Securities Commissions (IOSCO).[17] This institution has elaborated minimum standards that, in spite of being non-binding, have experienced widespread implementation by its members.[18]

Moreover, as D'Alessandro points out, 'the real guarantee of the efficiency of financial markets and of the protection of minority shareholders goes mainly through the reinforcement of the powers of the supervisory authorities'.[19] The globalisation of the economy and the main distinctive characteristic of today's evolution of markets, necessarily produces a continuous confrontation between various forms of market regulation, including the resort to criminal law, traditionally refractory to sharing any field under the power of the legislator. The recommendations, communications and guidelines elaborated by international economic organisations, under the form of 'soft law' have repercussions on national systems in the form of 'hard law'.[20]

The stock markets of New York and London today represent an obligatory point of reference for all the economic systems of the world. For this reason, D'Alessandro takes especially into account the American and British legal orders in his research on the criminal law protection of financial markets, particularly on the discipline regulating the supervisory authorities. These legal orders operate on the financial markets as a useful point of comparison given that they govern the more complex and advanced systems of the world and represent an ideal model even for the European community legislator, as well as an inspiration for the regulation and sanctioning of the phenomenon of market abuse.[21]

[14] See ch 1, section II.

[15] See ch 1, section III.

[16] See ch 1, section IV.

[17] C Brummer, *Soft Law and the Global Financial System: Rule Making in the 21st Century* (New York, Cambridge University Press, 2012) 77, explains with respect to the origins of IOSCO that 'as financial globalization enabled greater mobility of fraudsters, authorities wanted to ensure both robust (and common) approaches to securities regulation and sufficient cooperation to enforce national rules when criminals, evidence and witnesses were in other countries', and how IOSCO expanded from a Western hemispheric coordinator to include 50 other countries to the point that today this soft law organisation facilitating enforcement cooperation has near 150 members (ibid, 78).

[18] U Sieber, 'Rechtliche Ordnug in einer Globalen Welt' (2010) 41 *Rechtstheore* 159.

[19] F D'Alessandro, *Regolatori del Mercato, Enforcement e Sistema Penale* (Turin, Giappichelli Editori, 2014) 2.

[20] ibid, 3.

[21] ibid, 4.

II. Securities Fraud as a Criminal Offence

A. The Concept of 'Securities'

To address the internationalisation of securities fraud-related criminal law, it is first necessary to define securities fraud as a criminal offence. To do so, the first step is to explain the meaning of the term 'securities'. The 1933 Securities Act and the 1934 Securities and Exchange Act do not actually define it but enumerate an open list of instruments, including some well-known terms such as 'note', 'stock', 'bond' and 'debenture', as well as others that are not as broadly known, extending the list to 'any interest or instrument commonly known as a "security"'.[22]

Justice Jackson considered that the definition of the term 'securities' under the Securities Act is not exhaustive. He concludes that in general, the term 'security' refers to those instruments 'in which there is common trading for speculation or investment'.[23] Further, in utilising the legislative intent as the method to interpret the Securities Act, he concludes that besides the terms contained in the Securities Act, the statutory definition should be read to include 'novel, uncommon, or irregular devices … if it be proved as [a] matter of fact that they were widely offered or dealt in under terms or courses of dealing which established their character in commerce as "investment contracts" or as "any interest or instrument commonly known as a security"'.[24]

[22] According to the Securities Act 1933, 15 USC, s 77a, a security is 'Any note, stock, treasury stock, security future, security-based swap, bond, debenture, evidence of indebtedness, certificate of interest or participation in any profit-sharing agreement, collateral-trust certificate, preorganization certificate or subscription, transferable share, investment contract, voting-trust certificate, certificate of deposit for a security, fractional undivided interest in oil, gas, or other mineral rights, any put, call, straddle, option, or privilege on any security, certificate of deposit, or group or index of securities (including any interest therein or based on the value thereof), or any put, call, straddle, option, or privilege entered into on a national securities exchange relating to foreign currency, or, in general, any interest or instrument commonly known as a "security", or any certificate of interest or participation in, temporary or interim certificate for, receipt for, guarantee of, or warrant or right to subscribe to or purchase, any of the foregoing.' According to the Securities and Exchange Act 1934, 15 USC, s 78a, a security is 'Any note, stock, treasury stock, security future, security-based swap, bond, debenture, certificate of interest or participation in any profit-sharing agreement or in any oil, gas, or other mineral royalty or lease, any collateral-trust certificate, preorganization certificate or subscription, transferable share, investment contract, voting- trust certificate, certificate of deposit for a security, any put, call, straddle, option, or privilege on any security, certificate of deposit, or group or index of securities (including any interest therein or based on the value thereof), or any put, call, straddle, option, or privilege entered into on a national securities exchange relating to foreign currency, or in general, any instrument commonly known as a "security"; or any certificate of interest or participation in, temporary or interim certificate for, receipt for, or warrant or right to subscribe to or purchase, any of the foregoing; but shall not include currency or any note, draft, bill of exchange, or banker's acceptance which has a maturity at the time of issuance of not exceeding nine months, exclusive of days of grace, or any renewal thereof the maturity of which is likewise limited.'

[23] *Securities and Exchange Commission v CM Joiner Leasing Corporation*, 320 US 344, 351 (1943).

[24] ibid.

B. The Concept of 'Securities Fraud' in American Law

Having addressed the meaning of 'securities', the next step is to determine what 'securities frauds' actually are. This requires an inquiry into the federal statutes that regulate such frauds and into their interpretation. First, it is crucial to understand the function of the Securities and Exchange Commission (SEC)[25] in enforcing the legislation against market abuse.[26] Its historical background is represented by the stock market crash of 1929 and the consequent great depression that persisted until the early 1940s, when the development of the war industry to provide for American military needs to fight the Second World War brought about a revitalisation of the economy. Among the measures taken by President Franklin Delano Roosevelt to bring back confidence and trust to investors were to prompt Congress to enact first the Securities Act of 1933,[27] followed by the Securities and Exchange Act of 1934. The task to protect investors against market abuse begins with Section 10(b) of the Securities and Exchange Act authorising the SEC to establish rules necessary for the protection of investors as follows:

> [I]t shall be unlawful for any person, directly or indirectly, by the use of any means or instrumentality of interstate commerce or of the mails, or of any facility of any national securities exchange … (b) To use or employ, in connection with the purchase or sale of any security registered on a national securities exchange or any security not so registered, or any securities-based swap agreement any manipulative or deceptive device or contrivance in contravention of such rules and regulations as the Commission may prescribe as necessary or appropriate in the public interest or for the protection of investors.[28]

This statutory text is not self-executing and does not in itself prohibit anything.[29] It only grants the SEC rulemaking authority to prohibit the invention of 'any other cunning devices'[30] besides those already prohibited. As shown as follows, a criminal violation of Section 10(b) presupposes a violation of Rule 10b-5.

[25] Section 4a of the 1934 Securities and Exchange Act establishes the SEC 'to be composed by five commissioners to be appointed by the President with the advice and consent of the Senate'. It also secures the professional independence of commissioners by precluding them to 'engage in in any other business, vocation, or employment than that as serving as commissioner, nor shall any commissioner participate, directly or indirectly, in any stock-market operations or transactions of a character subject to regulation by the Commission'. The SEC has its central office in Washington and has 11 Regional Offices distributed throughout the United States territory.

[26] See JR Doty, 'The Role of the Securities and Exchange Commission in an Internationalized Marketplace' (1992) 60 *Fordham Law Review* 77.

[27] The Securities Act of 1933, under the title 'truth in securities law', aims both at requiring the possibly maximum information from the issuer offering new securities and prohibiting false and misleading information or any fraud connected with the offer of securities to the market.

[28] 15 USC, s 78(b).

[29] SM Bainbridge, *Insider Trading Law and Policy* (St Paul, MI, West Academic, Foundation Press, 2014) 26.

[30] Thomas Corcoran, member of President Roosevelt's administration, quoted by Bainbridge (ibid).

The SEC issued Rule 10b-5 in 1942 as a regulation to implement the will of Congress under Section 10(b) in the following terms:

> It shall be unlawful for any person, directly or indirectly, by the use of any means or instrumentality of interstate commerce, or of the mails or of any facility of any national securities exchange,
>
> (a) To employ any device, scheme, or artifice to defraud,
> (b) To make any untrue statement of a material fact or to omit to state a material fact necessary in order to make the statements made, in the light of the circumstances under which they were made, not misleading, or
> (c) To engage in any act, practice, or course of business which operates or would operate as a fraud or deceit upon any person, in connection with the purchase or sale of any security.[31]

This Rule prohibits not only false statements of fact or omissions that make truthful affirmative statements misleading, but also schemes and artifices to defraud and acts or practices that operate as frauds or deceit.

The United States Supreme Court in *Ernst & Ernst v Hochfelder*[32] gave precedence to Section 10(b) of the Exchange Act over Rule 10b-5 on the basis that an administrative rule could not exceed the power granted to the SEC by Congress under Section 23.[33] This opinion was applied in *Stoneridge Investment Partners LLC v Scientific Atlanta, Inc*, in which the Supreme Court rejected scheme liability[34] under Rule 10b-5.

C. Criminal Securities Fraud in American Law

Under Section 32(a) of the Exchange Act, the Department of Justice may bring criminal actions when the securities frauds involve a wilful violation of Rule 10b-5 either at its own initiative or at the request of the SEC as authorised by Section 21(d)(1) of the Exchange Act. The Act empowers the SEC not only to regulate the area, but also to prosecute all violations and impose civil or administrative

[31] 17 CFR 240.10b-5.

[32] *Ernst & Ernst v Hochfelder*, 425 US 185 (1976).

[33] SEC, s 23(a)(1). 'The Commission, the Board of Governors of the Federal Reserve System, and the other agencies enumerated in section 3(a)(34) of this title shall each have power to make such rules and regulations as may be necessary or appropriate to implement the provisions of this title for which they are responsible or for the execution of the functions vested in them by this title, and may for such purposes classify persons, securities, transactions, statements, applications, reports, and other matters within their respective jurisdictions, and prescribe greater, lesser, or different requirements for different classes thereof. No provision of this title imposing any liability shall apply to any act done or omitted in good faith in conformity with a rule, regulation, or order of the Commission, the Board of Governors of the Federal Reserve System, other agency enumerated in section 3(a)(34) of this title, or any self-regulatory organization, notwithstanding that such rule, regulation, or order may thereafter be amended or rescinded or determined by judicial or other authority to be invalid for any reason.'

[34] Scheme liability derives from the Rule 10b-5 prohibition to employ any device, scheme or artifice to defraud.

sanctions in order to respond to the challenges posed by a dynamic market. In addition, the Exchange Act includes certain violations such as accepting funds from security-based swap customers without registering as broker or dealer (Section 78c-5); effecting transactions on unregistered exchange (Section 78e); trading unregistered securities on exchange (Section 78f(h)); prohibiting exchange member's trading on exchange for own account (Section 78k-1(b)); and acting as a broker or dealer without registration (Section 78o(a)).

There are criminal provisions both in the Securities Act and in the Securities and Exchange Act. Section 24 of the 1933 Securities Act prescribes that:

> Any person who willfully violates any of the provisions of this title, or the rules and regulations promulgated by the Commission under authority thereof, or any person who willfully in a registration statement filed under this title, makes any untrue statement of a material fact or omits to state any material fact required to be stated therein or necessary to make the statements therein not misleading, shall upon conviction be fined not more than $10,000 or imprisoned not more than five years, or both.

Section 32 (a) of the Securities and Exchange Act provides that:

> Any person who willfully violates any provision of this title (other than section 30a), or any rule or regulation thereunder the violation of which is made unlawful or the observance of which is required under the terms of this title, or any person who willfully and knowingly makes, or causes to be made, any statement in any application, report, or document required to be filed under this title or any rule or regulation thereunder or under- taking contained in a registration statement as provided in sub- section (d) of section 15 of this title, or by any self-regulatory organization in connection with an application for membership or participation therein or to become associated with a member thereof, which statement was false or misleading with respect to any material fact, shall upon conviction be fined not more than $5,000,000, or imprisoned not more than 20 years, or both, except that when such person is a person other than a natural person, a fine not exceeding $25,000,000 may be imposed; but no person shall be subject to imprisonment under this section for the violation of any rule or regulation if he proves that he had no knowledge of such rule or regulation.

III. Critical Statutory Interpretation

A. Shortcomings of American Legal Scholarship in the Field of Criminal Securities Frauds

Samuel Buell criticises the doctrinal failure to define the notion of fraud, let alone to determine what securities frauds are and, more specifically, to clarify when such frauds turn out to be criminal.[35] He further emphasises the paucity of the law on

[35] SW Buell, 'What is Securities Frauds?' (2011) 61(3) *Duke Law Journal* 511, 555.

securities frauds to specify the conditions of fault and harm that makes imprisonment and other forms of criminal punishment available.[36] After underscoring the centrality of the mental state to understand securities fraud, Buell lists 12 significant law review articles that fail to develop 'a comprehensive analysis of the concepts of fraud and securities fraud as routes to rethinking and reforming the doctrine across the fields of criminal, regulatory and private civil liability'.[37] Throughout his thorough analysis of American law, Buell denounces that the notion of 'fraud' in securities remains undefined, that courts are not clear enough about the mens rea of securities fraud, and that the legal system has put in place a massive sanctioning machinery without identifying its purpose and objectives, making it impossible to measure its outcomes.[38] Other American scholars express similar opinions about insufficiencies of the American legal system to build a coherent doctrine to characterise criminal frauds. Jeremy Miller points out 'that severe confusion as to mens rea is the rule – not the exception in every jurisdiction',[39] and Michael L Siegel denounces the massive confusion related to the interpretation of the phrase mens rea and undertakes a review of the multiple and conflicting interpretations of this key phrase, which determines whether the actor has committed a securities-related offence or not.[40]

A comparative perspective provides American scholarship with the intellectual instrument to better understand how the statute criminalises behaviour otherwise considered to be a mere civil or administrative wrong.

B. The Use of Comparative Criminal Law to Rethink and Reform the Doctrine of Criminal Liability in American Securities Law

Resorting to foreign law to gain insight into the most complex issues surrounding the theory of the criminal offence is justified by the present paucity of categorisations of the Anglo-American doctrine and jurisprudence. The origin of what can be called an internationalisation of scholarship[41] in the civil law world can be traced to the German model. The German model consists of a set of abstract criminal

[36] ibid, 519.

[37] ibid, 525, fn 28.

[38] ibid, 517.

[39] JM Miller, 'Mens Rea Quagmire: The Conscience or Consciousness of the Criminal Law?' (2001) 29 *Western State University Law Review* 21, 56.

[40] ML Seigel, 'Bringing Coherence to Mens Rea Analysis for Securities-related Offenses' 2006 *Wisconsin Law Review* (2006) 1563, 1564.

[41] F Von Liszt, 'Zur Einführung: Rückblick und Zukunftspläne' in F Von Liszt (ed), *Das Strafrecht Der Staten Europas, Im Auftrag der Kriminalistischen Vereignung* (Berlin, Otto Liebmann, 1894) xxiv; HJ Hirsch, 'Internationaliesierung des Strafrechts und Strafrechtswissenschaft' (2004) 116 *Zeitschrif für die gesamte Strafrechtswissenschsaft* 835, 839–40; S Kesper Biermann and P Overath (eds), *Die Internationalisierung von Strafrechtswissenschaft und Kriminalpolitik (1870–1930)* (Berlin, Berliner Wissenschafts-Verlag, 2007).

law categories adopted by most of Continental Europe, Latin America and diverse parts of the world. This model is based on a comprehensive and consistent methodology that 'lends itself to application to any system of criminal law regardless of its legislative foundations'.[42]

Traditionally, German jurisprudence is regarded as a science that shares the scientific status of the social and behavioural sciences.[43] Indeed, a prominent Spanish criminal law scholar considers the German system of criminal law to be an achievement of the human sciences.[44]

This is all the more promising given the doctrinal confusion existing within the American scholarly commentaries to resolve issues presented by the interpretation of the criminal law side of securities fraud.

Comparison with the civil law[45] criminal law system, based on the German model, can prove to be an arsenal of possible solutions to fill the existing gaps of American law in the field of criminal securities fraud.

This comparative task is undertaken in this book to warrant the extraterritorial criminal enforcement of US law on securities fraud, specifically using the notion of blanket criminal laws and in the interpretation of the adverb 'willfully' in Section 30(a) of the Securities Exchange Act.[46] Furthermore, comparative criminal law will be used to explain the internationalisation of US criminal securities fraud through diffusion and/or legislative convergence as illustrated in the sections devoted to Swiss, French, Italian and German laws.

As an introductory matter, it is important to examine how different legal systems address the tension existing between the peculiar demand for flexibility in the area of business crimes and the principle of legality.[47]

[42] F Muñoz Conde, '"Rethinking" the Universal Structure of Criminal Law' (2004) 39 *Tulsa Law Review* 941.

[43] MD Dubber, 'The Promise of German Criminal Law: A Science of Crime and Punishment' (2005) 6 *German Law Journal* 1049, 1050–51.

[44] E Gimbernat Ordeig, 'Sind die bisherigen dogmatischen Grunderfordernisse eines Allgemeinen Teils geeignet, dem heutigen Stand der Kriminalität, der Strafzumessung und des Sanktionensystems zu genügen?' in HJ Hirsch (ed), *Krise des Strafrechts und der Kriminalwisensschaften?* (Berlin, Duncker & Humblot, 2000) 151, 165.

[45] The expression 'civil law' is used to demarcate those systems of law derived from Roman law, including private and public law, and that are mainly located in Western Europe and Latin America but can be also found in numerous other parts of the world. Among other sources, see HJ Berman and WR Greiner, *The Nature and Functions of Law* (New York, Foundation Press, 1980) 571–72.

[46] The notion of blanket criminal norms is explained in ch 3, section V.B, specifically in the text corresponding to nn 140 to 146. The application of the categories drawn from the German criminal law model to the interpretation of the word 'willfulness' in s 30(a) of the Securities Exchange Act is developed in ch 3, section V.C.

[47] According to the principle of legality, *stricto sensu*, the law (statute) is the only source of criminal law and nobody can be punished without a law (statute) enacted before the facts that have motivated the prosecution. It is both a constitutional safeguard and a condition for the effectiveness of criminal sanctions. In the US, this principle, often expressed as *nullum crimen, nulla poena sine praevia lege*, is mentioned by criminal law scholarship as a fundamental one. However, the US Constitution limits its formulation to the prohibition of *ex post facto* laws and to the prohibition of vague criminal norms,

In the US, the need to adapt criminal norms to the dynamism of economic life and to the creativity of white-collar offenders led Congress through the Exchange Act to assign the SEC broad regulatory powers to the point that through Rule 10b-5 courts generated 'a judicial oak which has grown from little more than a legislative acorn'.[48] Furthermore, in the particular case of the prohibition of insider trading, the most iconic form of securities fraud, a prominent specialist considers it to be the product of a federal common law.[49]

Although the troubling legislative technique of the Exchange Act's activating Rule 10b-5 defies a strict interpretation of the principle of legality it has survived earlier scholarly attacks.[50]

In the civil law world, a large number of countries following the German model have developed a specialised legislative technique to enact business-related criminal legislation compatible with the principle of legality.[51]

precluded by the due process clause of the 5th Amendment. Due process requires that a criminal statute be declared void when it is so vague that 'men of common intelligence must necessarily guess at its meaning and differ as to its application' (*Connally v General Construction Co* 269 US 385, 391 (1926)). There is no litmus paper test to determine whether a criminal statute is void for vagueness. The questions commonly considered by the Supreme Court to decide on this issue are: (1) Does the statute in question give fair notice to those persons potentially subject to it? (2) Does it adequately guard against arbitrary and discriminatory enforcement? (3) Does it provide sufficient breathing space for First Amendment rights?

[48] US Supreme Court Chief Justice William Rehnquist in *Blue Chip Stamps v Man*or *Drug Stores*, 421 US 723, 737 (1975).

[49] Bainbridge, *Insider Trading Law and Policy* (n 29) 29, underscores that 'the modern insider trading prohibition … is a creature of SEC administrative actions and judicial opinions, only loosely tied to the statutory language and its legislative history'. He further emphasises the almost non-existent minuscule legislative acorn on which rests the judicial oak. However, the legislative acorn is crucial given that to create federal offences by the judiciary is at odds with *United States v Hudson and Goodwin*, 7 Cranch 32 (1812). The US Supreme Court does not base its decision on the principle of legality but on the rejection of federal judicial power to recognise common law crimes. This decision was contested and in fact federal courts continued to hold significant common law powers and continued to make law in criminal cases. See RH Fallon, JF Manning, DJ Melzer and DL Shapiro, *Hart and Wechsler, The Federal Courts And The Federal System* (New York, Foundation Press, 2009) 610 ff. After *United Sates v Coolidge*, 14 US.(1 Wheat) 415 (1816), however, non-statutory prosecutions ended. At the state level common law crimes are today a relic of the past and only conceivable in the form of misdemeanours.

[50] See DJ Bacastow, 'Due Process and Criminal Penalties under Rule 10b-5: the Unconstitutionality and Inefficiency of Criminal Prosecutions for Insider Trading' (1982) 73 *Journal of Criminal Law & Criminology* 96. SB Duke, in 'Legality in the Second Circuit' (1983) 49 *Brooklyn Law Review* 911, emphasised (at 931) that 'the quintessential purpose of criminal law is to ceremonialize and to solidify the core values of society. It loses its moral force, and hence undermines its primary purpose, when those values are not democratically determined. There is little reason to respect judge-made criminal law and no per se basis to condemn those who are caught up in it.'

[51] This principle often attains constitutional rank. For example, s 103(2) of the Basic Law for the Federal German Republic establishes that 'An act may be punished only if it was defined by a law as a criminal offence before the act was committed.' Art 9(3) of the Spanish Constitution prescribes that the Constitution guarantees the principle of legality and Art 25(1) 'No one may be convicted or sentenced for actions or omissions which when committed did not constitute a criminal offence, misdemeanor or administrative offence under the law then in force.' The principle of legality is stated in modern times through the Latin phrase *nullum crimen, nulla poena sine previa lege*. It is derived from the Magna Carta (1215). After a long period of elaboration, it was subdivided as: (a) *Nullum crime sine lege scripta*, this means that criminal laws must be written. Custom is thus excluded as a source of law; (b) *Nullum*

Klaus Tiedemann, one of the most prominent German criminal law scholars and a pioneer in building business-related criminal law as a scientific discipline, points out the particularities of this special branch of the law. The main characteristics of these offences are the use of broad general clauses to describe and cover ever-changing varieties of business-related criminal behaviours; the protection of supra-individual or collective social values (*Rechtsgut*),[52] such as the integrity of capital markets, beyond the individual property interests of the direct victims; the punishment of behaviours for their mere endangerment of the values protected by the respective norms including those in which the actual endangerment does not need to be proven (offences of abstract endangerment); and, most important, the use of blanket criminal offences as characterised in depth in Chapter 3, section III.B of this book.

Tiedemann points out that blanket criminal offences and their incorporation by reference of behaviours defined in other statutes or administrative regulations are typical in business-related criminal law.[53] Generally these blanket definitions defer to administrative regulations to provide the description of the penalised behaviour according to changing situations and needs, especially at times of economic emergency and crisis. The legislative statute remains at a very abstract level, while the concrete content of the prohibition or mandate is defined by an administrative regulation and only then is the criminal punishment applicable.[54] The incorporation by reference can also be internal, a legislative technique in which the criminal penalty is established within the same statute that regulates the business-related behaviour.[55] These are called improper blanket laws, which have to be distinguished from what the civil law countries, following the German model, call 'normative elements of the definition' of the criminal offence, as for example the lack of ownership of the property that is taken and carried away in the crime of larceny. These implicit inclusions of value judgments or norms from other legal branches do not raise the constitutional problems of the blanket offences that expressly incorporate external norms by reference.

crimen sine lege praevia, this means to exclude retroactivity or ex post facto laws. In some civil law countries this principle is expressed as a command to apply the law most favourable to the accused; (c) *Nullum crimen sine lege certa*, this means that criminal offences should be clearly defined, not in a vague or uncertain manner. They would otherwise fall under the 'void-for-vagueness' doctrine in the US; (d) *Nullum crimen sine lege stricta*, this means the exclusion of analogy in the application of criminal statutes. Everything that is not strictly forbidden is permitted and cannot constitute a crime.

[52] German criminal law considers the theory of *Rechtsgut* as the basic tenet of criminal law. '*Rechtsgut*' can be defined as the vital interests and values of the individual and society that are protected by criminal law. According to Jescheck and Weigend, the '*Rechstgut*' is the basis for both the structuring and the interpretation of criminal law, it gives sense and purpose to the content of its provisions and plays an essential role in its systematisation. See H-H Jescheck and T Weigend, *Lehrbuch des Strafrechts: Allgemeiner Teil* (Berlin, Duncker & Humblot, 1996) 257.

[53] K Tiedemann, *Wirtschaftsstrafrecht. Einführung und Allgemeiner Teil mit wichtisten Rechtstexten*, 4th edn (Munich, Verlag Franz Vahlen, 2014) 87.

[54] ibid, 87, 88.

[55] ibid.

The use of blanket criminal norms may raise constitutional issues when they infringe upon paragraph 103, Section 2 of the German Basic Law[56] requiring definiteness and certainty in the definitions of criminal offences, inherent in the principles of *nullum crimen sine lege stricta* and *nullum crimen sine lege certa*.[57]

Blanket criminal norms have been challenged before the Federal Constitutional Court when the reading of the principal provision together with the referenced statute or regulation does not provide the sufficient definiteness for a fair warning. Among other examples, Tiedemann mentions paragraph 20a, Section 2 of the Securities Trading Act delegating to the Federal Ministry of Finances the definition of deceptive actions in cases of manipulation of exchange rates and securities. However, as Tiedemann points out, the provision maintained its constitutionality because its contents attained sufficient concretisation through the European Community's Directive on insider dealing and market manipulation of 28 January 2003.[58]

Even though broad concepts and incorporation by reference are typical of business-related criminal law, Jose Hurtado underscores that one cannot infer that the principle of legality should be abandoned or relaxed to the point of rendering it superfluous. 'The legal text, despite its imprecisions constitute always a limit to interpretation.'[59]

[56] ibid, 89 ff.

[57] See n 51.

[58] Tiedemann, *Wirtschaftsstrafrecht* (n 53) 90.

[59] J Hurtado Pozo, 'Droit Pénal Économique: Questions de la Partie Générale' in J Hurtado Pozo and O Thormann (eds), *Droit Pénal Économique* (Zurich, Schultess, 2011) 92.

3

Extraterritorial Application of United States Law

I. Introduction

The extraterritorial application of US law is an elementary form of the internationalised criminal law protection of capital markets. Other forms, such as the diffusion of the American model and harmonisation, are dealt with in Chapter 4, concerning insider trading, and Chapter 5, regarding market manipulation, as the most relevant examples of securities frauds experiencing the aforementioned forms of internationalisation.

In August 2013, the Court of Appeal for the Second Circuit in the case of *United States v Vilar* denied extraterritorial application of the criminal law anti-fraud provisions contained in the Securities Exchange Act. The specific object of this chapter is to criticise this decision and negate its premises.[1]

After delving in depth into the notion of extraterritoriality, this chapter offers a dynamic interpretation of the 1922 Supreme Court's decision in *United States v Bowman*, which is still the governing precedent on the extraterritorial application of criminal laws. Furthermore, it criticises the application of the 2010 Supreme Court's decision in *Morrison v National Australia Bank* to criminal cases and explains the Dodd-Frank Act's failed attempt to overrule it.

Chapter 3 undertakes a detailed analysis of each of *United States v Vilar*'s supporting arguments, using concepts extracted from the German criminal law model to identify some of this decision's significant shortcomings. It begins with a discussion of the extent and significance of the *Bowman* exception to the presumption against extraterritoriality in light of the need to protect the integrity of a delocalised capital market. Next, it interprets section 32(a) of the Securities Exchange Act in accordance with modern developments of criminal law theory. It consequently analyses the significant distinctions between criminal and civil law in contrast with their erroneous equation made by the *Vilar* court. The discussion ultimately leads to a justification of the Securities Exchange Act's extraterritorial enforcement through a contextual and dynamic interpretation of section 32(a),

[1] Most of this chapter is drawn from my article, E Rotman, 'Extraterritorial Criminal Enforcement of Securities Fraud Regulations after United States v. Vilar' (2015) 70 *University of Miami Law Review* 53.

taking into consideration the transnational nature of market integrity and public wealth values protected by this provision.

II. The Crucial Role of Extraterritorial Enforcement of the United States Criminal Law in the Prevention and Repression of Financial Fraud

A. Evolution of the Notion of Extraterritoriality

In the past, extraterritorial application of national criminal laws was very limited.[2] Extraterritoriality grew with the emergence of modern forms of globalisation.[3] In the field of securities laws, the comments to section 416 of the Restatement (Third) of Foreign Relations explain that '[a]s organized securities markets in different states are increasingly connected through electronic and institutional links', territorial factors in the exercise of prescriptive jurisdiction may become less relevant and extraterritorial factors more important.[4]

In early English common law, a court could not hear a case if any of what we currently call 'elements of a crime' occurred outside of England.[5] For example, in 1583, a murder committed on the foreshore came within the exclusive jurisdiction of the criminal Admiralty court only 'because it occurred on the seabed owned, by the Crown under the Royal Prerogative'.[6]

[2] David Hume wrote that Scottish courts 'are not instituted to administer justice over the whole world, but in our country, or a particular district of it only'. D Hume, *Commentaries on the Law of Scotland Respecting Crimes*, vol II (1797) 52, quoted in M Hirst, *Jurisdiction and the Ambit of the Criminal Law* (Oxford, Oxford University Press, 2003) 29. John Austin considered extraterritorial applications of jurisdictional rules 'anomalous cases' in *The Province of Jurisprudence Determined* (London, John Murray, 1832), cited by G Handl, J Zekoll and P Zumbansen, *Beyond Territoriality: Transnational Legal Authority in an Age of Globalism* (Leiden, Martinus Nijhoff Publishers, 2012) 17. In *MacLeod v Attorney-General for New South Wales* [1891] AC 455, 458 (Australia), the court asserted that 'all crime is local' and 'the jurisdiction over the crime belongs to the country where the crime is committed'. With respect to the US, Cedric Ryngaert points out that 'Throughout the history of US law, US courts have time and again pointed out the importance of the territorial principle.' C Ryngaert, *Jurisdiction in International Law* (New York, Oxford University Press, 2008) 59. In their contributions to a book on the harmonisation of criminal law, Mireille Delmas-Marty points out that the right to punish 'is traditionally considered an emblem of national sovereignty', and Mark Pieth expresses that he was astonished that criminal law is developing into one of the driving forces of harmonisation of law, 'even though it was always considered a traditional stronghold of national sovereignty'. M Delmas-Marty, M Pieth and U Sieber, *Les Chemins de l'Harmonisation Pénale/Harmonising Criminal Law* (Paris, Société de Legislation Comparée, 2008) 19 and 225, respectively.

[3] For earlier historical precedents of globalisation, see E Rotman, 'The Globalization of Criminal Violence' (2000) 10(1) *Cornell Journal of Law and Public Policy* 2, 2 ff.

[4] *Restatement (Third) of Foreign Relations Law of the United States* s 416 cmt at 298 (1987).

[5] KS Gallant, 'What Exactly is "Extraterritorial Application" of a Statute?' *Jurist Forum* (28 May 2013) available at ssrn.com/abstract=2271267.

[6] *Lacy's Case* (1583) 74 Eng Rep 246 (KB), cited in RJ Gillis, *Navigational Servitudes: Sources, Applications, Paradigms* (Leiden, Brill-Nijhoff, 2007) 76.

In the US, the notion of extraterritoriality experienced dramatic changes since its early formulation in the 1824 *Appollon* case.[7] According to this decision, a nation is entirely precluded from extending its laws beyond its own borders, 'except so far as regards its own citizens'.[8]

In the present era of globalisation, the exercise of extraterritorial jurisdiction has been deemed inevitable.[9] 'The expansion of commercial and financial interstate links has increased the vulnerability of States to adverse domestic effects of foreign activities.'[10] In the field of securities law, the extraterritorial reach of national law may become necessary when some states set low standards to attract investors, refuse to criminalise certain fraudulent activities such as insider trading, or avoid stringent corporate governance regulations.[11]

There is a certain parallel between the evolution of American law and German law on the subject, especially in light of how these laws' extraterritorial reach expanded from the end of the nineteenth century onwards.

To understand this evolution, I turn to a late nineteenth-century classic text on extraterritoriality from Ernst Beling, one of the most prestigious German scholars of that period.[12] In 1896, extraterritorial questions were limited to the legal status of governments, diplomats, and their propertyships, and certain German representatives abroad.[13] In sharp contrast, Peter Roegele's 2014 book, significantly entitled *German Criminal Law Imperialism*, shows how German criminal law today applies extraterritorially in manifold ways.[14]

Globalisation of crime, the intensification of interstate relations, and the need to protect transnational vital interests and values have determined the continuing expansion of German criminal law beyond its national borders since 1871.[15]

B. Extraterritoriality of Business-Related Criminal Law in a Globalised Economy

Although criminal law, as 'the most parochial of legal disciplines',[16] has traditionally been a stronghold of territoriality, the challenge of transnational business

[7] *The Appollon*, 22 US 9 Wheat 362 (1824).

[8] ibid, 370.This exception was confirmed by J Story, *Commentaries on the Conflict of Laws: Foreign and Domestic, in regards to Contracts, Rights, and Remedies* (Boston, MA, Hilliard, Gray & Co, 1834) 22 (expressly stating that every nation has a right to bind its own citizens by its own laws in every place beyond its boundaries).

[9] See Ryngaert, *Jurisdiction in International Law* (n 2) 187.

[10] ibid.

[11] ibid.

[12] See generally E Beling, *Die Strafrechtliche Bedeutung der Exterritorialität* (Breslau, Scheletter'sche Buchhandlung, 1896).

[13] ibid 169 ff.

[14] See generally P Roegele, *Deutscher Strafrechtsimperialismus: Ein Beitrag zu den völkerrechtlichen Grenzen extraterritorialer Strafgewaltausdehnung* (Hamburg, Verlag Dr Kovac, 2014).

[15] ibid 2 and 236.

[16] MD Dubber, 'Criminal Law in Comparative Context' (2006) 56 *Journal of Legal Education* 433.

crimes in today's interconnected world requires the extraterritorial application of business-related criminal laws as an indispensable condition of their effectiveness.

Globalisation of financial markets, advances in communications and transportation technologies, decreasing relevance of national borders, emergence of computer networks, reduced state authority, increasing cyber finance and offshore banking, and high demand for American securities abroad and vice versa, have increased the potential for transnational criminal securities fraud.

The extraterritorial application of national laws constitutes an immediate response to such challenges. Other forms of internationalisation of business-related criminal law that would presumably eliminate safe havens and prevent securities fraud[17] are: a) international treaties requiring an expanding number of nations to criminalise certain business crimes; b) preventive efforts by a number of international financial institutions, and standard-setting and trans-governmental regulatory networks;[18] and c) 'soft law' harmonisation of national legislations eventually resulting in convergent national business-related criminal law systems.

C. The Pros and Cons of Extraterritorial Enforcement of Business-Related Criminal Law

An inquiry into the normative aspects of extraterritorial enforcement of geographically ambiguous statutes will facilitate the understanding of specific aspects of the *Vilar* decision.

The extraterritorial application of criminal law provisions governing securities fraud raises significant normative issues relating to respect of the sovereignty of other nations and established principles of international law, such as non-intervention, comity and sovereign equality.[19] Also, such extraterritorial application may infringe upon the domestic constitutional principle of separation of powers.[20] Moreover, from the viewpoint of democracy, extraterritorial jurisdiction may impose national laws on foreign legal subjects who did not participate in their enactment.[21]

However, as John C Coffee, Jr points out, curtailments of extraterritoriality, when not expressly mandated by statutory provisions, 'miss much, and the

[17] See Part 1, section I, 'The Concept of Legal Internationalisation'.

[18] See SK Park, 'Guarding the Guardians: The Case for Regulating State Owned Financial Entities in Global Finance' (2014) 16 *University of Pennsylvania Journal of Business Law* 739, 740–56; see also K Raustiala, 'The Architecture of International Cooperation: Transgovernmental Networks and the Future of International Law' (2002) 43 *Virginia Journal of International Law* 1, 28–35.

[19] Ryngaert, *Jurisdiction in International Law* (n 2) 188.

[20] ibid.

[21] ibid.

unfashionable word – "extraterritorial" – cannot be avoided'.[22] He mentions four basic reasons that weigh heavily to support his conclusion: (1) the extreme mobility of major financial institutions and their ability to park abroad their high-risk operations, thus escaping the regulatory reach of their national legal systems; (2) because major financial institutions are 'too interconnected to fail', regulation of systemic risk requires extending regulations beyond domestic financial institutions to their foreign counterparts as well; (3) the preference of some countries to keep 'soft law' standards 'aspirational and ineffable' because they profit from extremely risky unregulated havens; and (4) the assertion of extraterritorial authority by the major financial nations as the best way to spur international bodies to develop a high consensus leading to meaningful 'soft law' standards.[23]

Another set of normative arguments supporting the extraterritorial application of national statutes can be drawn from the customary international law justifications of extraterritoriality, especially from the protective principle. Transnational securities fraud may cause serious damage to the integrity of financial markets, affecting vital economic interests of a nation. Such territorial impact justifies the extraterritorial reach of national laws under international law.

In addition, to support the extraterritoriality of securities fraud-related criminal provisions, it is useful to draw from the area of competition law: the extraterritorial reach of national criminal sanctions 'enables states to protect their domestic market[s] from anti-competitive activities which, while taking place elsewhere, adversely affect the home jurisdiction'.[24] This basic argument can be applied by analogy to the field of securities fraud. Also, here, extraterritoriality adds a deterrent effect by addressing violations unchallenged by the home jurisdiction due to lack of legislation or enforcement powers.[25] As in the case of competition law, 'extraterritoriality of criminal sanctions [for securities law violations] may supplement administrative procedures in other jurisdictions'.[26]

In the area of competition law, the extraterritorial reach of antitrust prohibitions makes a conceptual contribution to the public perception of the need for delivering markets from restrictive practices. In this respect, the extraterritorial application of competition law-related criminal provisions has been praised for its export of 'competition values'.[27] The extraterritorial application of securities, fraud-related criminal provisions may similarly contribute to a global consensus on a

[22] JC Coffee, Jr, 'Extraterritorial Financial Regulation: Why E.T. Can't Come Home' (2014) 99 *Cornell Law Review* 1259, 1260.

[23] ibid, 1260 and 1261.

[24] A Ezrachi and J Kindl, 'Cartels as Criminal? The Long Road from Unilateral Enforcement to International Consensus' in C Beaton-Wells and A Ezrachi (eds), *Criminalising Cartels: Critical Studies of an International Regulatory Movement* (Haywards Heath, Bloomsbury Professional, 2011) 419, 424.

[25] ibid.

[26] ibid.

[27] ibid, 425.

fair and efficient securities market. Furthermore, the extraterritorial application of criminal law provisions to countries operating in the global market force-feeds the criminalisation agenda to jurisdictions that resist extraterritoriality.[28]

Austen L Parrish advocates resolving global challenges through multilateral agreements rather than through unilateral domestic action.[29] He recognises, however, that '[e]xtraterritorial regulation is not always a bad idea. In under-regulated areas, extraterritoriality can sometimes fill a gap. And it may be that extraterritorial regulation can serve as a placeholder before more comprehensive international agreement can be reached.'[30]

Also, the rigid application of the presumption against extraterritoriality ignores some positive effects created by the extraterritorial application of US law, such as 'promot[ing] international negotiation and cooperation'.[31] A similar, positive effect had been noted in the extraterritorial application of anti-bribery laws, based on the Organisation for Economic Cooperation and Development on Combating Bribery of Public Officials in International Business Transactions, by generating mechanisms that should help firms do ethical business and comply with this type of legislation.[32]

Sarah C Kaczmarek and Abraham L Newman carried out an empirical study showing that the extraterritorial application of the Foreign Corrupt Practices Act dramatically increases the likelihood that foreign countries enforce their own anti-bribery norms.[33] Through econometric analysis, Kaczmarek and Newman determined that 'the odds of a country enforcing its first [anti-corruption] case are twenty times greater if a country has experienced extraterritorial application of the [United States Foreign Corrupt Practices Act]'.[34] By the same token, some pre-*Morrison* federal court decisions gave credit to the extraterritorial application of US antifraud provisions for encouraging Americans to achieve a high standard of business ethics in the securities industry.[35]

[28] ibid. The idea of force-feeding is used in the field of competition law.

[29] AL Parrish, 'Morrison, The Effects Test, and the Presumption Against Extraterritoriality: A Reply to Professor Dodge' (2011) 105 *American Society of International Law Proceedings* 399, 401–02.

[30] ibid, 402.

[31] WS Dodge, 'Extraterritoriality and Conflict-of-Laws Theory: An Argument for Judicial Unilateralism' (1998) 39 *Harvard International Law Journal* 101, 163–68, cited by WS Dodge, 'Understanding the Presumption Against Extraterritoriality' (1998) 16 *Berkeley Journal of International Law* 85, 117 (emphasis omitted).

[32] B Hock, 'Intimations of Global Anti-Bribery Regime and the Effectiveness of Extraterritorial Enforcement: From Free-Riders to Protectionism?' 9 *Tilberg Law and Economic Center, Discussion Paper No 2014-009* (13 February 2014) available at ssrn.com/abstract=2395156.

[33] SC Kaczmarek and AL Newman, 'The Long Arm of the Law: Extraterritoriality and the National Implementation of Foreign Bribery Legislation' (2011) 65(4) *International Organization* 745, 760.

[34] ibid.

[35] E Reuveni, 'Extraterritoriality as Standing: A Standing Theory of the Extraterritorial Application of the Securities Laws' (2010) 43 *University of California, Davis Law Review* 1071, 1082.

On the negative side, the extraterritorial application of business-related criminal sanctions in one jurisdiction may undermine administrative or compliance programmes in another.[36] Also, extraterritorial application of this type of criminal norm may bring about a host of double-jeopardy problems.[37]

Mireille Delmas-Marty warns that a unilateral expansion of internal law under the guise of combating impunity risks becoming an 'internationalization of hegemonic type'.[38] Also, Stephen Kim Park recognises that the possibility of this unilateral extraterritorial reach is 'contingent on highly concentrated state power',[39] and that 'the project[ion] [of a state's] regulatory rules … depends on its status as an economic hegemon'.[40]

While recognising the superiority of multilateral solutions, the extraterritorial application of US securities fraud-related criminal norms cannot be dismissed merely because of their characterisation as 'hegemonic'. The immediate extraterritorial reach may be indispensable not only to protect investors and punish unscrupulous manipulators, but ultimately to protect the integrity of financial markets intimately related to the protection of public wealth.[41] For instance, market integrity has a constitutional rank in Italy as a condition of the market economy.[42] In this regard, Salvatore Panagia believes that Article 41, section 2, in combination with Article 47 of the Italian Constitution, demonstrates that without criminal law protection of the integrity of financial markets against abuses and speculative excesses, these illegal abuses would not only destroy people's savings, but also the private will to invest.[43]

The most damaging effects of securities fraud, like those of other business-related crimes, are that they create distrust toward the system and its healthy components. Sutherland underscores that the most important damage resulting from white-collar crimes is the one caused in social relations by destroying trust, depressing social morale, and producing disorganisation.[44] Because public trust constitutes the vital sapping of international commerce,[45] an attack

[36] Ezrachi and Kindl, 'Cartels as Criminal?' (n 24) 425.

[37] ibid.

[38] M Delmas-Marty, 'Aplanir le terrain de jeu' in 'Les Figures de l'Internationalisation en Droit Pénal des Affaires' (2005) 4 *Revue de Science Criminelle et de Droit Pénal Comparé* 735, 737.

[39] Park, 'Guarding the Guardians' (n 18) 754.

[40] ibid.

[41] F Consulich, *La Giustzia e il Mercato: Miti e Realtà di una Tutela Penale dell' Investimento Mobiliare* (Milan, Dott A Giuffrè, 2010) 405.

[42] S Panagia, *La Tutela dei Mercati Finanziari: La Fatispeccie Penale a Rischio di Default* (Turin, G Giappichelli, 2011) 72.

[43] ibid.

[44] E Sutherland, *White Collar Crime* (New York, Holt, Reinhardt & Winston, 1949) 13.

[45] E Rotman, *Los Fraudes al Comercio y a la Industria* (Buenos Aires, Abeledo-Perrot, 1974) 30.

on it by white-collar crime affects the economy as a whole, posing a challenge that justifies the extraterritorial application of national criminal laws.

III. Overview of *United States v Vilar*'s Fundamental Precedents

A. *United States v Bowman*

In *Bowman*,[46] the Supreme Court decided a fraudulent fuel oil claim brought by a US-owned corporation for one of its ships. The fraud consisted of purchasing 1,000 tons of fuel oil and delivering only 600 tons.[47] The money paid for the undelivered 400 tons was then divided among four defendants.[48] Bowman – the ship's engineer – and the master concocted the fraud aboard the ship with the participation of two other co-conspirators based in Rio de Janeiro.[49]

In *Bowman*, the Supreme Court established that the presumption against extraterritoriality does not apply to criminal statutes that are not 'logically dependent on their locality for the government's jurisdiction, but are enacted because of the right of the government to defend itself against obstruction, or fraud, wherever perpetrated'.[50] Limiting the locus of some criminal offences, the Court explained, would greatly 'curtail the scope and usefulness of the statute and leave open a large immunity for fraud' committed in a foreign country.[51] In other words, *Bowman* held that the presumption against extraterritoriality is not applicable when it undermines the statute's purpose.[52]

B. *Morrison v National Australia Bank*

In June 2010, the US Supreme Court decided *Morrison*,[53] a case of obvious abuse of American judicial resources by Australian plaintiffs through a foreign-cubed[54] securities fraud class action. As pointed out by Stevens J in his Concurring Opinion, the 'case has Australia written all over it'.[55]

[46] *United States v Bowman*, 260 US 94 (1922).
[47] ibid, 95.
[48] ibid, 95–96.
[49] ibid, 95.
[50] ibid, 98.
[51] ibid.
[52] ibid, 102.
[53] *Morrison v National Australia Bank* 561 US 247 (2010).
[54] Foreign-cubed is defined as cases where there is a foreign plaintiff suing a foreign defendant for acts committed on foreign soil. See *Morrison v National Australian Bank Ltd*, 547 F3d 167, 172 (2d Cir 2008).
[55] *Morrison* (n 53) 286 (Stevens, J, concurring).

Morrison significantly limited the extraterritorial scope of the antifraud provisions contained in section 10(b) of the Securities Exchange Act[56] and SEC Rule 10(b)(5),[57] finding that these provisions do not create a private right of action for foreign purchasers of foreign securities outside of the US.[58] Prior to *Morrison*, the Court of Appeal for the Second Circuit required that the alleged wrongful conduct had to have substantial effects in the US in connection with securities and transactions abroad ('effects test') or that sufficient fraudulent conduct occurred in the US in connection with securities transactions abroad ('conduct test').[59] In *Morrison*, the Supreme Court knocked down nearly 40 years of federal court decisions, replacing their 'conduct' and 'effects' tests with a new 'transactional' test, limiting the scope of section 10(b) to causes of action that involve 'only transactions in securities listed on domestic exchanges and domestic transactions in other securities'.[60] The Court applied a strict presumption against extraterritoriality when the 'focus' of the relevant statute occurred outside the territory of the US. The Court concluded that the 'focus' of the Exchange Act 'is not on the place where the deception originated, but on purchases and sales of securities in the United States'.[61]

C. *Morrison's* Casualties

Morrison left investors unprotected in a number of situations. As explained in section IV, *Vilar* has compounded such flaws by depriving victims of criminal law protection.

Some of these consequences are mentioned by Stevens J in his Concurring Opinion in *Morrison*. He gives the imaginary example of an American investor buying shares of a foreign corporation that has a major American subsidiary with executives based in New York City.[62] The executives mastermind a massive deception inflating the corporation's stock, which is only listed on an overseas exchange, causing the price to plummet.[63] To this, Stevens J adds another imaginary situation in which the same executives persuade an unsophisticated retiree in Manhattan, on the basis of material misrepresentations, to invest her life savings in the company's doomed securities.[64] Steinberg and Flannigan give a similar example of 'a retiree, after being sold a doomed security in a door-to-door sale by an executive

[56] 15 USC, s 78l (2012).
[57] 17 CFR 240.10b-5 (2015).
[58] *Morrison* (n 53) 273.
[59] ibid, (n 54) 171.
[60] ibid, (n 53) 267.
[61] ibid, 266.
[62] ibid, 285 (Stevens J, concurring).
[63] ibid.
[64] ibid.

of a foreign owned US subsidiary, might be barred from bringing a section 10(b) action'.[65]

A group of 42 professors provide a list of dismissals of securities-fraud cases since *Morrison*, underscoring that this deficiency in investor protection would not have happened with a 'conduct' and 'effects' test because these tests captured the potential complexity of the relationships among investors and issuers.[66] Among these cases, I highlight one of a Norwegian securities firm and seven Norwegian municipalities that brought a suit against various Citigroup entities.[67] This case concerned the sale of fund-linked notes that were issued and traded outside of the US, but were structured, arranged and managed in the US by Citigroup's New York subsidiaries.[68] Applying the conduct test, the district court found that the essential core of the alleged fraud occurred in New York.[69] Six months later, after the Supreme Court decided *Morrison*, the district court reversed its previous decision and granted the defendant's motion to dismiss because the fund-linked notes were listed on European stock exchanges, notwithstanding the fact that the essential core of the alleged fraud occurred in New York.[70]

It is noteworthy that in transnational securities fraud cases covered in the past by circuit courts' 'conduct' and 'effects' tests, in both situations something happens in the US, and therefore Congress has an interest in them, and a presumption against such interest is unfounded.[71] Precisely, this circumstance is appropriately expressed in one of the earliest securities fraud Second Circuit decisions, where Judge Friendly pointed out '[t]he New Yorker who is the object of fraudulent misrepresentations in New York is as much injured if the securities are of a mine in Saskatchewan as in Nevada' and that Congress would not have wished protection to be withdrawn merely because the fraudulent promoter of the Saskatchewan mining securities took the buyer's cheque back to Canada and mailed the certificate from there.[72] This is precisely one of the situations deprived from protection in *Morrison*.[73] Federal courts adopted Judge Friendly's position for four decades without congressional reaction, while *Morrison*'s interpretation lasted less than four weeks until the Dodd-Frank Wall Street Reform

[65] MI Steinberg and K Flanagan, 'Transnational Dealings – Morrison Continues to Make Waves' (2012) 46 *International Lawer* 829, 863–64, fn 304.

[66] Comments from Robert P Bartlett et al, to Elizabeth M Murphy, Secretary, Securities and Exchange Commission 13–18 (18 February 2011) available at www.sec.gov/comments/4-617/4617-28.pdf.

[67] See *Terra Sec ASA Konkursbo v Citigroup, Inc*, 740 F Supp 2d 441 (SDNY 2010).

[68] ibid, 444–45.

[69] See *Terra Sec ASA Konkursbo v Citigroup, Inc*, 688 F Supp 2d 303 (SDNY 2010).

[70] See *Terra Sec ASA Konkursbo* (n 67) 740 F Supp 2d 444–47.

[71] JH Knox, 'The Unpredictable Presumption Against Extraterritoriality' (2011) 40 *Southwestern Law Review* 635, 648.

[72] *Leasco Data Processing Equip Corp v Maxwell*, 468 F 2d 1326, 1336–37 (2d Cir 1972), cited by Knox, ibid.

[73] Knox, 'The Unpredictable Presumption' (n 71).

and Consumer Protection Act attempted to reinstate both the 'conduct' and the 'effects' test for actions brought by the Securities and Exchange Commission (SEC) and the Department of Justice (DOJ).

D. The United States Congress Attempt to Overrule *Morrison*

Morrison left ambiguous the SEC and DOJ's authority to bring extraterritorial actions under section 10(b). In July 2010, Congress addressed this issue in sections 929P(b) and 929Y of the Dodd-Frank Wall Street Reform and Consumer Protection Act, the most important financial reform legislation since 1934.[74] These norms granted the SEC and DOJ jurisdiction over conduct within the US that constitutes significant steps in furtherance of the violation, even if the securities transactions occur outside of the US and involved only foreign investors, or conduct occurring abroad that had a foreseeable, substantial effect within the US.[75] In other words, Congress provided extraterritorial jurisdiction for SEC and DOJ actions under section 10(b) by using a 'conduct' and 'effects' test similar to the one used by the federal courts before *Morrison*.

In his floor statement, Representative Paul Kanjorski, chairman of the committee that drafted the Dodd-Frank Act, sections 929P(b) and 929Y in Title IX, expressed that the purpose of the reform was to grant authority to the SEC and DOJ to bring civil or criminal enforcement proceedings involving transnational securities fraud under both the 'conduct' and the 'effects' tests developed by the courts regardless of the jurisdiction of the proceedings.[76] Addressing the very recent Supreme Court decision in *Morrison*, Representative Kanjorski reaffirmed that the Bill's provisions concerning extraterritoriality are intended to rebut the presumption against extraterritoriality 'by clearly indicating that Congress intends extraterritorial application in cases brought by the SEC or the Justice Department'.[77]

Conversely, George T Conway III, the lawyer who argued and won the *Morrison* case for the defendant, concluded that section 929P(b) does not rebut the presumption against extraterritoriality because the provision addresses only the 'jurisdiction' of the 'district courts of the United States' to hear cases involving extraterritorial elements.[78] Conway points out that the drafters of the Dodd-Frank Act ignored the fact that in the *Morrison* decision the Supreme Court reiterated the

[74] Dodd-Frank Wall Street Reform and Consumer Protection Act, Pub L No 111–203, tit IX, ss 929P(b), 929Y (2010).

[75] ibid.

[76] 156 Cong Rec H5237 (daily edn 30 June 2010) (statement of Rep. Kanjorski).

[77] ibid.

[78] GT Conway III, 'Extraterritoriality after Dodd-Frank' *The Harvard Law School Forum on Corporate Governance and Financial Regulation* (5 August 2010) available at corpgov.law.harvard.edu/2010/08/05/extraterritoriality-after-dodd-frank/.

long-standing principle that the territorial scope of a federal law does not present a question of jurisdiction, but rather a question of substance.[79]

David He considers it unlikely that any lower court would interpret the statute in contradiction with Congress's objectives, 'because it is clear that Section 929P(b) intended to reinstate the conduct and effects approach for civil and criminal enforcement actions brought by the government against overseas violators'.[80] In addition, David He cites Painter,[81] expressing that '[m]ost judges will not be willing to tell Congress that, because of the way a statute is worded, it fails to accomplish anything at all.'[82]

If the SEC were free from *Morrison*'s jurisdictional limitations in civil actions, as the Dodd-Frank Act intended, the SEC investigations and DOJ prosecutions of criminal violations of the Securities Acts would unquestionably be free from the same restrictions. The following section challenges the *Vilar* decision that extends the *Morrison* jurisdictional limitations to criminal cases. *Vilar* implicitly assumes that the Dodd-Frank Act was ineffective. If the Dodd-Frank Act were effective, *Vilar* would become irrelevant.

IV. Critical Analysis of *United States v Vilar*

A. *United States v Vilar*

In *Vilar*, appellants Alberto Vilar and Gary Alan Tanaka were convicted of securities fraud, securities investment fraud and conspiracy, and they were sentenced respectively to 108 and 60 months' imprisonment, required to pay $35 million in restitution, and ordered to forfeit $54 million.[83] Exploiting their positions as prominent investment managers and advisors, Vilar and Tanaka solicited millions of people with the promise of investing the funds in predominantly safe, short-term deposits, but instead invested the money in highly volatile technology and biotechnology stocks.[84] The dot-com bubble burst of 2000 led to the precipitous fall of their investment.[85] In the midst of the catastrophe, they obtained $5 million dollars from a client by deceiving her with the false promise of an

[79] See ibid; see also WA Kaal and RW Painter, 'The Aftermath of Morrison v. National Australia Bank and Elliott Associates and Porsche' (2011) 8 *European Company & Financial Law Review* 77, 79; R Painter et al, 'When Courts and Congress Don't Say What They Mean: Initial Reactions to Morrison v. National Australia Bank and to the Extraterritorial Jurisdiction Provisions of the Dodd-Frank Act' (2011) 20 *Minnesota Journal of International Law* 1.

[80] D He, 'Beyond Securities Fraud: The Territorial Reach of US Laws after *Morrison v. N.A.B.*' 2013(1) *Columbia Business Law Review* 148, 168.

[81] Painter et al, 'When Courts and Congress don't say what they mean' (n 79) 12.

[82] He, 'Beyond Securities Fraud' (n 80) 169, fn 69.

[83] *United States v Vilar*, 729 F3d 62 (2nd Cir 2013).

[84] ibid, 68.

[85] ibid.

illusionary investment, while actually embezzling the entrusted funds to meet various personal and corporate obligations.[86] In this case, the Second Circuit held that securities fraud prohibitions section 10(b)[87] and Rule 10b-5[88] do not apply extraterritorially in criminal cases.[89] I will analyse the supportive reasons for this conclusion step-by-step in the critical analysis in section V. The German criminal law model plays a pivotal role in this analysis.

B. How a Comparative Analysis of the German Criminal Law Model can Help Identify Significant Shortcomings in *United States v Vilar*

As a consequence of the deficiencies in American legal doctrine on this point, enumerated in Chapter 2, section III.A and in section III.B of that chapter we proposed the use of comparative criminal law to rethink and reform the doctrine of criminal liability in American securities law.

Resorting to foreign law to gain insight into the most complex issues surrounding the theory of the criminal offence is justified by the present paucity of categorisations of the Anglo-American doctrine and jurisprudence.

The German model consists of a set of abstract criminal law categories adopted by most of Continental Europe, Latin America and diverse parts of the world.[90]

The use of a foreign model is justified by the paucity of categorisations existing within the common law to resolve issues presented by the *Vilar* case.[91] This conceptual dearth is decried by a number of American scholars. I will draw on the German model to develop my critical analysis of *Vilar*, and include references to American scholars' complaints about insufficiencies of US law in this field.

V. Discussion of Each of *United States v Vilar*'s Supporting Arguments

In the following sections I will cite in italics the relevant parts of the *Vilar* decision, followed by my respective rebuttal.

[86] ibid, 68–69.
[87] 15 USC, s 78l (2012).
[88] 17 CFR 240, r 10b-5 (2015).
[89] See *Vilar* (n 83) 98.
[90] F Muñoz Conde, '"Rethinking" the Universal Structure of Criminal Law' (2004) 39 *Tulsa Law Review* 941, 942.
[91] See ch 2, nn 35, 39, 40.

A. First Critique of *Vilar*

'[T]he presumption against extraterritoriality applies to criminal statutes, and section 10(b) is no exception.'[92]

i. Extent and Significance of the Bowman *Exception*

The *Bowman* decision excludes the presumption against extraterritoriality, as already explained, in criminal statutes that are not logically dependent on their locality for the government's jurisdiction but are enacted because of the right of the government to defend itself against obstruction or fraud, wherever perpetrated.

Relying on some lower court decisions, the government claimed in the *Vilar* case that *Bowman* excluded the presumption against extraterritoriality in *all* criminal law cases.[93] The *Vilar* court accurately rejected this incorrect interpretation.[94] Indeed, the *Bowman* decision excludes the presumption against extraterritoriality only in *some* cases.[95]

However, the *Vilar* court grievously misinterprets *Bowman* by excessively narrowing its exception to the point of making it inoperative. The *Vilar* court's erroneous interpretation of *Bowman* consists of limiting the exception to self-defence from attacks against government representatives or government property.[96] Indeed, the *Bowman* exception to the presumption against extraterritoriality also applies to governmental functions and to the vital social interests and goals served by the government.

To demonstrate the correctness of this argument, I will start with a grammatical interpretation. According to the 1922 *Bowman* decision, a limitation of the locus of some crimes to the strictly territorial jurisdiction would greatly 'curtail the scope and usefulness of the statute and leave open a large immunity for frauds as easily committed' in foreign states as in the US.[97] Furthermore, the decision refers only to criminal statutes 'enacted because of the right of the Government to defend itself against *obstruction*, or fraud wherever perpetrated'.[98]

The *Bowman* exception to the presumption against extraterritoriality should not be limited to natural persons that represent the government or to the government's property but should be extended to the government's functions as well as to its vital interests and goals. In a democratic system, the government is a means to achieve highly important social interests. This teleological interpretation is

[92] *Vilar* (n 83) 74.
[93] ibid, 72.
[94] ibid.
[95] ibid, 73.
[96] ibid.
[97] *United States v Bowman* (n 46) 98.
[98] ibid (emphasis added).

also confirmed by the *Bowman* decision when it uses the word 'obstructions'.[99] The word 'obstructions' clearly refers to governmental functions.[100] This interpretation is also confirmed by the examples provided in the *Bowman* decision as cases in which 'Congress has not thought it necessary to make a specific provision in the law that the locus shall include the high seas and foreign countries, but allows it to be inferred from the nature of the offense.'[101] For instance, 'bribing a United States officer of the civil, military or naval service to violate his duty or to aid in committing a fraud on the United States'.[102]

It is also important that the *Bowman* decision was later used to protect higher governmental interests, such as the environment and the integrity of insolvency procedures. Consider the *Skiriotes v Florida*[103] decision. In this case, the Florida statute forbidding the use of diving equipment for the purpose of taking commercial sponges from waters within Florida's territorial limits was applied extraterritorially on the basis that the US is not limited by any rule of international law from extending its laws extraterritorially to protect vital national interests such as natural resources.[104] This happens on the high seas and in foreign countries, provided that the rights of another nation or its nationals are not infringed.

In *Stegeman v United States*,[105] the Stegemans were convicted of having transferred property from the state of Oregon to Canada after filing a petition for bankruptcy, thus knowingly and fraudulently concealing property belonging to the bankruptcy estate.[106] The court considered that, as in *Bowman*, 'Congress has not thought it necessary to make a specific provision in the law that the *locus* shall include the high seas and foreign countries, but allows it to be inferred from the nature of the offense.'[107] On this basis, the court considered that Congress enacted 18 USC, section 152 to serve important governmental interests and 'not merely to protect individuals who might be harmed by the prohibited conduct'.[108]

Under the exceptions to the presumption against extraterritoriality, my interpretation of *Bowman* therefore encompasses the criminal law provisions protecting the integrity of capital markets. Because of today's interconnectedness of capital markets through electronic and institutional links, the importance of their location plays such a reduced role that one can no longer speak of 'local' markets. The globalisation of capital markets requires a global system of investment protection;

[99] ibid.
[100] ibid.
[101] ibid.
[102] ibid, 99.
[103] *Skiriotes v Florida*, 313 US 69 (1941).
[104] ibid, 72–77.
[105] *Stegeman v United States*, 425 F2d 984 (9th Cir 1970).
[106] ibid, 985.
[107] ibid, 986 (quoting *United States v Bowman*, 260 US 94, 98 (1922)).
[108] ibid, 986.

as long as this does not exist, the extraterritorial application of American legal provisions remains necessary.

ii. The Presumption Against Extraterritoriality Called into Question

Another line of argument questions the merit and value of the presumption against extraterritoriality, which was challenged by some scholars after the 2010 *Morrison* decision. In fact, these publications followed an article published in 2010 by John H Knox in the *American Journal of International Law*.[109] Knox made a painstaking historical analysis of the presumption against extraterritoriality, showing its changing underlying rationale through time, and pointing to its contradictions and incoherent application by the US federal courts.[110] Dissatisfied with these jurisprudential inconsistencies, he proposed a new interpretive canon – a presumption against 'extrajurisdictionality', the most predictable of the possible options.[111]

Knox looked into the bases of jurisdiction under international law. In those cases where the US has sole or primary jurisdiction, the courts are free to construe statutes without any presumption against their application.[112] When international law provides US courts with only some basis of jurisdiction, the courts should apply a soft presumption against the application of the statute – that is, allow the courts to overcome it by indication of a legislative intent to do so.[113] It is only when the US entirely lacks any basis of jurisdiction under international law that a strict presumption against application of the law should be overcome by only express and clear legislative statement.[114]

In a subsequent 2011 article,[115] Knox addressed the *Morrison* decision, rebutting its claim that the presumption against extraterritoriality provides 'a stable background against which Congress can legislate with predictable effects'.[116] He explained how *Morrison* 'exacerbated longstanding confusions in the Court's treatment of extraterritoriality' and noted 'virtues of a presumption against extrajurisdictionality are illustrated by the very circuit court decisions that *Morrison* rejected'.[117] Knox renewed his proposal for a presumption against extrajurisdictionality, underscoring the need to return to the roots of the presumption in the international law of legislative jurisdiction[118] to bring the Supreme Court

[109] JH Knox, 'A Presumption Against Extrajurisdictionality' (2010) 104 *American Journal of International Law* 351.
[110] See generally ibid.
[111] ibid, 389.
[112] ibid, 353.
[113] ibid.
[114] ibid.
[115] Knox, 'The Unpredictable Presumption Against Extraterritoriality' (n 71) 648.
[116] *Morrison v National Australia Bank* (n 53) 561 US 248.
[117] Knox, 'The Unpredictable Presumption Against Extraterritoriality' (n 71) 635.
[118] ibid. Knox explains how a presumption against extrajurisdictionality would be more consistent with congressional intent and more predictable than the Court's strict presumption against extraterritoriality.

jurisprudence back 'into coherence and in better alignment with reasonable assumptions of congressional intent'.[119]

Knox pointed out that the Supreme Court showcased the presumption against extraterritoriality as predictable and stable; when in the Supreme Court's hands, however, the presumption was used neither predictably nor stably. He underscored that the Court missed the opportunity to resolve the ambiguity regarding extraterritorial actions that affects the US, compounding the confusion by emphasising the 'focus'[120] of the statute in determining its extraterritorial reach.[121]

More recently, Zachary D Clopton challenges the validity and meaningfulness of the presumption against extraterritoriality and proposes to replace it altogether.[122] Clopton makes an inventory of all the purported justifications of the presumption against extraterritoriality and concludes that none of them holds water.[123] These justifications from courts and scholars are based primarily on the need to avoid foreign conflicts and Congress's overriding concern with domestic conditions.[124] To a lesser degree, other justifications include the need to affirm the principle of separation of powers by avoiding judicial activism and the prevention of due process violations through extraterritorial suits.[125]

Clopton analyses in depth each of these purported justifications, showing that they are weakened by contradictory judicial decisions and that these decisions reveal 'the presumption is poorly attuned to either of these laudable goals'.[126]

It is significant for the purposes of my argument that Clopton negates the absolute and immutable status of the presumption predicated by the *Morrison* decision, reminding us that the presumption is a relative tool of federal statutory interpretation and not a constitutional principle.[127] In fact, Clopton indicates the possibility of replacing it altogether.[128]

It is equally important that Clopton emphasises that the rules regarding extraterritoriality should be different for civil, administrative and criminal statutes.[129] It is disappointing, however, that Clopton's proposed replacement for the presumption against extraterritoriality in criminal cases happens to be the rule of lenity,[130] a rule of interpretation that, though important within its narrow ambit of application, cannot be generalised to all cases of extraterritorial application of criminal

[119] ibid, 653.

[120] *Morrison v National Australia Bank* (n 53) 266. The Court concluded that the 'focus' of the Exchange Act 'is not upon the place where the deception originated, but upon purchases and sales of securities in the United States'.

[121] Knox, 'The Unpredictable Presumption Against Extraterritoriality' (n 71) 643.

[122] ZD Clopton, 'Replacing the Presumption Against Extraterritoriality' (2014) 98 *Boston University Law Review* 1.

[123] See generally ibid.

[124] See generally ibid, 10–15.

[125] See generally ibid, 15–20.

[126] ibid, 1.

[127] ibid, 3–8.

[128] ibid, 21.

[129] ibid, 22–45.

[130] ibid, 30–31.

law. The Supreme Court explains, 'The rule of lenity applies only if, "after seizing everything from which aid can be derived," [a court] can make "no more than a guess as to what Congress intended."'[131] It is necessary to distinguish the external geographical ambiguity of the field of application of a criminal statute from the intrinsic ambiguity relating to the prohibition and penalties contained in the definition of the criminal offence. Here, we are not dealing with an intrinsic grievous ambiguity of a criminal statute, but with a situation in which the extraterritorial purpose of the statute, although implicit, is clear and obvious to a point that makes it unnecessary to spell out.

The cases covered by the *Bowman* exception to the presumption against extraterritoriality interpret statutory silence in situations where the unexpressed statutory purpose is clear.[132] Without this provision, a misguided rule of lenity would eliminate all extraterritoriality of statutes that omit an express mention of their obvious purpose of extraterritorial application across-the-board, including the *Bowman* situation. Keeping the presumption against extraterritoriality limited by the exception introduced by *United States v Bowman* is a more adequate solution.

B. Second Critique of *Vilar*

The Supreme Court has already interpreted Section 10(b), and it has done so in unmistakable terms: 'Section 10(b) reaches the use of a manipulative or deceptive device or contrivance only in connection with the purchase or sale of a security listed on an American stock exchange, and the purchase or sale of any other security in the United States.' To permit the government to punish extraterritorial conduct when bringing criminal charges under Section 10(b) 'would establish … the dangerous principle that judges can give the same statutory text different meanings in different cases'.[133]

Refusing to apply *Morrison*'s decision to the criminal enforcement of securities fraud is not giving a statutory text two different meanings. Indeed, we speak about two different rules within the same statute.

Section 10(b),[134] in itself, is no more than a private law prohibition. It is only when this behaviour is carried out 'willfully' that it becomes part of the criminal law definition contained in section 32(a).[135] Section 32(a) is the proper criminal

[131] *Reno v Koray*, 515 US 50, 65 (1995) (quoting *Smith v United States*, 508 US 103, 108 (1993) and *Ladner v United States*, 358 US 169 (1958)).

[132] See cases cited by ES Podgor and DM Filler, 'International Criminal Jurisdiction in the Twenty-First Century: Rediscovering *United States v Bowman*' (2007) 44 *San Diego Law Review* 585, 589.

[133] *United States v Vilar* (n 83) 74–75 (citations omitted) (quoting *Clark v Martinez*, 543 US 371, 386 (2005)).

[134] 15 USC, s 78l (2012).

[135] ibid, ss 78ff (2012).

law norm.[136] It establishes a serious criminal penalty and the conditions that the conduct has to meet in order to become criminal.[137]

The court in *Vilar* ignored that section 32(a) contains the definition of the crime, while section 10(b) generates only civil and administrative responsibilities, playing only a supplementary role when it is incorporated by reference into a criminal law rule to complete section 32(a)'s definition.[138]

Here, among other instances, the German criminal law model provides an answer to an American legal question. In the present case, the answer comes from the category of blanket criminal norms. Incorporation by reference into a criminal norm has received considerable doctrinal development in countries belonging to the civil law system.[139] The doctrine of blanket criminal laws (*Blankettstrafgesetze, leyes penales en blanco, leggi penali in bianco, lois cadres*) basically consists of a special case of legislative drafting techniques that entail the incorporation by reference of a norm existing elsewhere in the legal system to complete a criminal provision.[140] Karl Binding coined the term *Blankettstrafgesetze* (blanket criminal laws) in his trailblazing work, *Die Normen und ihre Übertretung* (*Norms and their Transgression*). In the first volume of his 1922 five-volume edition, he defined blanket criminal laws as those that contained only the sanction and referenced a number of statutes and administrative or police regulations to complete the precept.[141] Until such secondary rules are enacted, the blanket law is 'like a wandering body searching for its soul'.[142] Further development of this doctrine included in the category of blanket criminal laws the incorporation by reference of provisions existing within the same statute. In 1931, Edmund Mezger expanded the concept of blanket criminal law to include situations where the same body of law contains the precept in another section.[143] These cases are called improper blanket criminal laws and cover precisely the situation of the Securities Exchange Act.[144] This category plays

[136] ibid.

[137] ibid.

[138] 15 USC, ss 78l, 78ff (2012).

[139] The expression 'civil law' is used to demarcate those systems of law derived from Roman law, including private and public law, and that are mainly located in Western Europe and Latin America, but can be also found in numerous other parts of the world. Among other sources, see HJ Berman and WR Greiner, *The Nature And Functions of Law* (Brooklyn, Foundation Press, 1980) 571–72.

[140] Among many examples, see Art 310 of the Peruvian Criminal Code: 'Whoever extracts aquatic flora and fauna species in prohibited times, quantities, and areas or uses prohibited fishing or hunting procedures shall be punished with imprisonment no less than one year and no more than three years.' See also Art 334 of the Colombian Penal Code: 'Whoever, without the permission of a competent authority or infringing existing norms, performs, experiments, introduces or propagates animals, vegetables, or hydro-biological species, or bio-chemical or biological agents that endanger the health or existence of those species or alter the animal or vegetable population shall be punished with imprisonment of two to six years and a fine of 50 to 200 minimum monthly salaries.'

[141] K Binding, *Die* Normen *und ihre Übertretung: eine Untersuchung über die rechtmässige Handlung und die Arten des Delikts* 4th edn (Munich, Scientia Verlag Aalen (ed), 1922, rep 1965) 161–62.

[142] ibid, 162.

[143] E Mezger, *Strafrecht: Ein Lehrbuch*, 3rd edn (Berlin, Verlag von Duncker & Humblot, 1949) 196.

[144] ibid.

a central role in business-related criminal law,[145] where the application of blanket statutes is not only frequent, but is also typical.[146] An example of the completion of a blanket provision is section 3 of the German law relation to business crimes (Wirtschftsstrafgesetz) dealing with the regulation of prices,[147] as well as with laws regulating wine (Weingesetz).[148] This theory perfectly applies to the Securities Exchange Act, where section 32(a) is the blanket criminal law norm that incorporates by reference section 10(b), which, in turn, references to Rule10b-5.

As a subsidiary argument, I underscore the relativity of the unitary principle invoked by the *Vilar* court; that is, that both civil and criminal liabilities should be dealt with in the same way when they arise from the same statute.[149] In addition, as Jonathan Siegel recognises, it is impossible to anticipate every possible circumstance in which a canon of construction might someday apply.[150] 'It is an error to believe that the process of statutory interpretation can ever be mechanized or reduced to a set of determinate, nondiscretionary rules.'[151] Furthermore, in *United States v Nippon Paper Industries*, Circuit Judge Lynch expressed in his concurring opinion that sometimes the same language in a statute should not necessarily be read the same way in all contexts to which the language applies: 'New content is sometimes ascribed to statutory terms depending upon context.'[152] In *Robinson v Shell Oil Co*, the Supreme Court explained that, depending on context, a statutory term might have different meanings in different sections of a single statute.[153] Furthermore, Stevens J has repeatedly recognised that the same word can have different meanings in the same statute.[154]

C. Third Critique of *Vilar*

I will next address the third ground of the *Vilar* decision. The government contended that section 10(b) had different requirements in private law and criminal law; therefore, they should be interpreted in a different way.[155] The 'government observe[d] that only private plaintiffs must prove reliance, economic loss, and loss causation,

[145] K Tiedemann, *Wirtschaftsstrafrecht. Einführung und Allgemeiner Teil mit wichtigen Rechtstexten*, 4th edn (Munich, Verlag Franz Vahlen, 2014) 87.
[146] ibid.
[147] ibid, 54.
[148] ibid, 56.
[149] See generally *United States v Vilar* (n 83).
[150] JR Siegel, 'The Polymorphic Principle and the Judicial Role in Statutory Interpretation' (2005) 84 *Texas Law Review* 339, 394.
[151] ibid.
[152] *United States v Nippon Paper Industries*, 109 F3d 1, 10 (1st Cir 1997).
[153] *Robinson v Shell Oil Co*, 519 US 337, 343–44 (1997).
[154] See *Gen Dynamics Land Sys v Cline*, 540 US 581, 595 (2004); see also *United States v Santos*, 553 US 507, 525 (2008) (Stevens J, concurring).
[155] *United States v Vilar* (n 83).

whereas only the government (in criminal cases) must prove that the fraud was committed willfully'.[156] Here is the *Vilar* response, followed by my critique:

> *Critically, however, none of these differences relate to the* conduct *proscribed by Section 10(b) ... As for the element of willfulness in criminal cases, it comes directly from Section 32 of the Securities Exchange Act of 1934, which permits criminal liability to attach to a violation of Section 10(b), only when the violation is willful. But like the elements relevant only to private plaintiffs, the requirement of proving willfulness has nothing to do with the text or interpretation of Section 10(b). In other words, Section 32 provides no basis for* expanding *the conduct for which a defendant may be held criminally liable under Section 10(b).*[157]

This is another instance in which the contribution of the German criminal law model is fundamental. We concede that the conduct described in Rule 10b-5 under delegation from section 10(b) of the Securities Exchange Act,[158] when read isolated from Section 32(a),[159] as a description of the external phase of a behaviour, is the same for criminal and private law. This external conduct corresponds in German law only to the objective phase of the definition.[160] The same external conduct, however, gains full significance when it is incorporated into a criminal law norm.[161] Criminalisation operates as King Midas. In the same way that everything King Midas touched became gold, criminalisation changes the nature of the behaviour it addresses. While the traditional understanding of US common law is that conduct relevant to criminal law is basically 'a willed muscular contraction',[162] this naturalistic notion of human action has long been abandoned in the majority of civil law countries.[163] Following the German criminal law model, most

[156] ibid.

[157] ibid.

[158] 15 USC, s 78l (2012).

[159] 15 USC, s 78ff (2012).

[160] Modern developments in criminal law theory following the German model structure the definition of the criminal offence in two phases: an objective and a subjective. See, eg, EC Urzúa, *Derecho Penal, Parte General*, vol 1, 2nd edn (Santiago, Editorial Juridica de Chile, 1992) 278–79, 294.

[161] When a certain behaviour is criminalised, its statutory definition entails a negative judgment value, technically called the 'disvalue of the action'. See H-H Jescheck and T Weigend, *Lehrbuch des Strafrechts: Allgemeiner Teil* (Berlin, Duncker & Humblot, 1996) 238–46.

[162] GP Fletcher, *The Grammar of Criminal Law: American, Comparative, and International*, vol 1: *Foundations* (New York, Oxford University Press, 2007) 269; see also GP Fletcher, *Basic Concepts of Criminal Law* (New York, Oxford University Press, 1998) 44–46, 50–53.

[163] See definition of 'civil law system' in n 139. Some examples of scholarship from the numerous civil law countries where a naturalist notion of conduct was overcome are from Peru, see JH Pozo, *Manual de Derecho Penal, Parte General*, 3rd edn ((Lima, Editora Jurídica Grijley, 2005) 381–94; from Colombia, see F Velazquez, *Derecho Penal, Parte General*, 4th edn (Medellin, Colombia, Comilibros, 2009) 508–22; from Costa Rica, see GC Mora and JL Rodriguez, 'Francisco Castillo Gonzalez y el Derecho Penal Costarricense' cited in *Homenaje Al Prof Francisco Castillo Gonzalez en sus 70 Años* (2014) 38–39; from Argentina, see ER Zaffaroni, *Tratado de Derecho Penal, Parte General*, vol 3, 97–134 (Buenos Aires, Ediar 1981); from Chile, see C Urzúa, *Derecho Penal, Parte General*, vol 1 (n 160) 249, 294; and from Spain, see SM Puig, *Introduccion a las bases del Derecho Penal*, 2nd edn (Montevideo, Uruguay, Editorial B de I, 2003) 221.

of these countries have developed a more comprehensive and deeper concept of the nature of conduct in criminal law, which is still evolving and undergoing scholarly inquiry.[164]

Since the first half of the twentieth century, human conduct is no longer regarded by most civil law system specialists as a simple muscular contraction, but rather as an indivisible blend of objectivity and subjectivity.[165] After a long process of theoretical transformation, especially since the normative theory of culpability,[166] and even more so since the goal-oriented theory of conduct[167] was formulated, intent and negligence are no longer considered forms of culpability, but part of the subjective phase of the definition of the criminal offence.

[164] C Roxin, *Strafrecht, Allgemeiner Teil*, vol 1 (Munich, Verlag CH Beck, 2006) 236–70.

[165] See Fletcher, *Basic Concepts of Criminal Law* (n 162) 50–53; see also H Welzel, *El Nuevo Sistema del Derecho Penal* (Barcelona, Ariel, 1964) 62. In Argentina, Professor Frías Caballero taught that the criminal offence is a set of interdependent elements, 'and that each element is a function of the other' and that 'each element has both an objective and a subjective aspect'. MC Libarona, 'Frias Caballero: su Cátedra sobre la Teoría del Delito' in *Homenaje Al Profesor Dr Jorge Frías Caballero* (Colegio de Abogados del Departamento Judicial La Plata, 1998) 139–41.

[166] The normative theory of culpability started with Reinhard Frank in 1907 (*Über den Aufbau des Schuldbegriffs* (Giessen, Alfred Töpelmann, 1907)) and was later developed by a string of scholars. For this theory, culpability is basically blameworthiness. The structure of culpability according to this theory is constituted by the following three elements: (1) capacity of being culpable (not being insane or an infant); (2) intent or negligence, which are the psychological links between actors and their conduct; and (3) the normality of the attendant circumstances. This means that in a concrete situation, actors should have the power to act lawfully so that one can blame them if they act wrongfully. In other words, the attendant circumstances must warrant a fair expectation that actors behave in accordance with the law.

[167] The theory of purposive action (teleological or goal-oriented action) was conceived by Hans Welzel, who defined it as an activity consciously oriented towards a goal. This theory became the basis of the modern characterisation of criminal offences. The advocates of the teleological or goal-oriented theory of action criticise the formulation of the normative theory of culpability mentioned in the previous footnote. They claim that since the normative theory includes intent and negligence as one of the elements composing the structure of culpability, it confuses the value judgment of culpability with the valued object (negligent or intentional action). Culpability therefore consists of a pure value judgment of blameworthiness, and intent and negligence are part of the conduct, which is the object of the value judgment. Therefore, intent and negligence are no longer elements in the structure of culpability, but elements belonging to the definition of the criminal offence to which the conduct should adjust. The teleological or goal-oriented theory of culpability revamps the structure of culpability, which is now composed of three elements. The first element is the capacity of culpability; that is, the general capacity to understand the significance of one's wrongdoing and to determine oneself according to such understanding (eg infants and the insane are not capable of culpability). The second element is the possibility to understand the significance of one's wrongdoing in a concrete situation. When actors not only lack the actual consciousness of their wrongdoing, but also lack the possibility of attaining it, they cannot be blamed (cases of mistake about the legal prohibition). The third element is the possibility to determine oneself in conformity with the requirements of the legal order. In other words, it is necessary that attendant circumstances warrant a fair expectation that actors act in harmony with the legal order to consider them blameworthy. In this respect, it is not fair to expect law-abiding behaviour in situations of duress, concealment of close relatives from criminal persecution and illegal superior orders. See generally H Welzel, *Derecho Penal Aleman, Parte General*, 11th edn (Santiago, Editorial Jurídica de Chile, 1970).

In addition to the correspondence of a particular conduct with the definition of the criminal offence, both in its objective and subjective phases, such conduct must also be wrongful and culpable in order to constitute a criminal offence.[168] A particular conduct is *wrongful* when it contradicts legal norms protecting vital legal interests and values[169] that are significant enough to justify retributive consequences instead of mere compensatory ones.[170] This is clear in the *Vilar* case, where the possible punishment may reach a 20-year sentence of imprisonment and criminal fines far exceeding the extent of the damages.[171] Moreover, such wrongful conduct must also be *culpable* in the sense that the perpetrator must be personally blameworthy for the wrongful conduct.[172]

Within the context of securities fraud, the specific word 'willfully' contained in section 32(a)[173] means that the action externally described in section10(b)[174] must be committed with the consciousness of its wrongfulness.[175] The *Vilar* court erroneously stated that 'willfulness' has nothing to do with the text or the interpretation of section 10(b).[176] Quite the contrary, 'willfully' indicates the specific subjective requirement needed for the structural transformation of the conduct externally described in section 10(b) into the complex combination of external and internal elements that actually constitute a particular criminal conduct.[177] To understand this transformative role of the expression 'willfulness', one should of course connect it with the high degree of wrongfulness of which the perpetrator should be aware.[178] In this context, the subjective requirement of 'willfulness'

[168] Jescheck and Weigend, *Lehrbuch des Strafrechts* (n 161) 218.

[169] German criminal law considers the theory of *Rechtsgut* as the basic tenet of criminal law. '*Rechtsgut*' can be defined as the vital interests and values of the individual and society that are protected by criminal law.

[170] Jescheck and Weigend, *Lehrbuch des Strafrechts* (n 161) 256–60.

[171] *United States v Vilar* (n 83) 95–97.

[172] Welzel, *Derecho Penal Aleman, Parte General* (n 167) 197.

[173] 15 USC, ss 78ff (2012).

[174] ibid, s 78l (2012).

[175] In the US, the term 'willfully' is surrounded with interpretive confusion. The Supreme Court has pointed out that the word 'willful' is a 'word of many meanings.' *Spies v United States*, 317 US 492, 497 (1943). In the context of securities fraud, however, the Ninth Circuit has interpreted this term correctly. The Ninth Circuit interpreted 'willful' as 'intentionally undertaking an act that one knows to be wrongful'. *United States v Tarallo*, 380 F3d 1174, 1188 (9th Cir 2004). This decision is case-specific and in the US, neither courts nor scholars have categorised this concept within a comprehensive theory of the criminal offence. 'Willfulness' has been related neither to the conduct nor to the values and interests protected by the criminalisation of such conduct, as is the case in the German model.

[176] See *United States v Vilar* (n 83) 75–76.

[177] See n 165.

[178] See n 161. The term 'willfulness' (see n 175), as defined by the Ninth Circuit in *United States v Tarallo*, 380 F3d 1174, 1183 (2004), links the intentionality with the high degree of wrongfulness needed to transform the securities fraud into a criminal offence. The decision of Congress to make a behaviour criminal implies the requirement of a serious culpable wrongdoing; that is, the wilful conduct should contradict basic vital social values consisting in this case in the integrity of the financial market as a crucial part of the economy. While civil and administrative actions are available for the infringement of any rule under the Securities Exchange Act, only a limited number are subject to criminal enforcement. For example, filing violations would be excluded from the latter. It is necessary that the culpability of the perpetrator should be based on a degree of wrongfulness enough to compromise the integrity of the financial market and to thus arouse the moral condemnation of society.

indicates a high degree of antisociality, enough to justify the application of the criminal justice system.[179] To criminally enforce a statute means that its infringement has attained such gravity that it deserves the moral condemnation of all society.[180] Wilfulness in itself is not sufficient to transform securities violations into a criminal offence. A certain entity of offensiveness or harm is also necessary for a behaviour to become a criminal offence. Although it is difficult to establish such a qualitative leap, section 32(a) provides some parameters by establishing a maximum penalty of 20 years of imprisonment and extremely high fines. By characterising securities fraud as a very serious felony, section 32(a) implies that the gravity of the harm should be commensurate with at least one year of imprisonment, which is the minimum penalty for felonies. Here the penalty helps to determine the magnitude of the fraudulent action that has to be committed wilfully in order to become a criminal offence.

Moreover, in the modern notion of a gradual culpability,[181] the measure of blameworthiness depends on the magnitude of the wrongfulness.[182]

We have already used theoretical German legal approaches to reformulate the notion of human conduct to challenge the Second Circuit's assumption that the notion of conduct is the same in both civil and criminal contexts[183] and to interpret the nature and scope of the word 'wilfully'.

The adverb 'wilfully' is given a pivotal role in section 32(a)'s definition of the crime.[184] It corresponds in American terminology to the mens rea of securities fraud.[185] As mentioned earlier, some American scholars have noted insufficiencies in American law regarding this concept. These well-founded scholarly complaints justify the present volume's reliance on foreign legal systems in search for conceptual clarification. Consider, for instance, Michael L Seigel's complaints.[186] Seigel denounces the massive confusion related to the interpretation of the phrase 'mens rea'[187] and undertakes a review of the multiple and conflicting interpretations of this key phrase, which determines whether the actor has committed a crime or not.[188]

[179] See n 178.

[180] J Dressler, *Understanding Criminal Law*, 5th edn (New York, LexisNexis, 2009) 2.

[181] Jescheck and Weigend, *Lehrbuch des Strafrechts* (n 161) 428, 470 and 471; H Welzel, *El Nuevo Sistema de Derecho Penal: una Introducción a la Doctrina de la Accion Finalista* (Barcelona, Ediciones Ariel, 1964) 131.

[182] Urzúa, *Derecho Penal, Parte General*, vol II (n 160) 13.

[183] *United States v Vilar* (n 83) 74.

[184] 15 USC, s 78ff (2012).

[185] See Leng-Chia Hung, 'Securities Markets – A Place to Get Rich Quick or a Quicksand Going Straight to Jail? The "Mens Rea" Required for Insider Trading Criminal Liability' (2010) 5 *National Taiwan University Law Review* 1, 2.

[186] ML Seigel, 'Bringing Coherence to Mens Rea Analysis for Securities-related Offenses' 2006 *Wisconsin Law Review* 1563, 1569.

[187] ibid, 1565.

[188] ibid; see also JM Miller, 'Mens Rea Quagmire: The Conscience or Consciousness of the Criminal Law?' (2001) *Western State University Law Review* 21, 52–55.

Seigel praises the Model Penal Code (MPC), published by the American Law Institute in 1962, for unifying and simplifying the common law's mens rea terminology, and he recommends emphatically its adoption in the field of securities-related criminal offences.[189] It is true that the MPC has improved and unified mens rea terminology; however, it has not reached the conceptual depth achieved by other legal systems since 1962.[190] A comparative perspective might provide American scholarship with the intellectual instrument to better understand the role and significance of a particle such as 'wilfully' within the context of a statute that criminalises behaviour otherwise considered to be a mere civil or administrative wrong. The need for such a contribution can be inferred from Joshua Dressler's insights into the ambiguity of the term mens rea.[191] Although apparently Professor Dressler is not aware of theoretical criminal law developments in the civil law world, or at least he does not refer to them, he intuitively understands some of the categories elaborated in these countries.[192]

Dressler clearly perceives that the words 'mens rea' hide two different meanings: the 'culpability' meaning and the 'elemental' one.[193] According to the former, mens rea denotes a morally blameworthy state of mind, while the latter indicates 'the particular mental state' elements included in the definition of certain criminal offences.[194] Such a perception has led to the reformulation of the concept of criminal offence in countries that follow the German model.[195]

In German legal literature, which has influenced most civil law countries in the last half of the twentieth century, the notions of 'action', 'behaviour' and 'conduct' are dealt with as inextricably linked with intent, as opposed to older approaches in which human beings were viewed as responsive machines.[196] The expression 'willfulness' cannot be seen, as in the *Vilar* decision, as a mere appendage that triggers the intervention of the criminal justice system; rather, it must be viewed as a crucial element in the definition of a crime, transforming the nature and substance of the defined conduct. In these new developments of criminal law theory, human conduct is no longer conceived as 'a willed muscular

[189] Model Penal Code, s 2.02 (Am Law Inst Proposed Official Draft 1962).

[190] Originally, culpability was conceived as a nexus or psychological link between the actor and the act. This link manifested itself in two forms: intent and negligence. In the latest developments of criminal law theory, culpability became a pure judgment of blameworthiness composed of three elements: capacity of culpability (ie sanity or age), the actual possibility of knowing the wrongfulness of the action, and the ability to conform the action to the requirements of the law. See Welzel, *Derecho Penal Aleman, Parte General* (n 167) 214.

[191] See Dressler, *Understanding Criminal Law* (n 180) 118–19.

[192] ibid.

[193] ibid.

[194] ibid.

[195] W Naucke, 'An Insider's Perspective on the Significance of the German Criminal Theory's General System for Analyzing Criminal Acts' 1984 (3) *Brigham Young University Law Review* (1984) 305, 306, 320–21. See also MD Dubber, 'The Promise of German Criminal Law: A Science of Crime and Punishment' (2005) 6 *German Law Journal* 1049, 1050 and 1086.

[196] See Fletcher, *Grammar of Criminal Law* (n 162) 289.

contraction' but as goal-oriented.[197] Intent, therefore, traditionally defined as a form of culpability, becomes an essential component of the notion of conduct.[198] Culpability, on the contrary, is a judgment about such conduct that takes place at a later stage of analysis.[199] It consists of determining the personal blameworthiness of the perpetrator, taking into account circumstances such as mental health, maturity, possibility of knowing the transgressed legal precept and absence of duress.[200] Dressler, as explained above, has picked up on the ambiguity of the term mens rea, used indifferently as a descriptive element of a particular state of mind or as culpability in the general sense of blameworthiness.[201] This is to a certain extent an approximation to similar modern doctrinal developments in the civil law system.[202]

The crime of securities fraud is actually defined in section 32(a), in which 'willfulness' is an essential element of this definition. For the rest, it incorporates section 10(b) by reference.[203] Accordingly, it is misleading to affirm, as Judge Cabranes does in *Vilar*, that the wilful commission of the fraud does not relate to the conduct prescribed by section 10(b).[204] Quite the contrary, 'wilfully' is an essential element of the conduct, transmuting section 10(b) after its incorporation by reference to section 32(a).[205]

The confusion of the court can be traced to the ambiguous nature of mens rea in the Anglo-American tradition and how this ambiguity 'loops back and undermines our understanding of human action'.[206]

Judge Cabranes erroneously concludes that proving wilfulness has nothing to do with the text or interpretation of section 10(b).[207] He ignores that wilfulness transforms the nature of the conduct. By using such an expression, the Exchange Act refers to a particular conduct that poses a social threat to the vital values and interests of the community and becomes the object of moral condemnation of a whole society.[208] This is, however, just the beginning of our argument. Any homicide, rape or larceny is criminal conduct subject to social condemnation and moral opprobrium, but the circumstances in themselves do not justify their

[197] ibid, 269; see Fletcher, *Basic Concepts of Criminal Law* (n 162) 51–53.
[198] Cury Urzúa, *Derecho Penal, Parte General*, vol 1 (n 160) 249, 294.
[199] Welzel, *Derecho Penal Aleman, Parte General* (n 167) 214.
[200] ibid.
[201] Dressler, *Understanding Criminal Law* (n 180) 118–19.
[202] In the modern civil law system developments, intent has been removed from the notion of culpability and has become part of the notion of conduct and therefore of the definition of the offence. Culpability, on the other hand, is a separate element of the criminal offence considered in the last stage of the crime's analysis consisting of a pure judgment of blameworthiness. As specified in n 190, Dressler understands that, on the one hand, the term mens rea means intent as part of the definition of the offence, while, on the other hand, it refers to a general judgment of blameworthiness.
[203] 15 USC, s 78ff (2012).
[204] *United States v Vilar* (n 83) 75–76.
[205] 15 USC, ss 78l, 78ff (2012).
[206] Fletcher, *Grammar of Criminal Law* (n 162) 288.
[207] *United States v Vilar* (n 83) 75–76.
[208] See Dressler, *Understanding Criminal Law* (n 180) 118–19.

extraterritorial application.[209] *Bowman* expressly underscores that many intrinsically local crimes fall within the territorial jurisdiction of the state and cannot be applied extraterritorially without an express mandate from Congress.[210]

Further inquiry into the governmental and social value protected by section 32(a) combined with section 10(b), that is, the integrity of the securities market, leads us to conclude that such a value is similar to those values protected by the Supreme Court in *Bowman* and used to affirm the will of Congress to apply the criminal provision extraterritorially.[211] The globalisation of securities markets has brought about its delocalisation, and therefore places it under the *Bowman* exception to the presumption against extraterritoriality.[212]

After having determined that 'willfulness' transforms the nature of the definition of fraud provided by section 10(b) into a criminal offence, the next step is to determine that the social value protected by such criminal provision rises to the nature of governmental interest that, according to *Bowman*, justifies its extraterritorial application. The Securities Exchange Act was basically enacted to protect investors; maintain fair, orderly and efficient markets; and facilitate capital formation necessary to sustain economic growth.[213] The delocalisation of securities markets requires the extraterritorial application of the Act to attain these goals.

D. Fourth Critique of *Vilar*

Here is *Vilar*'s last relevant proposition, followed by my critique:

> *The government argues that criminal statutes 'are concerned with prohibiting individuals … from defrauding American investors and from using the infrastructure of American commerce to defraud investors' and that applying the presumption against extraterritoriality to criminal statutes 'would create a broad immunity for criminal conduct simply because the fraudulent scheme culminates in a purchase or sale abroad.'*

[209] To justify their extraterritorial application without an express congressional mandate, it is necessary, using Chief Justice Taft's words, that these 'offences are such that to limit their [prosecution] to the strictly territorial jurisdiction would be greatly to curtail the scope and usefulness of the statute'. A Chehtman, *The Philosophical Foundations of Extraterritorial Punishment* (New York, Oxford University Press, 2010) 76 (internal citation omitted).

[210] See *United States v Bowman* (n 46) 98.

[211] As, for example, the environment in *Skiriotes v Florida* (n 103), and the integrity of the bankruptcy proceeding in *Stegeman v United States*, 400 US 837 (1970).

[212] See Podgor and Filler, 'International Criminal Jurisdiction' (n 132); see also Ryngaert, *Jurisdiction in International Law* (n 2) 187.

[213] 'The mission of the U.S. Securities and Exchange Commission is to protect investors, maintain fair, orderly, and efficient markets, and facilitate capital formation.' US Securities and Exchange Commission, *The Investor's Advocate: How the SEC Protects Investors, Maintains Market Integrity, and Facilitates Capital Formation*, available at www.sec.gov/about/whatwedo.shtml (last visited 22 October 2015). The Securities and Exchange Act of 1934 mentions in s 12 that the purposes of the Act are the maintenance of fair and orderly markets and the protection of investors and the public interest. See Securities Exchange Act 1934, Pub L No 112–158, s 12 (2012).

> *But much the same could be said of civil fraud statutes: Applying the presumption against extraterritoriality immunizes thieves and swindlers from civil liability for defrauding Americans abroad.*[214]

To justify the application of *Morrison* to criminal cases, the *Vilar* court considers that the strict application of the presumption against extraterritoriality has the same consequences in civil and criminal realms.[215] If it were the same to dispense civil wrongdoers from liability as to immunise perpetrators from criminal responsibility for a certain behaviour, there would be no reason to criminalise such behaviour in the first place. There is a fundamental difference between reduced protection of individuals against personal damages and reduced protection of society against attacks to its vital social interests and values, such as the integrity of financial markets. This qualitative difference is reflected in the difference between civil and criminal law procedures. Securities fraud can reach such gravity as to concern not only the direct victim, but also the entire society.[216] The award of compensatory damages results in a money transfer from one person to another, while a criminal law conviction implies the moral condemnation made by an entire society.

Business-related criminal law typically protects supra-individual vital interests and values, such as the integrity of securities markets.[217] In a globalised economy, these legally protected collective interests have experienced such a delocalisation that, to be meaningfully protected, they can hardly be constrained by strict territorial limitations.

Another aspect of the distinction between civil and criminal law that justifies its separate treatment regarding extraterritoriality is the motivation and purposes of private litigants as opposed to those of public prosecutors.[218] *Morrison*'s merit was to curtail the abusive use of the American judicial system by Australian plaintiffs in an intrinsically Australian case.[219] This case was an illustration of Lord Denning's remark, 'As a moth is attracted to the light, so is a litigant drawn to the United States.'[220] Foreign litigants often elect the US forum, searching for

[214] *United States v Vilar* (n 83) 74 (internal citations omitted).

[215] ibid.

[216] E Rotman, 'La Criminalidad Financiera en el Siglo XIX' *Revista de Derecho Penal y Criminolgia* (April–June 1969) 228, 234.

[217] Tiedemann, *Wirtschaftsstrafrecht* (n 145) 67.

[218] 'The enforcement for violation of federal securities law is carried out at the administrative, civil and criminal levels. The SEC has the authority to initiate investigations of potential violations and to prevent them through civil and administrative enforcement. The Department of Justice has sole jurisdiction over criminal proceedings.' CA Yaeger, 'Securities Fraud' (2014) 51 *American Criminal Law Review* 1720. In addition, a federal district court in Pennsylvania recognised a private right of action for violation of Rule 10b-5 in *Kardon v Nat'l Gypsom Co*, 73 F Supp 798 (ED Pa 1947). The federal case law developed on this subject was officially recognised by the Supreme Court in *Blue Chip Stamps v Manor Drug Stores*, 421 US 723 (1975). See DE Herz-Roiphe, 'Innocent Abroad?: Morrison, Vilar, and the Extraterritorial Application of the Exchange Act' (2014) 123 *Yale Law Journal* 1875, 1877 (provides important insights on the difference of securities fraud private and public actions).

[219] See generally *Morrison v National Australia Bank* (n 53) 248.

[220] *Smith Kline & French Lab Ltd v Bloch*, [1983] 1 WLR 730, 733 (CA) (Lord Denning MR).

handsome jury awards, punitive damages, contingency fees, ample discovery and other attractions offered by American courts.[221] In private actions, profit considerations command the forum selection and eclipse any public policy considerations.[222]

A criminal action initiated by a public plaintiff, such as the DOJ, is unlikely to ignore potential international conflicts and will try to avoid them. The main reason supporting the presumption against extraterritoriality is dispelled when a branch of the US government seriously concerned with avoiding international friction prosecutes the securities fraudsters.[223] This is the reason why the Dodd-Frank Act attempted to reintroduce the 'conduct' and 'effects' tests for public enforcement of US law, whether by the SEC or the DOJ.[224]

E. Conclusion

The *Vilar* decision incorrectly applies the *Morrison* holding to a very different factual and legal setting. *Morrison* is about a private law class action involving an evident abuse of the US judicial system by Australian litigants.[225] This abuse led to a unanimous rejection by the district and circuit federal courts as well as by the totality of the Supreme Court justices.[226] In contrast, *Vilar* is about an action brought by the DOJ against transnational criminals to preserve social values of the highest rank, such as financial market integrity and investors' trust.[227] The severity of the punishment, imprisonment of up to 20 years and significant fines, demonstrates the gravity of the crime for which Vilar and his accomplice were accused.[228] Unlike the National Australia Bank agents in *Morrison*, Vilar and his accomplice were not trying to gain US jurisdiction, but rather were attempting to avoid it.[229]

The Supreme Court's *Morrison* decision is silent on whether its interpretation of the Securities Exchange Act covers criminal prosecutions.[230] What is more, Justice Stevens's concurrence was in the understanding that public enforcement of the Exchange Act's antifraud provisions was not included in the holding.[231]

[221] A Bell, *Forum Shopping and Venue in International Litigation* (New York, Oxford University Press, 2007) 20, 29, 31; GB Born, *International Civil Litigation in the United States* (Deventer, Netherlands and Boston, MA, Wolters Kluwer, 1996) 3–5.

[222] On the strong monetary incentives for aggrieved investors in private enforcement, see generally NR Ramphal, 'The Role of Public and Private Litigation in the Enforcement of Securities Laws in the United States,' *Rand Dissertation Series* (Santa Monica, CA: Rand Corporation, 2007).

[223] For a similar argument, see Herz-Roiphe (n 218) 1879.

[224] Dodd-Frank Wall Street Reform and Consumer Protection Act, Pub L No 111-203 (2010).

[225] See generally *Morrison v Nat'l Austl Bank Ltd* (n 54) 247.

[226] See generally ibid; see also ibid, 172.

[227] See generally *United States v Vilar* (n 83).

[228] See generally ibid.

[229] See generally *Morrison v National Australia Bank* (n 53); *United States v Vilar* (n 83).

[230] See generally *Morrison v National Australia Bank* (n 53) 247.

[231] ibid, 274 (Stevens J, concurring).

The *Vilar* court extended *Morrison*'s restrictive holding to the criminal antifraud provisions of the Exchange Act, disregarding essential substantive and procedural differences between the civil and criminal law ambits.[232] The court further ignored the dynamic character and the purposes of the Securities Exchange Act in a world of internationalised financial markets.[233]

Despite its wholehearted adherence to *Morrison*'s interpretation of the Act, *Vilar* recognised that *United States v Bowman* had survived *Morrison*.[234] Such recognition opens a significant crack in the presumption against extraterritoriality, a seemingly iron wall in Justice Scalia's own statutory interpretative methodology.

After undermining the presumption against extraterritoriality by recognising the validity of the *Bowman* exception, *Vilar* tried to backtrack by giving the narrowest possible interpretation of *Bowman*.[235] This artificial conclusion betrays not only *Bowman*'s words, but also its spirit.

It is important to bear in mind that the presumption against extraterritoriality is not a constitutional principle; it is a canon of interpretation with dubious precedential value.[236] This is a case in which *Morrison*'s supportive rationale should not be binding, and its interpretative methodology should not be adopted – all the more so, as in this case, when they are applied to new and different factual contexts.

Statutory interpretative methodology is not part of the holding. '[U]nder the doctrine of *stare decisis* a case is important only for what it decides – for the "what," not for the "why," and not for the "how."'[237] In this respect, Randy J Kozel warns against precedents defined 'capaciously and inclusively in constraining future courts', as is often the case in contemporary federal practice.[238] *Morrison* is an example of this unwarranted broadening of the holding's scope.

Scalia himself believed that dicta are 'binding upon neither' the Supreme Court nor the inferior courts, and that they do not deserve *stare decisis* weight.[239] Moreover, as Judge Leval pointed out, '[t]he Supreme Court's dicta are not law,' and judges 'may not treat Supreme Court's dictum as dispositive'.[240] Although Scalia emphasised that the presumption against extraterritoriality has historical lineage,[241] such circumstance does not prove binding force.[242]

[232] See generally *United States v Vilar* (n 83).
[233] ibid.
[234] ibid.
[235] ibid.
[236] See AR Gluck, 'The Federal Common Law of Statutory Interpretation: Erie for the Age of Statutes' (2013) 54 *William & Mary Law Review* 753, 760–65; see also S Foster, 'Should Courts Give Stare Decisis Effect to Statutory Interpretation Methodology?' (2008) 96 *Georgetown Law Journal* 1863, 1910–11 (while actually advocating for giving *stare decisis* effect to statutory interpretation methodology, implicitly recognising that as of now, the state of the law does not accept it).
[237] *In re Osborne*, 76 F3d 306, 309 (9th Cir 1996).
[238] RJ Kozel, 'The Scope of Precedent' (2014) 113 *Michigan Law Review* 179, 230.
[239] ibid, 187 (citations omitted) (internal quotation marks omitted).
[240] PN Leval, 'Judging Under the Constitution: Dicta about Dicta' (2005) 81 *New York University Law Review* 1249, 1274.
[241] Parrish, 'Morrison, The Effects Test' (n 29) 98.
[242] Kozel, 'The Scope of Precedent' (n 238) 191.

Furthermore, sections 10(b) and 32(a) of the Securities and Exchange Act should be interpreted systematically and in accordance with the purposes of the Securities Exchange Act.[243] The definition of the crime prosecuted in *Vilar* is contained in section 32(a).[244] As a blanket provision, this section incorporates by reference section 10(b), which provides the external description of the criminalised behaviour.[245] Moreover, section 32(a) criminalises securities fraud by punishing it with a severity commensurate to the values protected by such criminal provision.[246]

The term 'willfully' in section 32(a) is inextricably related to the conduct externally described in section 10(b) and incorporated by reference into the criminal provision of section 32(a).[247] The law requires a specific state of mind when securities frauds have reached the magnitude that justifies their criminalisation (that is, threatening both market integrity and public wealth).[248] The protection of these vital social values that are instrumental to the workings of the economy led the legislator to create a new criminal provision. This provision includes the more stringent requirement of consciousness of a type of wrongfulness, the magnitude of which explains such criminalisation. Perpetrators must be aware of the contradiction of their behaviour with vital social values to an extent that justifies their criminal law protection under section 32(a) of the Securities Exchange Act.[249]

Therefore, in the context of securities frauds, the adverb 'wilfully' stands for a manipulative or deceptive device or contrivance made unlawful by section 10b of the Exchange Act, carried out with the awareness of its inherent highly detrimental nature. The magnitude of the action's harmfulness should be measured against its aptitude to compromise the integrity of the financial market, thus reaching the point that had led Congress to criminalise it in the first place.[250] 'Wilfully', therefore, is not a mere appendage disconnected from the conduct externally described by section 10(b), as *Vilar* shortsightedly believes.

Moreover, it is precisely the transnational nature of the values of market integrity and public wealth protected by section 32(a) that justifies the extraterritorial application of the Securities Exchange Act antifraud provisions. The globalisation of financial markets regulated by the Securities Exchange Act demands a dynamic interpretation of the Act, in light of its 'present societal, political, and legal context'.[251]

[243] See n 213.
[244] 15 USC, s 78ff (2012).
[245] 15 USC, ss 78l, 78ff (2012).
[246] 15 USC, s 78ff.
[247] 15 USC, ss 78l, 78ff (2012).
[248] See nn 161, 178.
[249] ibid.
[250] ibid.
[251] WN Eskridge Jr, 'Dynamic Statutory Interpretation' (1987) 135 *University of Pennsylvania Law Review* 1479.

Chapters 4 and 5 will respectively cover insider trading and market manipulation as foremost examples of legislative convergence: on the one hand through diffusion of the American legal model, and on the other, through a harmonisation process culminating with the regulation of market abuse in Europe.

4

The Internationalised Repression of Insider Trading

I. The United States Law on Insider Trading

Besides isolated examples offered by Tripodi (Italy – see section VII)[1] and the role of insider trading in the debacle of the South Sea Company,[2] the modern genesis of insider trading thinking started in the US, where it became of central relevance in American law, as a matter of the state law fiduciary duties of corporate directors and officers.[3] Even when the federal government adopted the Securities Act in 1933 and the Securities Exchange Act in 1934, it is only in the late 1960s that insider trading was recognised and 'emerged as a central feature of modern US securities regulation'.[4]

Mann and Lustgarten explained already in 1993 the challenge posed to the Securities and Exchange Commission (SEC) by the extraordinary increase in the internationalisation of the world's securities markets, and the need to undertake initiatives to promote international cooperation in the enforcement of insider trading.[5]

The diffusion of American law in a number of countries represents a prevailing form of internationalisation of the insider trading prohibition. Therefore, the analysis of this internationalisation process should start by an account of American insider trading law.

There is neither a legal definition of the term 'insider trading', nor a straightforward doctrinal definition. William KS Wang and Marc I Steinberg, in their treatise about insider trading,[6] limit themselves to describe its scope, rather than expressly

[1] AF Tripodi, *Informazione Privilegiati e Statuto Penale del Mercato Finanziario* (Padua, Casa Editrice Dott. Antonio Milani, 2012) xv, offers the following examples: Gnaeus Flavius, stealing and publicising the secret book of the *legis actionis* to gain political advantages; the administrators of the Dutch East Indies Company selling their shares on the advanced knowledge of dividends reduction; and Nathan de Rostschild's purchases with the advance knowledge of Napoleon's defeat in Waterloo.

[2] R Dale, *The First Crash: Lessons From The South Sea Bubble* (Princeton, NJ, Princeton University Press, 2004) 97 and 179.

[3] SM Bainbridge, 'An Overview of Insider Trading Law and Policy: an Introduction' in SM Bainbridge (ed), *The Research Handbook on Insider Trading* (Northampton, MA, Elgar Publishing, 2013) 1.

[4] ibid.

[5] MD Mann and LA Lustgarten, 'Internationalization of Insider Trading Enforcement: A Guide to Regulation and Cooperation', *Practising Law Institute*, Pli Order No B4-7024 (1993) 2.

[6] WKS Wang and MI Steinberg, *Insider Trading* (New York, Oxford University Press, 2010) 1.

defining this expression. Furthermore, they agree with other commentators that the term 'insider trading is actually a misnomer'.[7] Their use of the term 'insider trading' designates 'trading by *any* one (inside or *outside* of the issuer) on any type of material nonpublic information about the issuer or about the market for the security'.[8]

At the beginning of the twentieth century, insider trading was regulated in some States as part of state corporate law, mainly targeting corporate officers and directors who bought stock from shareholders of their company in face-to-face transactions.[9] Today, federal securities law has largely taken precedence over state law. Since the 1930s, with the advent of federal securities laws, state law kept only a subsidiary role, covering gaps in the federal laws.

The textual nucleus of US insider trading law, the point of departure of a vast process of internationalisation, consists of section 10(b) of the Exchange Act, and in the judicial derivations of SEC's adoption of Rule 10b-5.[10]

Moreover, the basic provisions contained in section 10(b) of the Exchange Act and Rule 10b-5 have been shaped by the interpretation of the US Supreme Court in a series of path-breaking decisions.

The first insider trading case under Rule 10b-5 was a 1961 ruling of the SEC in an administrative procedure: *In re Cady, Roberts & Co.*[11] Cheever Cowdin, a broker and board member of the broker-dealer firm, Cady, Roberts & Co, was also a member of the Board of Directors of the Curtiss-Wright Corporation. As such, he was informed of a reduction of a dividend that would determine a selling spree as soon as it reached the public knowledge. Before this information impacted the market, Cowdin relayed this insider information to another broker, Robert M Gintel, who entered two sell orders in anticipation of such event without disclosing the inside information. The SEC decided that corporate 'insiders', particularly officers, directors and controlling stockholders, have an affirmative duty to disclose material facts which are known to them by virtue of their positions in the corporation but which are not known to persons with whom they deal. Their silence amounts to a misleading or deceptive activity prohibited by Rule 10b-5. The SEC believed that when disclosure was not feasible, either for being improper or unrealistic, then the alternative should be to forgo the transaction. As a result of this administrative action, Gintel was fined and temporarily suspended from the New York Stock Exchange. Cowdin could not be prosecuted because he died

[7] ibid. See also SM Bainbridge, *Insider Trading Law And Policy* (St Paul, MI, West Academic, Foundation Press, 2014) 1.

[8] Wang and Steinberg, *Insider Trading* (n 6) 1.

[9] Bainbridge, *Insider Trading Law and Policy* (n 7) 2.

[10] The insider trading prohibition is also regulated in US law by SEC Rule 14e-3 under the Exchange Act, s 14(e) regarding tender offers; Exchange Act, s 16(b) prohibiting corporate directors, officers and shareholders owning more than 10% of the firm's stock from earning short-swing profits by buying and selling stock in a six-month period; and by 18 USC, s 1341 regarding wire and mail frauds, as well as by the Sarbanes Oxley Act, 18 USC, s 1348 regarding criminal prosecution of securities frauds. FA Gevurtz, 'The Globalization of Insider Trading' (2002) 15 *Transnational Law* 63, 65, fn 7.

[11] *Cady, Roberts & Co*, 40 SEC 907 (1961).

a year before the hearing. This case provided the rationale for the 'Traditional' or 'Classical Theory' that imposes liability on corporate insiders who obtain material, non-public information as a result of their positions in the corporation and use the information to trade their corporation's securities without disclosing such information.

The first influential judicial decision was *SEC v Texas Gulf Sulphur Co.*[12] After agents of the Texas Gulf Sulphur Co discovered an ore deposit in Ontario in 1959, the company's president gave express orders to the team members to maintain the discovery and exploration efforts strictly confidential. The discovery was followed up with further explorations, drilling and the acquisition of the land where the ore deposit belonged. The discovery was announced to the public in 1964.

In the previous years, a company's insiders bought stock and stock options, and tipped off outsiders, all benefitting from the stocks rising prices. The SEC reacted by suing the insiders for violation of Rule 10b-5. The cases culminated with a decision of the Second Circuit Court of Appeals holding that an insider possessing material non-public information must either disclose the information before trading or abstain from trading until the information had been disclosed. This disclose or abstain rule was backed by a policy of equality of access to information.

In the 1980s, the US Supreme Court radically narrowed the scope of the insider trading prohibition as formulated by the *Texas Gulf Sulphur* decision.

The stream of US Supreme Court cases recognising criminal liability for insider trading begins with *Chiarella v United States*,[13] which is the first criminal prosecution based on a violation of the Securities Exchange Act. This case involved the employee of a financial printer, Chiarella, who deduced the concealed names of the targets of takeover operations from coded and confidential papers that he had access to by virtue of his position in the company. The employee profited from his advanced knowledge through timely purchases and sales of the stock of the targeted corporations without disclosing his inside information. Indicted on 17 counts of violating section 10(b) of the 1934 Act and SEC Rule 10b-5, he was brought to trial and convicted on all counts. The Court of Appeal for the Second Circuit affirmed the conviction, which was eventually reversed by the US Supreme Court. The main issue faced by the Court was whether Chiarella's silence may have constituted a manipulative or deceptive device subject to the anti-fraud provisions of the Securities Exchange Act. The failure to disclose material non-public information, however, was not considered to give rise to fraud liability on the part of Chiarella because he was not under the duty to disclose. This duty only arises, Powell J pointed out, 'when one party has information 'that the other party is entitled to know because of a fiduciary or other similar relation of trust and confidence between them'.[14] In this case, no duty could arise from Chiarella's relationship with the sellers of the target company's securities since he had no prior

[12] *SEC v Texas Gulf Sulphur Co*, 401 F2d 833, 848 (2d Cir 1968), cert denied, 394 US 976 (1969).
[13] *Chiarella v United States*, 445 US 222 (1980).
[14] ibid, 231.

dealings with them. 'He was not their agent, he was not a fiduciary, and he was not a person in whom the sellers had placed their trust and confidence. He was in fact a complete stranger who dealt with the sellers only through impersonal market transactions.'[15] Chief Justice Burger dissented arguing that Rule 10(b) implies that *anyone* who misappropriates non-public information has an absolute duty to disclose (emphasis added). However, this opinion was not taken into consideration because it was beyond the instructions given to the jury. This issue was later addressed in the *O'Hagan* case, which considerably expanded the scope of the insider trading prohibition.[16]

In *Dirks v SEC*,[17] the Supreme Court further demarcated the boundaries of the insider trading's prohibition by defining the scope of tippees' liability. This case revolves around one of the largest corporate frauds of the 1970s, the downfall of Equity Funding of America.[18] Ronald Secrist, one of Equity's former officers, informed Raymond Dirks, the main protagonist in this case, that Equity Funding's assets were fraudulently overstated. Dirks was an analyst who specialised in insurance companies' securities. He worked for a New York brokership dealer firm who advised institutional investors. Taking into account that life insurance was one of the products sold by Equity Funding, the former officer, Secrist, prompted Dirks to verify the fraud and take the necessary steps so that the market would take notice and the authorities would investigate Equity Funding.

Consequently, Dirks visited Equity Funding's headquarters in Los Angeles, and for the purpose of his inquiry he interviewed both members of senior management and employees. Some employees confirmed the charges of fraud. This admission caused Dirks to disclose the fraud to a number of clients and investors, thus precipitating a sell-off of the corporation's holdings to the tune of $16 million. Dirks simultaneously contacted a bureau chief journalist at the *Wall Street Journal* in Los Angeles, asking him to publish the story, but the journalist refused because he feared that he would be sued for libel. The divulgation of the results of Dirks investigation led to the detection of the fraud, which ultimately led to the collapse of Equities Funds' shares, the impounding of the corporation's records by the California insurance authorities, the decision of the *Wall Street Journal* to publish the story, and the eventual consequent entry of the corporation into receivership.

After a subsequent investigation, the SEC found that Dirks had aided and abetted violations of section10(b) of the Securities Exchange Act of 1934 and SEC Rule 10b-5 by repeating the allegations of fraud to investors who later sold their Equity Funding stock. The Supreme Court again granted *certiorari* to decide the intricate issue presented by this case and reversed the SEC decision. As in *Chiarella*, Powell J gave the opinion of the Court.

[15] ibid, 232–33.
[16] See *United States v O'Hagan* later in this section.
[17] *Dirks v SEC*, 463 US 646 (1983).
[18] R Stelnick, *Mainframe: Madoff-size Money, Monstrous Misapplication* (2 November 2011) available at www.decodeqdscience.org/mainframe-madoff-size-money-monstrous-misapplication-logon/4918.

The main issue was to determine how a tippee acquires the *Cady, Roberts's* duty to disclose or to refrain from trading on inside information. The Court reaffirmed the principle that 'a duty to disclose arises from the relations between parties … and not merely from one's ability to acquire because of his position in the market'.[19]

The Court underscored that a broad duty to disclose merely based on the reception of the non-public information from an insider would endanger and thus inhibit the situation of market analysts, who perform a function essential for the preservation of a healthy market.[20] On the other hand, there is the danger that insiders may use the undisclosed information to their advantage through the use of an outsider. Thus, tipping may become an indirect means to violate the *Cady, Roberts* disclose or abstain rule.

According to *Dirks*, tippees who received improper inside information have a duty to disclose, which is derivative from that of the insider. The tippee assumes a fiduciary duty to the stockholders of a corporation not to trade on material non-public information only in specific situations: when the tippee knew or should have known that the tippers breached their fiduciary duty to the shareholders. However, an insider-tipper only breaches their fiduciary duty when that insider will personally benefit, directly or indirectly, from the disclosure.[21] Absent some personal gain there has been no breach of duty to stockholders and therefore there is no derivative breach from the tippee. In most cases, tipping does not necessarily involve a breach of fiduciary duty, when for example the recipient is a market analyst. Whether disclosure of inside information is a breach of duty depends on the purpose of the disclosure.

The Court applied its newly developed notion of tippee responsibility to the petitioner Dirks, finding that he had not violated the antifraud provisions of the Exchange Act. He was a stranger to Equity Funding, had no pre-existent fiduciary duty to its shareholders, and he did not create any expectation of confidentiality to obtain the information nor did he misappropriate it. Furthermore, Secrist and the Equity Funding employees received no monetary or personal benefit for revealing Equity Funding's secrets and Dirks played a major role in exposing the fraud to the appropriate authorities.

In *United States v O'Hagan*,[22] the Supreme Court announced the Misappropriation Theory as a new theory of liability under Rule 10b-5 by expanding the scope to reach those who traded in breach of a duty owed to the source of the information. The liability of traders is not founded upon their fiduciary relationship between the trader and the party with whom they trade, but on their deceptive conduct in connection with securities transactions. The undisclosed, self-serving use of the principal's information in order to buy or sell securities, in breach of a duty of loyalty and confidentiality, defrauds the principal of

[19] *Dirks v SEC* (n 17) 658. Citing *Chiarella* (n 13) 231–32.
[20] *Dirks v SEC* (n 17) 658.
[21] ibid, 662.
[22] *United States v O'Hagan*, 521 US 642 (1997).

the exclusive use of that information and therefore violates section 10(b) and Rule 10b-5.

James Hermann O'Hagan worked as a partner of the law firm Dorsey & Whitney in Minneapolis, Minnesota. In July 1988, Grand Metropolitan PLC (Gran Met) retained Dorsey & Whitney to represent Grand Met in negotiations for a potential tender offer for the common stock of the Pillsbury Company. Both Grand Met and Dorsey & Whitney took positive steps to maintain the secrecy of the tender offer. On September of 1988, Dorsey & Whitney withdrew from Gran Met's representation and in October, Grand Met publicly announced its tender offer for Pillsbury stock.

Since August of the same year, O'Hagan, who was not directly involved in Grand Met's representation, started purchasing call options for Pillsbury stock and continued until he owned more than any other individual investor, in addition to purchasing considerable amounts of shares of Pillsbury's common stock. In sum, when Grand Met announced its tender offer, the price of Pillsbury stock rose to nearly $60 a share, and O'Hagan sold his holdings in the company making a profit of more than $4.3 million. O'Hagan's wrongdoings were compounded by the destiny of the misappropriated funds: concealment of a previous embezzlement and conversion of unrelated trust funds. O'Hagan was investigated by the SEC, and indicted for multiple charges of securities fraud; namely defrauding his law firm and its client by using undisclosed non-public information regarding Grand Met's planned tender offer for his own benefit. In addition, O'Hagan was also indicted for mail fraud and money laundering, and was eventually convicted on all charges and sentenced to a 41-month term of imprisonment. On appeal, the Court of Appeal for the Eighth Circuit expressly rejected the misappropriation theory of insider trading-related securities fraud and reversed the conviction. The Supreme Court granted *certiorari* and reversed in turn the Eighth Circuit's judgment.

Ginsburg J, who delivered the opinion of the Court, considered that O'Hagan's behaviour constituted a fraudulent device in connection with the purchase and sale of securities, thus falling under the antifraud provisions of the Securities Exchange Act. A fiduciary who '[pretends] loyalty to the principal while secretly converting the principal's information into personal gain, "dupes" or defrauds the principal'.[23] A trustee acting as an agent may not use the property that has been entrusted to him, without consent. According to section 10(b) a misappropriator's deceptive use of information must be in connection with the purchase or sale of a security. The fiduciary's fraud is consummated not when the fiduciary gains the confidential information, but when, without disclosure to his principal, he uses the information to sell or purchase securities.[24] The securities transaction coincides with the breach of duty. Misappropriators who trade on the basis of material, non-public information, gain their advantageous market position through deception,

[23] ibid, 653–54.
[24] ibid, 643.

deceiving the source of the information and simultaneously harming members of the investing public.[25]

In the case where the misappropriator would put the information to another use, the statute's prohibition would not be implicated. The theory does not catch all forms of fraud; rather, it catches fraudulent means of capitalising on such information through securities transactions.

On 23 October 2000, Rule 10b5-1 became effective,[26] adopting a standard of mere awareness of material non-public information at the time of the trade as sufficient for insider trading liability and introducing three affirmative defences under certain conditions: before becoming aware of the information the person had: (1) entered into a binding contract to purchase or buy the security; (2) instructed another person to purchase or sell the security for the instructing person's account; or (3) adopted a written plan for trading securities.

In 2001, the SEC promulgated Rule 10b5-2 providing guidance about situations in which a person owes a duty of trust or confidence under the misappropriation theory.[27] This rule was considered 'a move in the right direction [but] … still woefully inadequate as a basis for criminal prosecution'.[28]

The misappropriation theory was criticised for its lack of clarity in defining the criminal liability under this theory.[29] Appellate courts including the Supreme Court 'have failed to define what kinds of relationships trigger liability for insider trading based on [this] theory' positing 'that the SEC should articulate in detail the parameters of the fiduciary duties that give rise to 10b-5 liability'.[30]

In December 2014, the US Court of Appeal for the Second Circuit, in *United States v Newman*,[31] introduced a substantial hurdle, preventing the SEC and the

[25] ibid, 643–44.

[26] 17 CFR, s 240.10b-5-1 – Trading 'on the basis of' material non-public information in insider trading cases.

[27] 17 CFR, s 240.10b5-2 (2001). The rule outlines three situations:

(1) Whenever a person agrees to maintain information in confidence;
(2) Whenever the person communicating the material nonpublic information and the person to whom it is communicated have a history, pattern, or practice of sharing confidences, such that the recipient of the information knows or reasonably should know that the person communicating the material nonpublic information expects that the recipient will maintain its confidentiality; or
(3) Whenever a person receives or obtains material nonpublic information from his or her spouse, parent, child, or sibling; *provided*, however, that the person receiving or obtaining the information may demonstrate that no duty of trust or confidence existed with respect to the information, by establishing that he or she neither knew nor reasonably should have known that the person who was the source of the information expected that the person would keep the information confidential, because of the parties' history, pattern, or practice of sharing and maintaining confidences, and because there was no agreement or understanding to maintain the confidentiality of the information.

[28] B Hang, 'The SEC's Criminal Rulemaking in Rule 10b5-2: Incarceration Should be Made of Sterner Stuff' (2002) 41 *Washburn Law Journal* 629, 631.

[29] ibid, 629.

[30] ibid, 630–32.

[31] *United States v Newman*, 773 F3d 438, 452 (2014), cert denied.

Department Of Justice targeting of remote tippees many levels removed from corporate insiders.

United States v Newman is a case in which the tippee received a tip from an analyst who was part of a chain of intermediaries exchanging non-public insider information, originated from a corporate insider. The main issue was to prove beyond a reasonable doubt the mens rea element of the crime. This mens rea consists in the tippee's knowledge of the tipper's breach of duty: trading non-public insider information provided in exchange for a benefit, without disclosure.

The defendants in this case, Doug Newman and Anthony Chiasson, were portfolio hedge fund[32] managers respectively at Diamond Capital Management LLC and at Level Global Investors LP. Both traded on the basis of information obtained from a group of analysts who were many steps removed from the analyst that actually received the inside information from the corporate insider. The defendants traded on the basis of this information and made a considerable profit.

Subsequently, the government charged the defendants for violating section 10(b) of the Securities and Exchange Act and SEC Rule 10b-5, arguing that the corporate insiders breached their duties of confidentiality by tipping material non-public information to others who traded on the basis of that information. Under *Dirks*, the defendants were derivatively liable if they knew or should have known that such a breach occurred. What the government failed to recognise was that *Dirks* specifically ruled that a fiduciary breach alone is not the securities fraud as proscribed by section 10(b) and Rule 10b-5. The breach must be coupled with the intent to defraud and the tipper's personal benefit as a quid pro quo for providing the information. In this case, the defendants did not know the tipper. Therefore, the defendants had no way of knowing if the information was accurate or if there had been a benefit exchanged for the tip. The Second Circuit Court criticised the government for ignoring the *Dirks* mens rea requirement: actual knowledge of the tippee of the tipper's breach of duty including their obtainment of a personal benefit.

United States v Newman is important because it clearly pinpoints the elements of the crime, rejecting the SEC's reliance on the excessive indeterminacy of the

[32] According to S Friese et al, *US Regulation of Hedge Funds* (Chicago, IL, American Bar Association Publishing, 2013) 1, 'The term "hedge fund" has no uniformly accepted meaning, but commonly refers to a professionally managed pool of assets used to invest and trade in equity securities, fixed-income securities, options, futures and other derivatives, and other financial instruments.' They underscore that the adjective 'hedge' has a classificatory value to distinguish these funds from other investment pools but no descriptive value because hedge funds may or may not hedge against risks. They further exemplify with a long list that includes funds that invest only in securities for the long term, funds that do not invest at all and only trade from market or security depreciation, long-short funds that sell securities short to guard against risks in their long-term investments, funds that sell securities short opportunistically to profit from expected declines in their prices, funds that trade in put and call options or future contracts to hedge, and funds that do so hoping to profit from directional security or market bets, funds that are fundamental investors, while others rely on technical analysis, funds that specialise in currency trading in contrast with others that exclude securities in US dollars, etc. They consequently infer that hedge funds do not represent an asset class or any particular style of porfolio management.

nature of the statute to prosecute remote tippees at the borderline of due process requirements.[33] The courts dislike the SEC's litigation strategy and want to maintain a high standard of proof, allow the market to flourish, and ensure that educated traders know what type of activity is illegal so that they may avoid criminal pitfalls. The government has filed a petition for rehearing. In the fiscal year of 2014, the SEC made $4.16 billion in disgorgements and penalties of their tenacious prosecutions of investors, including corporations who would prefer to settle than to have their name dragged through the mud.[34]

The *Newman* case emphasised the distinction between the permissible sharing of information and the illegal use of material non-public information.[35] After Newman, the knowledge of the tipper's personal benefit has become a core mens rea element for tippee liability.[36]

In the Supreme Court decision of *Bassam Yacoub Salman v United States* of 6 December 2016,[37] the unanimous opinion of the Court, delivered by Alito J, affirmed the 9th Circuit conviction of Salman. Salman was indicted for trading on inside information he received from a friend and relation-by-marriage, Michael Kara, who, in turn, received the information from his brother, Maher Kara, a former investor banker at Citigroup. Maher testified at Salman's trial that he shared inside information with his brother Michael to benefit him and that he expected him to trade on it, and Michael testified to sharing the information with Salman, who knew it was from Maher. Salman was convicted. While Salman's appeal to the conviction was pending, the Second Circuit Court decided that *Dirks* does not permit the fact finder to infer from a gift of confidential information to a trading relative or friend, unless there is proof of a meaningful close personal relationship between tipper and tippee that generates an exchange that is objective, consequential and represents at least a potential gain of a pecuniary or similarly valuable nature.[38]

In a similar way the April 1999 *Report of the President's Working Group on Financial Markets, Hedge Funds, Leverage, and the Lessons of Long-Term Capital Management* affirms that 'the term "hedge fund" is commonly used to describe a variety of different types of investment vehicles that share some common characteristics. Although it is not statutorily defined, the term encompasses any pooled investment vehicle that is privately organized, administered by professional money managers, and not widely available to the public.'

[33] On constitutional aspects of legality in securities frauds, see DJ Bacastow, 'Due Process and Criminal Penalties under Rule 10b-5: The Unconstitutionality and Inefficiency of Criminal Prosecutions for Insider Trading' (1982) 73 *Journal of Criminal Law & Criminology* 96; RH Fallon, JF Manning, DJ Melzer and DL Shapiro, Hart and Wechsler, *The Federal Courts and the Federal System*, 6th edn (New York, The Foundation Press, 2009) 609, 610.

[34] R Harasimowicz, 'Nothing New, Man – The Second Circuit's Clarification of Insider Trading Liability in United States v. Newman Comes at a Critical Juncture in the Evolution of Insider Trading' (2016) 57 *Boston College Law Review* 765, 797.

[35] JK Strader, '(Re)conceptualizing Insider Trading: United States v. Newman and the Intent to Defraud' (2015) 80 *Brooklyn Law Review* 1410, 1421.

[36] *Newman* (n 31) 450–51.

[37] *Bassam Yacoub Salman v United States*, 580 US__ (2016) (*more*), 137 SCt 420, 196 LEd 2d. 361.

[38] *United States v Newman* (n 31).

While the evidence established that Maher made a gift of trading information to Michael and that Salman knew it, there is no evidence that Maher received anything of a 'pecuniary or similarly valuable nature' in exchange or that Salman knew of any such benefit. The Court reasoned that the case was governed by the *Dirks* holding. The 9th Circuit Court decided not to follow *Newman's* requirement of an additional gain for the tipper in cases of confidential information for family or friends. The Supreme Court accepted this interpretation, whose tension with the Second Circuit Court's *Newman* decision motivated the granting of *certiorari* in the first place.

In particular, the Supreme Court held that 'the elements of fiduciary duty and exploitation of nonpublic information also exist when the insider makes a gift of confidential information to a trading relative or friend'. In such cases 'the tip and trade resemble trading by the insider followed by a gift of the profits to the recipient'. To the extent that the Second Circuit Court held that the tipper must also receive something of a 'pecuniary or similarly valuable nature in exchange to a gift to the family or friends (*Newman*, 773 F. 3d. at 452)', the Supreme Court in *Salman* agreed with the Ninth Circuit Court that this requirement is inconsistent with *Dirks* and that 'the personal benefit incudes the benefit that one would obtain from simply making a gift to a trading relative'.

On 23 July 2017, the Second Circuit Court decided in the appeal of Matthew Martoma against his insider trading conviction[39] that *Salman* altered the analysis underlying *Newman*'s 'meaningfully close personal relationship' additional[40] requirement and that making a gift of inside information to a relative is little different from trading on the information, obtaining the profits and giving them out. Furthermore, the Court concluded that the logic of gift giving in *Dirks*, strongly reaffirmed by *Salman*, is that a corporate insider personally benefits whenever he is disclosing inside information as a gift with the expectation that the recipient would trade 'on the basis of that information or would otherwise exploit it for his pecuniary gain'.

On 25 June 2018, the Second Circuit amended its decision affirming Matthew Martoma's conviction. In *Martoma I*, the Court found that *Newman*'s additional[41] requirement that the tipper and tipee in gift cases 'should have a meaningfully close

[39] Martoma was a hedge funds manager dealing with between $400 million and $500 million of pharmaceutical investments. Two doctors working on an experimental drug against Alzheimer's revealed to Martoma confidential information about the trial results. As a consequence of receiving such information, Martoma sold part of the holdings of the SAC company that he was managing. After a presentation of the trial results at a drugs conference, the drug companies' share prices dropped considerably, and Martoma's trading ahead of time earned the SAC company approximately $80 million in profits and avoided losses of approximately $165 million. His transactions led to his prosecution for insider trading and to a conviction in February 2014.

[40] Additional to the basic requirement challenged by *Salman* of an additional gain for the tipper in cases of confidential information for family or friends.

[41] In *Martoma I* (*US v Martoma*, No 14-3599, (2d Cir Aug 23, 2017), the Court found that *Salman* contradicted *Newman*'s additional requirement that the tipper and tipee in gift cases 'should have a meaningfully close personal relationship'.

personal relationship' was inconsistent with *Salman*. In the amended decision the Court concluded that *Newman*'s 'meaningfully close personal relationship' did no more than 'cabin the gift theory using to other freestanding personal benefits that have long been recognized by our case law' (referring to *Dirks* and its progeny). Consequently, it reached the same results of the amended decision, while avoiding to challenge *Newman*'s second requirement of a 'close personal relationship'.

II. The Internationalisation of Insider Trading Law

Although in 1967, France had already adopted a statute outlawing insider trading[42] and a 1966 ordinance in the Canadian province of Ontario imposed civil and administrative sanctions to insider traders,[43] laws against insider trading started to proliferate only in the 1980s and became a generalised phenomenon in the 1990s.[44] Bhattacharya and Daouk's comprehensive study showed that of 103 countries that had stock markets, 87 had insider trading laws but were enforced in only 38 of them. They added that before 1990 the proportion was 9 out of 34.[45]

The primary cause of these developments lies in the growth of securities markets and on the automation of securities transactions.

Most of the internationalisation is a result of the diffusion of the American model starting in the 1980s. Although there were isolated provisions prohibiting insider trading in the past, in countries such as France and the UK,[46] the modern wave of internationalisation through diffusion started in Switzerland in 1988. This trend of internationalised diffusion of the American model led to European Union (EU) directives and regulations, which influenced a number of European countries. Therefore, after dealing with Switzerland, this chapter will successively address EU law and four of the main countries that adjusted their legislations accordingly: France, UK, Italy and Germany.

III. Switzerland

As pointed out in section II, the internationalisation of the insider trading prohibition, mainly through diffusion of the American model, intensified at the close of

[42] See R Irving, 'French Insider Trading Law: a Survey' (1990) 2 *University of Miami Inter-American Law Review* 41, addressed the offence of insider trading for the first time, creating the COB (Commission organising the stock market). Art 162-b of the Ordinance required that the stipulated insiders disclosed any securities transaction within 60 days of its occurrence. The actual criminalisation took place in 1970 with Law L 451 of the Monetary and Financial Code.

[43] Gevurtz, 'The Globalization of Insider Trading' (n 10) 65, fn 7.

[44] U Battacharya and H Daouk, 'The World Price of Insider Trading' (2002) LVII(1) *The Journal of Finance* 75.

[45] ibid.

[46] SR Bazley, *Market Abuse Enforcement: Practice and Procedure* (Haywards Heath, Bloomsbury Professional, 2013) 10 ff.

the 1980s.[47] Switzerland had a pioneer role in these developments when it included an insider trading provision in its criminal code that made possible extradition procedures to the US, blocked until then by the lack of dual criminality.[48] This new development was particularly important, given the high amount of transactions with foreign shares purchased by the Swiss banks from the American Stock Exchange.[49]

At the time, the US authorities were investigating a number of securities transactions carried out by persons who were in possession of material non-public information concerning the securities involved, using Swiss bank accounts as intermediaries.[50] To be able to reach these offenders, the US authorities exercised great pressure on Switzerland to criminalise insider trading.[51] This concern of the US had already manifested in the past, resulting in a 1977 treaty[52] providing for cooperation between the law enforcement agencies of both countries in the investigation or prosecution of criminal offences. This cooperation was conditioned, however, by the requirement of dual criminality.

Finally, on 18 December 1987, the Council of the Swiss Confederation introduced the crime of insider trading in Article 161 of the Criminal Code, which entered into force in July 1988. This article removed the past extradition difficulties and had therefore a crucial significance for international cooperation between the US and Switzerland.[53]

Given the pressure from the US authorities in the enactment of this legislation, Swiss critics dubbed the new norm as 'Lex Americana', because it was suggested that the real purpose of the promulgation of Article 161 'had little to do with concerns of insider dealings in the Swiss market, but the insider dealings which occurs on the United States financial markets'.[54] This explains why the prohibition was a paper tiger at the beginning.[55] However, later on, insider transactions turned out to be an actual problem in Switzerland.[56] The main rationale of the norm was

[47] A Nieto Martin, 'Americanisation or Europeanisation of Corporate Crime' in M Delmas-Marty, M Pieth and U Sieber (eds), *Les Chemins de l'Harmonisation Pénale/Harmonizing Criminal Law* (Paris, Société de Législation Comparée, 2008) 327, 346.

[48] Switzerland and the US were already parties to a bilateral treaty. The Treaty on Mutual Assistance in Criminal Matters between the Swiss Confederation and The United States was signed on 25 May 1973 and was the first mutual assistance treaty of its kind to which the US was a party. This treaty was followed by a series of other criminal mutual legal assistance treaties (MLATS) with a number of other countries.

[49] Nieto Martin, 'Americanisation or Europeanisation of Corporate Crime' (n 47) 335.

[50] P May and M Weber, 'Insider Dealing Legislation and Switzerland' (1989) 7(8) *International Banking Law* 153.

[51] A Kern, 'The Law of Insider Dealing: A Tale of Two Jurisdictions' (2013) 112 *Zeitschrift für vergleichende Rechtswissenschaft* 263, 265.

[52] *Treaty Between the United States of America and the Swiss Confederation on Mutual Assistance in Criminal Matters* 27 UST 2019, TIAS 8302.

[53] N Schmid, *Schweiserisches Insiderstrafrecht* (Bern, Stämpfli, 1988) 227.

[54] May and Weber, 'Insider Dealing Legislation and Switzerland' (n 50).

[55] B Bruppacher, 'Schweiz als Eldorado für Insider-Deals' in *20 Minuten*, retrieved from www.20min.ch/finance/news/story/29474512.

[56] P Forstmoser, 'Die neue Schweizerische Strafnorm gegen *Insider*-Geschäfte' (1989) *Zeitschrift für Unternehmens- und Gesellschaftsrecht* 124, 125.

to maintain the equal chances of investors as a necessary requirement for a viable capital market.

In its original version, under the label of 'exploitation of confidential information', Article 161 either punished with imprisonment of up to three years or fined the action of a list of specific insiders of procuring a pecuniary benefit for themselves or others by exploiting confidential information. This information had to be foreseeably capable of influencing the price of a number of securities or options. This crime was extended to whoever made this information known to a third party.

Formerly, the Swiss legislator limited the scope of Article 161 through its paragraph 3. The term 'confidential information' relating to share prices was restricted by paragraph 3 of the article to forthcoming issues of new shares, to mergers or acquisitions or to 'similar circumstances with comparable implications'. Thus circumstances that did not come under the insider criminal law provisions were, for example, sales of securities that were carried out in the run-up to a profit warning to cushion an expected fall in price.[57] The purpose of the restriction was to criminalise only significant abuses of confidential information and to exclude minor or trivial offences.[58] The Federal Council recommended the repeal of paragraph 3 of Article 161 of the Swiss Criminal Code without replacement. With this repeal, the ban on exploiting confidential information was be extended to any insider information relating to prices.[59]

Article 161 of the Swiss Criminal Code encompassed two offences.[60] The first prohibited the exploitation of inside information or its transmission to third persons by organs, officers and members of the administration and auxiliary personnel. The second offence punished tippees but only when they exploited the inside information. Even though anybody could be a tippee, the scope of application of the prohibition was considerably narrowed by the fact that the tippees were subject to criminal punishment only when it was proven that the inside information was transmitted deliberately by an authentic insider.[61] Given that the globalisation of securities markets brought about a massive technological progress in the field of communications and information transmission, Article 161 of the Criminal

[57] *State Secretariat for International Financial Matters* (SIF), available at www.sif.admin.ch/dokumentation/00509/00510/00622/00627/00678/index.html?lang=en.

[58] Schmid, *Schweiserisches Insiderstrafrecht* (n 53) 111.

[59] *Swiss Federal Finance Administration*, available at www.sif.admin.ch/dokumentation/00509/00510/00622/00627/00678/index.html?lang=en.

[60] 'Whoever as member of a board of directors, business management, auditing agency or as an agent of a corporation or of a company dominated by or dependent from such corporation, as a government agency or as a public official, or as employees of the above-mentioned individuals, procures a pecuniary benefit for himself or for another by exploiting the confidential information, which disclosure can in a foreseeable manner considerably influence listed or pre-listed shares, other securities, or the corresponding book entry securities, or options on any of the aforementioned securities, or whoever makes such information known to a third party, shall be punished with imprisonment up to three years or fines.'

[61] W Wohlers, '§ 14 Finanz-und Kapitalmarktstrafrecht' in G Ackermann and G Heine (eds), *Wirtschaftsstrafrecht in der Schweiz* (Bern, Stämpfli, 2013) 369.

Code turned out to be insufficient. The globalisation of financial crimes also led to the provision of the enforcement authorities with an expanded surveillance and investigation instrumentarium. Finally, the recent financial crisis brought about a decisive thrust to the legal enforcement and public attitude regarding insider dealing.[62] In 2012, the rules against insider trading were modified and transferred from the Criminal Code to the Stock Exchange Act, aiming at the transparency and effectiveness of the stock market as well as the equal treatment of the investors. In the Stock Exchange Act, insider trading was regulated in Article 40.[63]

On 1 January 2016, Switzerland experienced a new legislative development in the field of capital markets. The new Financial Markets Infrastructure Act[64] regulated the organisation and functioning of the financial market infrastructure. The scattered provisions of various federal statutes were merged into a single statute and adapted to transformed markets interrelations and exchanges and to international standards.[65] The text of Article 40 of the Stock Exchange Act was transferred to the new statute without significant changes. Under the title 'Exploitation of Insider Information', Article 154 of the Financial Markets Infrastructure Act now provides the following:

> 1. Whoever as a body or as a member of a managing or supervisory body of an issuer or of a company controlling or controlled by him or her, or as a person who

[62] K Lorez and G Dobrauz-Saldapenna, 'Die revidierte Schweizer Insiderhandels und Marktmissbrauchsregulierung' in (2014) 86 *Zeitschrift für Wirtschafts- und Finanzmarktrecht* 38.

[63] This was the text:

> '1 Whosoever as a body or a member of a managing or supervisory body of an issuer or of a company controlling or controlled by him or her, or as a person who due to his or her holding or activity has legitimate access to insider information, is liable to imprisonment of up to three years or a fine if he or she gains a pecuniary advantage for him- or herself or for another with insider information by: exploiting it to acquire, sell securities admitted to trading on a stock exchange or an institution which is similar to an exchange in Switzerland or to use financial instruments derived from such securities; disclosing it to another; exploiting it to recommend to another to acquire or sell securities admitted to trading on a stock exchange or an institution which is similar to an exchange in Switzerland or to use financial instruments derived from such securities.
>
> 2 Whosoever through activities as detailed in paragraph 1 gains a pecuniary advantage of more than one million Swiss Francs is liable to imprisonment of up to five years or a fine.
>
> 3 Whosoever gains a pecuniary advantage for him- or herself or for another by exploiting insider information disclosed to them by a person as detailed in paragraph1 or acquired through a crime or an offence to acquire or sell securities admitted to trading on a stock exchange or an institution which is similar to an exchange in Switzerland or to use financial instruments derived from such securities is liable to a imprisonment of up to one year or a fine.
>
> 4 Whosoever does not belong to the persons referred to in paragraphs 1–3 yet gains a pecuniary advantage for him- or herself or for another by exploiting insider information to acquire or sell securities admitted to trading on a stock exchange or an institution which is similar to an exchange in Switzerland or to use financial instruments derived from such securities is liable to a fine.'

[64] *Finanzmarktinfrastrukturgesetz*, SR 958.1.

[65] Press release, *Bundesrat verabschiedet Botschaft zum Finanzmarktinfrastrukturgesetz*, available at www.news.admin.ch/message/index.html?lang=de&msg-id=54305.

because of his or her holding or activity has legitimate access to insider information, is liable to imprisonment of up to three years or a fine if he or she gains a financial gain for him- or herself or for another with insider information by:

- a. Exploiting it to acquire, sell securities admitted to trading on a Swiss stock exchange or to use equity derivatives derived from such securities;
- b. Disclosing it to another;
- c. Exploiting it to recommend to another to acquire or sell securities admitted to trading on a stock exchange or an institution, which is similar on a Swiss stock exchange, or to use equity derivatives derived from such securities.

2. Whosoever through activities as detailed in paragraph 1 gains a financial advantage of more than one million Swiss Francs is liable to imprisonment of up to five years or a fine.
3. Whosoever gains a pecuniary advantage for him- or herself or for another by exploiting insider information or a related recommendation disclosed to them by a person as detailed in paragraph 1 or acquired through a crime or an offense, to acquire or sell securities admitted on a Swiss stock exchange or to use equity derivatives derived from such securities is liable to an imprisonment of up to one year or a fine.
4. Whosoever does not belong to the persons referred to in paragraphs 1–3 yet who gains a pecuniary advantage or a related recommendation for him- or herself or for another by exploiting insider information to acquire or sell securities admitted on a Swiss stock exchange or to use equity derivatives derived from such securities is liable to a fine.

As Mark Pieth points out, the characterisation of the perpetrators has been considerably extended.[66] Primary insiders (Section 1) are now divided in three subcategories: (a) 'Organ insiders', that is, persons who are organs or member of a directive or supervisory organ, issuers or companies controlled by issuer, who in all cases have access to the inside information; (b) 'Function insiders', that is, persons that acquired the information through their functions, including auxiliary personnel; (c) most recently, persons who according to their participation in the company, such as large shareholders, it is agreed to give them access to information for important decisions. The law excludes people who are not specifically intended to acquire the information and obtain it by mere coincidence.

In addition, as Mark Pieth indicates, the law includes secondary insiders (Section 2) and other persons that profit from inside information.[67]

Secondary insiders (Section 3), while not encompassed by paragraph 1, receive either inside information or a recommendation based on such information and use it to obtain for themselves or for others a financial profit. Those who obtain this information by chance are not included in the prohibition.

Section 4 contains a general misdemeanour provision punishing other persons not belonging to the groups described as primary or secondary insiders who use

[66] M Pieth, *Wirtschaftsstrafrecht* (Basel, Helbing Lichtenhahn, 2016) 121.
[67] ibid, 122.

inside information or recommendations based on such information, to act and thus obtain a profit for themselves or for others.

Article 2, Section j of the Financial Market Infrastructure Act defines inside information as confidential information, the disclosure of which is apt to considerably influence the price of securities admitted to negotiation in Switzerland.

Article 154(1) of the Financial Markets Infrastructure Act punishes not only the official organs of large joint companies (*Aktiengesellschaften*) such as members of the board of directors or supervisory board, but also the managers and controllers of partnerships and other forms of enterprise organisations, including de facto managers.[68]

This provision includes as insiders, employees that are apprised of relevant information because of their contractual functions, such as lawyers, notaries and tax or financial advisors. The law also encompasses other persons, as far as they have access to inside information within the scope of their professional activities. Examples are financial analysts, members of rating agencies and persons who are involved in the design or printing of information brochures.[69] According to Article 29 of the Swiss Criminal Code, the actions of corporate entities can be attributed to natural persons when such persons act as organs or as members of a collective organ of a legal entity; as company members; as employees with independent decision-making authority in their field of activity within either a legal entity, a company or a sole proprietorship; or as de facto managers.

Article 154(1) provides that auxiliary personnel can only be considered perpetrators when they obtain the inside information in the context of their specific duties in the company.[70] Also, shareholders can be possible perpetrators when they obtain the information as a result of their participation in the corporation activities.[71]

Furthermore, managers, members of a supervisory body, and persons mentioned in Article 154(1) must obtain the relevant information within the scope of their insider official position and not simply by chance, that is, the inside information should be the result of their position as insiders. It is, therefore, not enough for the completion of the offence when the information is obtained through a mistaken e-mail or though friendly conversations with colleagues. The situation of the firm's legal counsel who obtain the information outside of their mandate is also excluded.[72]

Article 154(1) presupposes that the insider exploits or transmits inside information, which released to the public would be apt to influence the price of securities traded in the Swiss stock exchange or an institution which is similar to the Swiss stock exchange.

[68] With respect to the similar Art 40 of the Swiss Stock Exchange Act, see Wohlers, '§ 14 Finanz-und Kapitalmarktstrafrecht' (n 61) 370.

[69] ibid, 371.

[70] ibid.

[71] ibid, 373.

[72] ibid.

The concept of inside information encompasses past or present events. These can consist of events related to the enterprise such as the resignation of a board director or the discovering of a new product, but not appreciations and prognoses, rumours and speculations. However, the factual circumstances under which such prognoses, appreciations, rumours and speculations are built are relevant inside information.[73]

The notion of inside information also includes intentions and plans that are not available to the public even though they have transcended within the ambit of the corporation. Plans that remain in the mind of the entrepreneurs are not considered as inside information because 'no one can be his own insider'.[74] However, this catchphrase is an oversimplification, because there are cases in which self-created circumstances, undisclosed to the public, become the basis of an actual transaction. According to Wohlers, one should only exclude from the prohibition of insider trading, cases in which the insider information consists in the pure intent of the perpetrator.[75]

The insider trading prohibition should protect the equal chances of investors as a necessary requirement for a viable capital market.[76] However, the protection of equal chances does not require that the investors disclose their intent before they undertake a transaction, because, as Wohlers points out, 'the realization of their own intended transaction does not unjustifiably favor the investors with regard to others'.[77] This is also valid for cases in which the investor carries out the transaction through third persons. These third parties are not punishable, providing that they do not get an additional profit from the transaction.[78] Of course, if the intent of the investor is formed through the receipt of inside information from others, the prohibition would apply, as for example, when the president of the board of directors exploits the situation that in the next days he would publicise his own resignation, thus influencing the price of the shares of the corporation.[79]

The provision prohibiting insider trading presupposes that inside information should be confidential. Information is confidential when it is known by a limited number of persons. Mere rumours cannot be considered as confidential information.[80] Neither is the information confidential when it is accessible to the public even though it requires specialised endeavours to obtain it.[81]

Moreover, in order to materialise the prohibition of insider trading, it is necessary that the information should influence the price of the corporation's shares in a considerable way.

[73] ibid, 374. See also Pieth, *Wirtschaftsstrafrecht* (n 66) 123.

[74] Bundesgerichtsentscheid 1A. 110/2002 of 26 November 2002, Erwägung 4.4.

[75] With respect to the similar Art 40 of the Swiss Stock Exchange Act, see Wohlers, '§ 14 Finanz-und Kapitalmarktstrafrecht' (n 61) 375. See also Pieth, *Wirtschaftsstrafrecht* (n 66) 123.

[76] Bundesgerichtsentscheidung 118 Ib 547 E. 4e/bb.

[77] With respect to the similar Art 40 of the Swiss Stock Exchange Act, see Wohlers, '§ 14 Finanz-und Kapitalmarktstrafrecht' (n 61) 376.

[78] ibid.

[79] ibid.

[80] Bundesgerichtsentscheidung 118 Ib 448 E. 6b, 455.

[81] With respect to the similar Art 40 of the Swiss Stock Exchange Act see, Wohlers, '§ 14 Finanz-und Kapitalmarktstrafrecht' (n 61) 377.

The determination of when insider information is apt to considerably influence the price of securities poses difficult evidentiary problems.[82] A Swiss commentator[83] favours the adoption of the reasonable Investor Test, as well as the Probability Magnitude Test developed in US law. According to the first test, inside information is relevant for the price formation of the security when there is a considerable likelihood that reasonable investors would use this information as part of the basis of their investment decision. The Probability Magnitude Test considers that the significance of the circumstances to take into account depends on the probability that the information would form the basis of the investor's decision.

The behaviour defined in Article 154(1) consists: (a) in the exploitation of an insider information to personally carry out a transaction; (b) recommending another to carry out the same; or (c) transmitting the insider information to another. The alternative contained in Article 154(1)(a) punishing the exploitation of information related to confidential facts, encompasses cases in which the perpetrator purchases or sells securities in the stock market or over the counter. Exploitation takes place when the knowledge of the insider information constitutes one of the causes of the purchase or sale. The behaviour is not punishable when the order to carry out the transaction took place before acquisition of the inside information. The Financial Markets Infrastructure Act does not define as insider trading, situations in which the inside information leads to abstaining from a planned transaction or to cancelling it when it is already ordered. With respect to the similar Article 40 of the Swiss Stock Exchange Act, Wohlers points out that in these cases there is no criminal omission because the prohibition refers only to active behaviour given that the efficient function of capital markets as protected legal interest is not affected when no transaction takes place. The exploitation of inside information through an omission is only possible when the perpetrator abstains to act in order to obstruct a transaction executed by others. Therefore, the omission is only punishable when there is a duty to act.[84]

Article 154(1) punishes primary insiders when they exploit the inside information or when they communicate it to others. Both tippees and those who misappropriated the information through either a felony or a misdemeanour are only punishable when they exploit such information through the undertaking of a transaction. If the tippee passes the information to a third person, the original tipper, that is the original insider, is punishable under Article 154(1) when the third person exploits the inside information, and this exploitation was encompassed

[82] ibid, 381.

[83] C Leuenberger, 'Die materielle kapitalmarktstrafrechtliche Regulierung des. Insiderhandels de lege lata und de lege ferenda' in *Schweizer Schriften zum Handels- und Wirtschaftsrecht*, vol 296 (Basel, Zürich, Dike Verlag, 2010). See also Pieth, *Wirtschaftsstrafrecht* (n 66), who emphasises the lack of precision of the criteria to determine the relevance of the information, which is derived not only from new issues of shares, and mergers and acquisitions, but also from profit warnings, management changes or enterprise restructuring.

[84] Bundesgerichtsentscheidung of 2 February 2000, 2A.230/1999 E. 5a. With respect to the similar Art 40 of the Swiss Stock Exchange Act, see Wohlers, '§ 14 Finanz-und Kapitalmarktstrafrecht' (n 61) 383.

within the intent of the original insider. The tippees are not punishable for the mere transmission of the information to a third party, but they may be punished as instigators[85] when the third person actually exploits such information.[86]

In general, the alternative contained in Article 154(1)(b) that punishes the disclosure of inside information to a non-insider, presupposes the actual communication of inside information and not the mere tip to buy or to sell. On the other hand, Article 154(1)(c) punishes the communication of a tip to buy or to sell given on the basis of inside information.[87]

It is irrelevant whether the transmission of the inside information or the delivery of the tip as such was in return for payment or gratuitously. What really counts is that the transmitter of the inside information or the tipper should have the intent to enrich themselves or to enrich a third person.[88] Examples of the latter are benefiting a person closely related to the perpetrator such as a friend or family member or benefiting the enterprise where the perpetrator works. The enrichment may consist of either making a profit through the rising prices of the securities or of avoiding a loss in the case of falling prices. Moreover, Article 154 requires that the profit should be the direct result of exploiting the advanced insider information and that the insider information has not yet become public.[89]

Furthermore, when in the context of Article 154(1)(b) and the seller of the information receives the payment, this payment constitutes the profit required by the provision to commit the offence, even if the receiver of the inside information does not exploit it. The tipper is also punishable when he transmits the information gratuitously in case that the receiver exploits the information to obtain a pecuniary advantage.[90]

Insider trading is an intentional crime in Swiss law. The prevailing opinion in Switzerland that the old Article 40 of the Swiss Stock Exchange Act can be committed through *dolus eventualis*[91] regarding the desired economic profit is also applicable to Article 154 of the Financial Markets Infrastructure Act.

[85] Pieth, *Wirtschaftsstrafrecht* (n 66) 124 agrees with this possibility. Art 24 of the Swiss Criminal Code defines instigation as follows: '(1) Any person who has willfully incited another to commit a felony or a misdemeanour, provided the offence is committed, incurs the same penalty as applies to the person who has committed the offence. (2) Any person who attempts to incite someone to commit a felony incurs the penalty applicable to an attempt to commit that felony.'

[86] With respect to the similar Art 40 of the Swiss Stock Exchange Act, see Wohlers, '§ 14 Finanz-und Kapitalmarktstrafrecht' (n 61) 387.

[87] ibid, 383.

[88] ibid.

[89] ibid, 384.

[90] ibid. See also Pieth, *Wirtschaftsstrafrecht* (n 66) 124, who emphasises the problematic nature of investment tips, given that for secondary insiders only the exploitation makes the transmission punishable.

[91] Perpetrators act with *dolus eventualis* when having represented themselves the result described in the definition of the offence as the possible consequence of their behaviour, they accept this possibility in case it would hypothetically happen. The attitude of the perpetrator is indifference regarding the occurrence of the prohibited result: The criminal result is ratified ex ante and the perpetrator does not believe in the possibility of avoiding the result. Pieth, *Wirtschaftsstrafrecht* (n 66) 124 reminds that some scholars demand direct intent regarding the falseness and misleading quality of the information.

Article 154(3) encompasses two kinds of perpetrators: (a) tippees who exploit insider information or a related recommendation disclosed to them by a person as detailed in Article 154(1); and (b) persons who received the information through a felony or misdemeanour.[92] In the case of tippees belonging (a), Article154(3) presupposes that the information was not legally obtained but provided by an insider – a proposition often difficult to prove. This prohibition also encompasses the situation of a chain of tips (*Kettentipp*) regarding the inside information. The conviction of original insiders is not a necessary element of the crime. Neither it is mandatory to prove that the primary insider committed a wrongful violation of Article 154(1) through the transmission of the information.[93] It is necessary that the tippee knows that the information came from an original insider (enumerated in Article 154(1)), but it is not mandatory to prove the existence of collusion.

Article 154(4) punishes whoever exploits inside information in order to carry out a transaction. This is significant for persons who receive information that was not directed to them, including the possibility of a mere chance, as for example, a cleaning person who finds the information accidently left by the insider.[94] The prohibition contained in Article 154(4) also includes the inside information casually overheard in a restaurant or train or from a taxi passenger.[95] The same provision covers situations in which the tipper does not directly communicate the inside information as such, but the tippee implies it, as for example when the tippee derives the inside information from a mere recommendation. Article 154(4) also applies when the tippee does not know that the information comes from an insider.[96]

A conviction according to Article 154(4) presupposes that the tippees use the information for the completion of transactions. In the case of those who are not primary insiders, and merely transmit the information without exploiting them personally, they are not punishable except in the case of complicity. It is possible that tippers fall under the provision of Article 24 of the Swiss Criminal Code, punishing instigation.

Swiss criminal law is based on the territorial principle combined with the ubiquity principle.[97] This means that criminal norms apply either in the place where the perpetrator acted or in the place where the result requested by the statutory definition of the offence occurs. In the case of insider trading the place of the

[92] With respect to the similar Art 40 of the Swiss Stock Exchange Act, see Wohlers, '§ 14 Finanz-und Kapitalmarktstrafrecht' (n 61) 386.

[93] ibid.

[94] ibid, 388.

[95] ibid, 386

[96] ibid, 387.

[97] In Switzerland and in Germany the ubiquity principle represents what in the US is the combination of the objective territoriality principle (the effects doctrine) and the subjective territoriality principle. (See ch 1, section II, '*territorial jurisdiction* over offences completed in the territory of the claimant country (objective territoriality) or over offences commencing in its territory (subjective territoriality)'.)

commission of the crime is where the perpetrator ordered the transaction or the place in which an innocent intermediary executed the order.[98]

IV. European Union

The internationalisation of securities frauds in Europe is the result of both the diffusion of the American model and the significant efforts of harmonisation, and more recently, of unified regulation by the EU authorities. It is, therefore, necessary to refer to the European legal framework on the subject, before analysing the adoption of national laws on insider trading by major European countries as well as their successive reforms. European nations have ceded to the European legislator a considerable part of their autonomy in the regulation of financial markets.

During the 1980s, the Securities and Exchange Commission brought a number of important insider trading cases involving international fraudulent activity, using a variety of methods to gather evidence and reach unlawfully obtained funds even when the evidence or funds involved were located outside of the US.[99] The Council of the European Communities introduced the 1989 Insider Dealing Directive,[100] opening the way for large European companies to enter American markets without being subject to legal barriers.[101] Americanisation in this area of corporate crime 'is as much the consequence of pressure, as it is of the conviction that these types of norms are both necessary and useful for the market'.[102] Insider dealing legislation was also enacted in other important financial centres, including South Africa and China.[103] In 1979, Rider and French, in their global study *The Regulation of Insider Trading*[104] covered 40 jurisdictions on every continent except South America.

The European Union Insider Trading Directive is the obvious result of US influence. Eric Engle undertook the comparison with US law, pointing out that some terms and consequences of the EU law directives are more clearly defined than in the US, and also indicated that the possibility of private law actions is wider than in Europe.[105]

[98] Art 3 and Art 8 of Swiss Criminal Code.

[99] MD Mann and LA Lustgarten, *Internationalization of Insider Trading Enforcement – A Guide to Regulation and Cooperation* (New Orleans, LA, American Bar Association–National Institute on White Collar Crime, 1990) 523.

[100] Council Directive 89/592/EEC of 13 November 1989 coordinating regulations on insider dealing.

[101] Nieto Martin, 'Americanisation or Europeanisation of Corporate Crime' (n 47) 335–36.

[102] ibid, 336.

[103] RCH Alexander, *Insider Dealing and Money Laundering in the EU: Law and Regulation* (Burlington, VT, Ashgate Publishing Company, 2007) xv.

[104] BAK Rider and HL French, *The Regulation of Insider Trading* (Dobbs Ferry, NY, Oceana Publications, 1979).

[105] E Engle, 'Insider Trading in US and EU Law: A Comparison' (2010) 26 *European Business Law Review* 490.

The prohibition from 'taking advantage' represented a strict standard of interpretation demanding that perpetrators not only used their inside information but must 'take advantage' of such information. Since such a restrictive standard resulted in low enforcement, the 2003 EU Directive on Insider Trading and Market Manipulation (Market Abuse Directive or 'MAD')[106] corrected this situation.

According to Article 2(1) of Directive 2003/6:

> member states shall prohibit any person referred to in the second sub-paragraph who possesses inside information from *using* that information by acquiring or disposing of, or by trying to acquire or dispose of, for his own account or for the account of a third party, either directly or indirectly, financial instruments to which that information relates.

Article 2(1) of the predecessor Directive 89/592 prohibited *taking advantage* of the inside information. In Directive 2003/6, the term 'taking advantage of' was replaced by the term 'from using'.

Carolyn Silane[107] explains that the purpose of the EU Directive was to achieve market fairness and transparency for investors. The Council Directive 2003/6 expressly prohibited trading on insider information regardless of how such information was obtained.[108] In this way, Silane points outs out the EU's statutory scheme of liability would encompass more than the US with respect to electronic data thieves. In the US, the mere possession of inside information when a trade occurs is not enough without the proof of a breach of duty.

On 23 December 2009, the European Court of Justice (Third Chamber) decided Case C-45/08 *Spector Photo Group NV and Chris Van Raemdonck v Commissie voor het Bank-, Financie-en Assurantiewezen (CBFA)* interpreting the meaning of Article 2(1) of Directive 2003/6 in the sense that whenever an insider makes a transaction with a related financial instrument, he is presumed to have 'used' inside information. By requiring the mere 'use' of the information, the 2003 MAD eased the proof of the violation demanded by the 1989 Directive on Insider Trading, in which Member States were supposed to 'take advantage' of the inside information. The European Court of Justice interpreted Article 2(1) of Directive 2003/6 on market abuse as meaning that the fact that a person, as referred to in the second paragraph of that provision (basically administrators, shareholders, professionals and criminal perpetrators), in possession of inside information, acquires or disposes of, or tries to acquire or dispose of, for his own account or on account of a third party, either directly or indirectly, the financial instruments to which that information relates, implies that the person has 'used that information' within the

[106] In January 2003, the EU published an official Directive on Insider Trading and Market Manipulation aiming at increasing investor confidence and securing market integrity. Council Directive 2003/6/EC, [2003] OJ L69/16.

[107] CA Silane, 'Electronic Data Theft: A Legal Loophole for Illegally Obtained Information – A Comparative Analysis of US and EU Insider Trading Law' 5 *Seton Hall Circuit Review* 333.

[108] ibid, 351.

meaning of that provision, but without prejudice to the rights of the defence, and, in particular, to the right to be able to rebut that presumption.

The ECJ decision underscores that the Directive has deliberately eliminated all reference to intention in the definition and that the presumption of intent can be implied if the objective elements of the definition are present does not infringe the principle of the presumption of innocence. Moreover, the European Court explained that the infringement of the provision prohibiting insider trading must be analysed in light of the purpose of the Directive: protect the integrity of financial markets and the consequent confidence of investors.

In accordance with the purpose of the Directive, the information must have a significant effect on the price of the financial instruments to which it relates or on the price of related derivative financial instruments. In addition, the ECJ points out that the capacity to have such significant effect must be assessed a priori, in the light of the content of the information at issue and the context in which it occurs. Therefore, to determine whether information is inside information, it is not necessary to examine whether its disclosure actually had a significant effect on the price of the financial instruments to which it relates.

The decision of the European Court of Human Rights (ECtHR) of 4 March 2014, in *Grande Stevens and others v Italy*[109] profoundly impacted European countries' legislation on market abuse. The seven judges composing the Second Chamber unanimously decided that the double repression of market abuse, administrative and criminal, existing in Italy contradicted the principle *non bis in idem* contained in Article 4 of Protocol 7 to the European Convention of Human Rights. Consequently, if the administrative procedures led to an administrative sanction, this precluded all later criminal convictions for the same facts.

The EU increasingly abandoned its original scepticism regarding insider trading, as the American cultural attitude toward the prohibition gained traction in Europe.[110] In Europe the basic concern behind the regulation of insider trading is the equal access to securities markets, considering that insider dealing 'prevents full and proper market transparency, which is a prerequisite for trading for all economic actors in integrated financial markets'.[111] Given that investor confidence and efficient market functioning are the dominant objectives of the regulation of insider trading, the source of the inside information is immaterial, unlike in the US where the prohibition is based on fiduciary concepts.[112] The Market Abuse Directive of 2003 defines inside information as one of a 'precise nature that has not been made public relating, directly or indirectly, to one or more issuers or one or more securities'.[113]

[109] *Grande Stevens and others v Italy* App no 18640/10, Final Judgment (Merits) (ECtHR, Second Section, 4 March 2014).

[110] M Ventoruzzo, 'Comparing Insider Trading in the United States and In the European Union: History and Recent Developments', *Max Plank Institute for International, European, and Regulatory Procedural Law, MPI Lux, Working Paper 5* (2014) 5.

[111] ibid, 23.

[112] ibid.

[113] ibid, 23–24.

The requirement of 'precise information excludes rumours and refers to a set of circumstances, which exists or may reasonably be expected to come into existence, or an event that has occurred or may reasonably be expected to occur and is specific enough to allow a conclusion on the possible effects of the price of the securities'.[114]

Given the 'legislative, market and technological developments since the entry into force of that Directive which have resulted in considerable changes to the financial landscape',[115] the European Parliament and the Council issued on 16 April 2014, EU Regulation No 596/2014 on market abuse (MAR) and repealed the 2003 MAD. This Regulation was based on a report of 25 February 2009 of the EU High Level Group on Financial Supervision, chaired by Jacques de Larosière.

A more uniform and stronger market abuse framework for the EU was necessary to 'remove the remaining obstacles to trade, and significant distortions of competition resulting from divergences between national laws'.[116] MAR, therefore, shapes the market abuse requirements in the form of a regulation to ensure their direct application, thus providing 'more legal certainty and less regulatory complexity'.[117]

The direct application of the MAR has created a simultaneous coexistence of two normative systems: MAR and the existing national regulations on emission of financial instruments and on the financial market. Since some of the national norms are incompatible with the European ones, the combination of national and European rules on market abuse require an effort of coordination. For this purpose, it is necessary to take into account that Article 2, paragraph 1 of the Regulation extends the application of the rules governing market abuse, to the following:

(a) Financial instruments admitted to trading on a regulated market or for which a request for admission to trading on a regulated market has been made;
(b) Financial instruments traded on an MTF (multilateral trade facility), admitted to trading on an MTF or for which a request for admission to trading on an MTF has been made;
(c) Financial instruments traded on an OTF (organised trading facility);
(d) Financial instruments not covered by point (a), (b) or (c), the price or value of which depends on or has an effect on the price or value of a financial instrument referred to in those points, including, but not limited to, credit default swaps and contracts for difference.

The Regulation also extended the application of Article 2, paragraph 1 to behaviour or transactions, including bids, relating to the auctioning on an auction platform

[114] ibid, 24.
[115] Recital (3) of MAR.
[116] Recital (5) of MAR.
[117] Recital (4) of MAR.

authorised as a regulated market of emission allowances[118] or other auctioned products based thereon, including when auctioned products are not financial instruments, pursuant to Regulation (EU) No 1031/2010. Without prejudice to any specific provisions referring to bids submitted in the context of an auction, any requirements and prohibitions in this Regulation referring to orders to trade shall apply to such bids.

According to Article 2, paragraph 2, Articles 12 (market manipulation) and 15 (prohibition of market manipulation) also apply to:

(a) Spot commodity contracts,[119] which are not wholesale energy products, where the transaction, order or behaviour has or is likely or intended to have an effect on the price or value of a financial instrument referred to in paragraph 1.
(b) Types of financial instruments, including derivative contracts or derivative instruments for the transfer of credit risk, where the transaction, order, bid or behaviour has or is likely to have an effect on the price or value of a spot commodity contract where the price or value depends on the price or value of those financial instruments; and
(c) Behaviour in relation to benchmarks.

According to Article 2, paragraph 3, the Regulation applies to any transaction, order or behaviour concerning any financial instrument as referred to in paragraphs 1 and 2, irrespective of whether or not such transaction, order or behaviour takes place on a trading venue.

Pursuant to Article 2, paragraph 4, the prohibitions and requirements in the Regulation shall apply to actions and omissions, in the Union and in a third country, concerning the instruments referred to in paragraphs 1 and 2.

As the result of this provision the market abuse legal regulation not only applies to financial instruments admitted for negotiation on a regulated market and to

[118] The European Union Emission Trading Scheme trades primarily in EU allowances. Emissions trading is a market-based approach to control pollution. In an emission trading system the government sets an overall limit on emissions and issue allowances or authorisations equal to each participant pollution baseline calculated on each participant's historical emissions in a way that to comply, the pollution emitted should equal the pollution allowances. Participants that pollute less can sell their allowances to those who need to increase their pollution levels. To avoid the risk that polluters who receive their allowances for free may maintain their pollution levels to receive more allowances in the future, the allowances are auctioned. Commission Regulation EU No 1031/2010 governs the timing, administration and other aspects of auctioning of greenhouse gas emission allowances. Art 38 prohibits insider trading proscribing the relevant persons who possess inside information to submit, modify or withdraw a bid for an auctioned product to which that information relates. Art 39 also prohibits to disclose inside information outside the normal course of the exercise of its employment, profession, or duties, and to recommend or induce another person on the basis of inside information, to submit, modify or withdraw the bid for auction products to which that information relates.

[119] According to Investopedia, 'A spot commodity is a commodity up for immediate trade, as opposed to a commodity under contract for trade at a future date. A commodity is a necessary good, which is used in commerce that is interchangeable with other commodities of the same type. Spot commodities are traded on the spot market with an expectation of delivery at settlement. In contrast, commodities traded on the futures market have a delivery set at a future date.'

those for which a request for admission in a regulated market has been made, but it also extends to financial instruments negotiated on qualified markets, such as multilateral trading facilities as well as in over the counter trading facilities.[120]

Chapter II, Article 7 of the EU Regulation defines 'inside information' as a notion central not only for insider trading, but also for market manipulation.[121] According to Article 7, paragraph 1 of MAR, 'inside information' is:

> information of a precise nature, which has not been made public, relating, directly or indirectly, to one or more issuers or to one or more financial instruments, and which, if it were made public, would be likely to have a significant effect on the prices of those financial instruments or on the price of related derivative financial instruments.

This 'price sensitivity' is so when it is information that 'a reasonable investor would be likely to use as part of the basis of his or her investment decisions' (Article 7, paragraph 2 of MAR).

The efforts of the 2014 reform, as of previous ones, was to tie down the norms about insider trading within parameters of certainty and strict legality and to overcome their past characteristic of vagueness and indeterminateness. Therefore, the central elements of 'inside information', also referred to as 'privileged information', became having a precise distinctive character, a non-public nature, pertaining to an issuer or to a financial instrument and the so-called 'price sensitivity'.[122]

The element of precision excludes simple rumours, vague and uncontrolled, and mere conjectures not grounded on in-depth knowledge.[123] Moreover, also the writings of financial analysts and consultants, their evaluations, research and statistics are not characterised by the necessary precision. Miedico points out that this characteristic reflects the fundamental idea that the repression of insider trading is derived from cognitive advantages obtained from a position in the corporation and not from cognitive advantages derived from a greater capacity to organise and interpret data available to the public. This conclusion is, however, upturned when the elaborations of analyst and consultants is based on non-public data obtained from regular encounters with insiders who have shared it mostly for promotional purposes.[124]

In accordance with recital 18 of MAR:

> Legal certainty for market participants should be enhanced through a closer definition of two of the elements essential to the definition of inside information, namely the precise nature of that information and the significance of its potential effect on the prices of the financial instruments, the related spot commodity contracts, or the auctioned products based on the emission allowances. For derivatives which are wholesale energy products, information required to be disclosed in accordance with Regulation (EU) No 1227/2011 of the European Parliament and of the Council of 24 October 2011 on

[120] M Miedico, 'La Disciplina Penalistica degli Abusi di Mercati' in A Alessandri (ed), *Reati In Materia Economica* (Turin, Giappichelli Editore, 2017) 319.

[121] ibid.

[122] ibid, 321.

[123] ibid.

[124] ibid.

> wholesale energy market integrity and transparency should, in particular, be considered as inside information.

This recital encompasses the two basic characteristics of inside information: precision and potential impact on the price of financial instruments. The information covered by the Regulation includes 'corporate information' produced by the issuer and 'market information' generated by external sources.[125]

The information may consist in a future event as long as it is apt to allow an investment decision on the securities market that makes it price sensitive, such as about a future public offer of acquisition of the shares of a company.[126]

Moreover, the information does not need to be absolutely detailed and exhaustive. It is enough if it contains a general orientation representing an advantage for the investor who has to decide about the sale or acquisition of a financial instrument and, thus, such information is reflected on its price.

The information must be non-public, that is, not known by an indeterminate number of people. The inside information includes information obtained through a long-term process. According to recital 16 of MAR:

> Where inside information concerns a process which occurs in stages, each stage of the process as well as the overall process could constitute inside information. An intermediate step in a protracted process may in itself constitute a set of circumstances or an event which exists or where there is a realistic prospect that they will come into existence or occur, on the basis of an overall assessment of the factors existing at the relevant time. However, that notion should not be interpreted as meaning that the magnitude of the effect of that set of circumstances or that event on the prices of the financial instruments concerned must be taken into consideration. An intermediate step should be deemed to be inside information if it, by itself, meets the criteria laid down in this Regulation for inside information.

Recital 17 of MAR clarifies that:

> Information which relates to an event or set of circumstances which is an intermediate step in a protracted process may relate, for example, to the state of contract negotiations, terms provisionally agreed in contract negotiations, the possibility of the placement of financial instruments, conditions under which financial instruments will be marketed, provisional terms for the placement of financial instruments, or the consideration of the inclusion of a financial instrument in a major index or the deletion of a financial instrument from such an index.

Article 20 of MAR, expresses that:

> Persons who produce or disseminate investment recommendations or other information recommending or suggesting an investment strategy shall take reasonable care to ensure that such information is objectively presented, and to disclose their interests or indicate conflicts of interest concerning the financial instruments to which that information relates.

[125] ibid, 322.
[126] ibid.

And that 'Public institutions disseminating statistics or forecasts liable to have a significant effect on financial markets shall disseminate them in an objective and transparent way.'

Market soundings, in turn, are 'important for the proper functioning of financial markets and market soundings should not in themselves be regarded as market abuse' (Recital 32 of MAR). However, 'the person receiving the market sounding shall assess for itself whether it is in possession of inside information or when it ceases to be in possession of inside information' (Article 11 of MAR, paragraph 7).

Article 8, paragraph 1 of MAR determines that insider dealing arises 'where a person possesses inside information and uses that information by acquiring or disposing of, for its own account or for the account of a third party, directly or indirectly, financial instruments to which that information relates', and also considers to be insider dealing 'the use of inside information by cancelling or amending an order concerning a financial instrument to which the information relates where the order was placed before the person concerned possessed the inside information'. In relation to auctions of emission allowances or other auctioned products based thereon that are held pursuant to Regulation (EU) No 1031/2010, the use of inside information shall also comprise submitting, modifying or withdrawing a bid by a person for its own account or for the account of a third party.[127]

Article 8, paragraph 2 defines insider dealing through recommendation or inducement. This happens when the person who possesses inside information:

(a) recommends, on the basis of that information, that another person acquire or dispose of financial instruments to which that information relates, or induces that person to make such an acquisition or disposal, or
(b) recommends, on the basis of that information, that another person cancels or amends an order concerning a financial instrument to which that information relates, or induces that person to make such a cancellation or amendment.

According to Article 8, paragraph 3, the use of the recommendations or inducements referred to above amounts to insider dealing 'where the person using the recommendation or inducement knows or ought to know that it is based upon inside information.'

Article 8, paragraph 4 enumerates persons to whom this article applies. These are those who possess inside information as a result of:

(a) being a member of the administrative, management or supervisory bodies of the issuer or emission allowance market participant;
(b) having a holding in the capital of the issuer or emission allowance market participant;
(c) having access to the information through the exercise of an employment, profession or duties; or
(d) being involved in criminal activities.

[127] See n 118.

This paragraph extends the subjective qualification to become insider dealers to 'any person who possesses inside information under circumstances other than those referred above where that person knows or ought to know that it is inside information', and paragraph 5 extends the qualification of insider dealer to 'natural persons who participate in the decision of legal persons to carry out the acquisition, disposal, cancellation or amendment of an order for their account'.

Directive 2014/57/EU of the European Parliament and of the Council of 16 April 2014 on criminal sanctions for market abuse (market abuse Directive) declares in its first recital that:

> an integrated and efficient financial market and stronger investor confidence requires market integrity. The smooth functioning of securities markets and public confidence in markets are prerequisites for economic growth and wealth. Market abuse harms the integrity of financial markets and public confidence in securities, derivatives and benchmarks.

And in Recital 3 the Directive explains that:

> The report of 25 February 2009 by the High-Level Group on Financial Supervision in the EU, chaired by Jacques de Larosière (the 'de Larosière Group') recommended that a sound prudential conduct of business framework for the financial sector must rest on strong supervisory and sanctioning regimes. To that end, the de Larosière Group considered that supervisory authorities must be equipped with sufficient powers to act and that there should also be equal, strong and deterrent sanctions regimes against all financial crimes and that such sanctions should be enforced effectively, in order to preserve market integrity. The de Larosière Group concluded that 'Member States' sanctioning regimes are in general weak and heterogeneous.

Furthermore, on Recital 8, the Directive expresses that 'the introduction by all Member States of criminal sanctions for at least serious market abuse offences is therefore essential to ensure the effective implementation of Union policy on fighting market abuse'.

On Article 3 the Directive deals with insider trading under the title 'Insider dealing, recommending or inducing another person to engage in insider dealing', mandating Member States to take the necessary measures to ensure that insider dealing, recommending or inducing another person to engage in insider dealing as referred to in paragraphs 2 to 8, constitute criminal offences at least in serious cases and when committed intentionally.

According to paragraph 2, coinciding in this respect with Article 8, paragraph 1 of MAR, 'insider dealing arises where a person possesses inside information and uses that information by acquiring or disposing of, for its own account or for the account of a third party, directly or indirectly, financial instruments to which that information relates'.

Paragraph 3 of the Directive mirrors Article 8, paragraph 2 of MAR in identifying the persons to whom the prohibition of insider trading applies, that is, those who possess inside information as a result of:

(a) being a member of the administrative, management or supervisory bodies of the issuer or emission allowance market participant;

(b) having a holding in the capital of the issuer or emission allowance market participant;
(c) having access to the information through the exercise of an employment, profession or duties; or
(d) being involved in criminal activities.

Article 3 of the Directive also applies to any person who has obtained inside information under circumstances other than those referred to in the first subparagraph where that person knows that it is inside information.

Paragraph 4 of Article 3 also mirrors the part of Article 8, paragraph 1 of MAR, that considers insider dealing to be 'the use of inside information by cancelling or amending an order concerning a financial instrument to which the information relates where the order was placed before the person concerned possessed the inside information', and paragraph 5 mirrors the part of Article 8 of MAR providing that:

> In relation to auctions of emission allowances or other auctioned products based thereon that are held pursuant to Regulation (EU) No 1031/2010, the use of inside information referred to in paragraph 4 of this Article shall also comprise submitting, modifying or withdrawing a bid by a person for its own account or for the account of a third party.

Paragraph 6 of Article 3 of the Directive also exactly mirrors Article 8, paragraph 2 of MAR, recommending that for the purposes of the Directive, another person engaged in insider dealing, or inducing another person to engage in insider dealing, arises where the person possesses inside information and:

(a) recommends, on the basis of that information, that another person acquire or dispose of financial instruments to which that information relates, or induces that person to make such an acquisition or disposal; or
(b) recommends, on the basis of that information, that another person cancels or amends an order concerning a financial instrument to which that information relates, or induces that person to make such a cancellation or amendment.

While in Article 8, paragraph 3 of MAR the use of the recommendations or inducements amounts to insider dealing 'where the person using the recommendation or inducement knows or ought to know that it is based upon inside information', Article 3, paragraph 7 of the Directive strictly requires thatthe use of the recommendations or inducements referred to in paragraph 6 the person using the recommendation or inducement actually know that it is based upon inside information to amount to insider dealing.

Article 3, paragraph 8 justifies persons who are or have been in possession of inside information and used that information, engaging in insider dealing on the basis of an acquisition or disposal, where their behaviour qualifies as legitimate behaviour under Article 9 of MAR. Among the exemptions, Article 9 mentions, for example, the situation in which the person used the information in the normal course of his function as a market maker, as well as the situation where the person is authorised to execute orders on behalf of third parties, and the acquisition or disposal to which the order relates, is made to carry out such an order legitimately in the normal course of the exercise of that person's employment, profession or duties.

In agreement with the purposes of the Directive, Article 7, paragraph 1 prescribes that Member States must take the necessary measures to ensure that the offences referred to in Articles 3 to 6 (insider dealing, recommending or inducing another person to engage in insider dealing; unlawful disclosure of inside information; market manipulation; and inciting, aiding and abetting, and attempting these offences) are punishable by effective, proportionate and dissuasive criminal penalties, and that insider dealing, recommending or inducing another person to engage in insider dealing and market manipulation are punishable by a maximum term of imprisonment of at least four years, while unlawful disclosure of inside information shall be punished with a maximum term of imprisonment of at least two years.

Unlawful disclosure of inside information is dealt with in Article 4 of MAR, which prescribes in paragraph 1 that it constitutes a criminal offence at least in serious cases and when it is committed intentionally. Paragraph 2 determines that unlawful disclosure arises where a person possesses inside information and discloses that information to any other person, except where the disclosure is made in the normal exercise of an employment, profession or duties.

Market manipulation, proscribed by Article 5 of the Directive, is dealt with in Chapter 5, section VII.

With respect to legal persons, Article 8 of the Directive establishes their liability as follows:

> 1. Member States shall take the necessary measures to ensure that legal persons can be held liable for offences referred to in Articles 3 to 6 committed for their benefit by any person, acting either individually or as part of an organ of the legal person, and having a leading position within the legal person based on:
>   (a) power of representation of the legal person;
>   (b) an authority to take decisions on behalf of the legal person; or
>   (c) an authority to exercise control within the legal person.
> 2. Member States shall also take the necessary measures to ensure that legal persons can be held liable where the lack of supervision or control, by a person referred to in paragraph 1, has made possible the commission of an offence referred to in Articles 3 to 6 for the benefit of the legal person by a person under its authority.
> 3. Liability of legal persons under paragraphs 1 and 2 shall not exclude criminal proceedings against natural persons who are involved as perpetrators, inciters or accessories in the offences referred to in Articles 3 to 6.

Article 9, in turn, focuses on sanctions to legal persons, establishing that:

> Member States shall take the necessary measures to ensure that a legal person held liable pursuant to Article 8 is subject to effective, proportionate and dissuasive sanctions,

which shall include criminal or non-criminal fines and may include other sanctions, such as:

(a) exclusion from entitlement to public benefits or aid;
(b) temporary or permanent disqualification from the practice of commercial activities;
(c) placing under judicial supervision;
(d) judicial winding-up;
(e) temporary or permanent closure of establishments which have been used for committing the offence.

V. France

A. Historical and Institutional Background

Until 1967, insider trading was rampant in France despite the existence of Article 419 of the French Penal Code, prohibiting the use of fraudulent schemes to influence supply and demand in the marketplace.[128] According to a tolerant and complacent attitude toward French capital markets,[129] Article 419 was not enforced in the area of stock markets and securities trading. This changed in 1966 and 1967, when the legislator became aware of the need to moralise the stock markets and to make them transparent.[130] In order to prevent the inequality between the different stock market players, the legislator enacted Law No 66-537 of 24 July 1966 on Commercial Companies and Ordinance No 67-833 of 28 September 1967,[131] creating the Commission des Opérations des Bourses (COB) (Stock Exchange Operations Commission) as an independent regulating administrative authority, following the American example of the Securities Exchange Commission. The attributions of this French market authority grew over time from a regulating power to a sanctioning power of administrative infringements to its regulations, respectively by Law No 85-1321 of 14 December 1985 and by Law No 89-531 of

[128] Art 419 of French Penal Code of 1810, from the Napoleon Series Org (Transcribed by Tom Holmberg): 'Those who, by false or slanderous reports, purposely spread among the people; or by offering higher prices than those which were asked by the venders themselves; or by coalitions or combinations among the principal holders of the same kind of merchandize or provisions, tending to prevent such goods being sold at all, or being sold under a certain price; or by any fraudulent ways or means whatever, shall have effected the enhancement or reduction of the price of provisions or merchandize; or of the public securities and stocks, above or below the prices which would have been determined by the free and natural competition of trade; shall be punished with an imprisonment of not less than one month, nor more than one year, and a fine of from 500 to 10,000 francs. The offenders may, moreover, be placed, by sentence or judgment, under the superintendence of the high police, during not less than two years, nor more than five years.'

[129] R Irving, 'French Insider Trading Law: A Survey' (1990) 22(1) *The University of Miami Inter-American Law Review* 47.

[130] M Giacopelli and N Catelan, 'Délit et manquement d'initiés' in *Répertoire de Droit Pénal et de Procedure Pénale* (initiated in 1970) (Paris, Dalloz, May 2015) section 1 (under title 'Géneralités').

[131] ibid.

2 August 1989. The COB became the Monetary and Financial Authority after Law No 2003-706 of 1 August 2003, setting up a more efficient repression of market abuse and empowering the Authority to double the number of stock market offences and administrative infringements to its regulations. The Monetary and Financial Authority was the result of the fusion of the COB, the Council of Financial Markets (Commission des Marches Financiers) and the Council for Discipline of the Financial Management (Commission de Discipline de la Gestion Financière) with the power to establish its own Regulations, to investigate its violations, and to judge the violators and sanctioning them for the administrative infringements (*manquements*) of its own regulations, including international functions of cooperation with the market authorities of other states that have concluded agreements of international cooperation with France.

With regard to criminal offences, Law No 2013-1117 of 6 December 2013, in its mission to reinforce the fight against tax fraud and major economic and financial criminality, established a new financial public prosecutor, with national jurisdiction, specialising with complex financial crimes with many perpetrators, accomplices and victims.

B. Past Developments on the Insider Trading Prohibition

Returning to the evolution of insider trading legislation in France, Ordinance No 67-833 of 28 September1967 required members of the board of the company, administrators, members of the supervisory board and permanent representatives exercising any of these functions to disclose securities transactions within six days of their execution. The COB would compile and publish these transactions as a matter of public record and the government would use them to deter insider trading.[132] The underlying governmental policy was based on the belief that disclosing corrupt insiders to their peers would arouse public hostility and shame. Insider trading was not prohibited per se, but non-disclosure would result in criminal sanctions and forfeiting of profits.[133]

Given the overwhelming flood of insider reports, the COB openly admitted in 1969 that it was unable to process the majority of them. In addition, the COB recognised its incapacity of investigating the staggering number of insiders that were ignoring the reporting obligations altogether.[134] Consequently, the COB proposed to the government to amend the legislation, abandoning the disclosure approach in favour of a complete prohibition on insider trading.

Finally, on 23 December 1970, at a time in which insider trading was altogether unregulated in the rest of Europe, France enacted Law No 70-1203, criminalising insider trading per se under Article 10-1, in order to create confidence and attract

[132] Irving, 'French Insider Trading Law: A Survey' (n 129) 47.
[133] ibid, 48.
[134] ibid.

investors during a market crisis. The Statute redefined the specified insiders (*initiés internes*) as directors and certain officers of a company; their permanent representatives, as for example accountants and attorneys; their spouses, unless separated under judicial decree; and their non-emancipated minor children. Insiders were obliged to hold their shares in nominative form or to deposit shares in bearer form in a bank, giving notice of this deposit to the COB.[135] Article 162-161 applied to both listed and non-listed securities.

In addition to the internal insiders, Article 10-1(1) included the category of external insiders (*initiés externs*), referring to all other persons 'who have at their disposal while exercising their professional functions privileged information on the technical, commercial, or financial circumstances and operations of a company'.[136] The penalty for this violation was imprisonment from two months to two years and/or a fine of up to four times the profits obtained.

In 1976, the Chief Executor Officer of the European joint venture of Otis Elevator, Inc (Otis Europe) flew to the US to persuade Otis Elevator, Inc to acquire the company BDR. With the knowledge of this transaction, he placed an order of 71,179 francs of BDR securities. Upon his return to Paris, the takeover announcement triggered a sharp surge in the price of BDR shares. Otis Europe's Chief Executive was consequently prosecuted as an external insider (*initié extern*) under Article 10-1(1). The defendant argued that the crime of using confidential information while trading, Article 10-1(1), required a specific intent of using the information for the unlawful purpose of gaining an unfair financial advantage on the stock market and that the prosecutor had not met this requirement. The court, on the basis of an absence in the legal text of any express allusion to a specific intent, ruled that Article 10-1(1) did not require it and that the mere possession of inside information regarding a company, while trading in that company's securities, was sufficient to prove that the insider 'exploited'[137] the information, in accordance with the purpose of the insider trading laws. To inspire confidence in the stock markets, the crime defined in Article 10-1(1) consisted not in the profit derived from the use of inside information or the intention to make it profitable, but rather that the perpetrator 'tilted an otherwise level playing field in his advantage through his use of inside information'.[138]

Later, in 1977, another case involving the former CEO of a public works corporation (Compagnie Française d'Entreprise) exemplified the doctrine of 'complete abstention' as a means of maintaining a 'level playing field'.[139] Although the French company's CEO had been demoted from the CEO position, the defendant had remained privy to inside information from the company and therefore learned

[135] ibid, 49.
[136] ibid, 51.
[137] The French text used the word *exploited* to describe the offence.
[138] Irving, 'French Insider Trading Law: A Survey' (n 129) 54.
[139] Decided on 26 May 1977, 1978 DS Jur, 379. See Irving, 'French Insider Trading Law: A Survey' (n 129) 54.

that the corporation's ventures in Morocco lost considerably more money than previously estimated.

With this knowledge, the defendant sold his shares before the information became public, avoiding a considerable loss. The trial court dismissed the charges for lack of evidence that the defendant had exploited the information because his bank had pressured him to sell his shares.

The Court of Appeal reversed the decision after discovering that the defendant had not entered the transaction under the 'most pressing necessity' because he had access to other stocks to guarantee his debts. Indeed, the Court of Appeal decision implied a presumption of unlawfulness regarding any transaction involving an insider in which the trader of securities retains material, undisclosed information. Once, the 'most pressing necessity' exception was discarded, and the insider was found to be under a general obligation to completely abstain from transactions where he has had any inside information related to the relevant securities. This is what has been named the 'complete abstention doctrine'. The French legislator also adopted this doctrine in 1983.[140]

The crime of insider trading was modified several times until the creation of the Council of Financial Markets (Conseil des Marchés Financiers (CMF)). The crime of insider trading, originally introduced by the Law of December 1970, was included in the Monetary and Financial Code (Code Monétaire et Financier) under Article L 465-1 after the changes introduced by Law No 2005-842 of 26 July 2005 on the Confidence and Modernisation in the Economy, and Law No 2013-672 of 26 July 2013 on Separation and Regulation of Banking Activities.

Only a limited circle of insiders enumerated in Article L 465-1 could commit this criminal offence. Initially, only corporate leaders were considered insiders. This quality was later extended to other persons who participated in insider operations, creating a distinction between primary and secondary insiders. The new MAR blurs this distinction and refers in Article 8 to 'persons who possess privileged information and use it to acquire or transfer on their own account or account of a third person, directly or indirectly, the financial instruments of which this information refers'.

It is important to point out that an American investor, convicted in France for insider trading, challenged the definition of the second circle of insiders made by Article L 465-1(1). The defendant appealed to the European Court of Justice for the lack of predictability of the legal text and its consequent violation of the principle of legality. In this case, *Soros v France*,[141] the ECtHR considered that the use of general qualifications in the definition of criminal offences was inevitable and that it did not violate the principle of legality.[142] With respect to the predictability,

[140] Irving, 'French Insider Trading Law: A Survey' (n 129) 57.

[141] *Soros v France* [2011] ECtHR 172 (6 October 2011).

[142] S Soler, *Las Palabras De La Ley* (Mexico City, Fondo de Cultura Económica, 1969) 176, 177, explains the need of the legislator to typify in order to regulate, that is, to construct abstract patterns to regulate legal situations.

the Court expressed that Article 10-1 of the 1967 Ordinance[143] was sufficiently predictable to the extent that the case law defined the notion of insider in situations that were sufficiently close to the point that Soros could not have any doubt that his behaviour was reprehensible, all the more because he was an institutional investor.

The criminal offence contained in Article L 465-1 punished the carrying-out of illegal operations on the stock market by legally defined insiders who had access to privileged information.

Having defined insiders as one of the elements of the crime, it was necessary then to define the notion of privileged information as another element.[144] Insider information in the context of that provision consisted in the privileged information possessed by a circle of insiders who obtained such information by virtue of their position in the enterprise. Information obtained through the markets' rumour pipeline was not criminalised.[145] The privileged information needed to be sufficiently precise, confidential and have the aptitude to influence the price of stocks. The information ceased to be confidential when it was made known to the public and not through the mere enlargement of the circle of insiders. The *Cour de Cassation* (Court of Cassation) decided on 26 June 1995 that the privileged nature of information did not result from an analysis made by those who receive it and use it, but it had to be appreciated in an objective way, excluding any arbitrariness and in function of its sole content.[146] The relevant information referred either to the prospects or the situation of an issuer, whose securities were negotiated on the regulated markets, or to the prospects of a security listed on the regulated market.[147]

[143] Art 10-1 of the Ordinance 67-833 of 28 September 1967 punished with two years of imprisonment and a fine of 10 million francs – an amount that could be increased in proportion to the profit obtained by the offence without ever being inferior to such profit – the fact that certain corporate officers and persons who on occasion of their profession or their functions were in possession of privileged information about the prospects or situation of issuers of securities negotiated in a regulated market or about the prospects of the evolution of a security admitted in a regulated market, to carry out or to knowingly allow to carry out, directly or through an intermediary, one or more transactions before the public became aware of such information. The Ordinance also punished with six months of imprisonment and a fine of 100,000 francs the communication of the same information to a third party outside the normal framework of his (her) profession or function. Moreover, the Ordinance punished with the penalties established in the first part of the provision, to spread among the public by any means false or misleading information of the same nature as described in such provision.

[144] Giacopelli and Catelan, 'Délit et manquement d'initiés' (n 130) (under title s 2 'Éléments constitutifs').

[145] See M Véron, *Droit penal des affaires*, 10th edn (Paris, Dalloz, 2012); P Conte, 'Marchés d'instruments financiers – Activité des marchés d'instruments' in *Juris-classeur Droit Pénal des Affaires* (Paris, Lexis-Nexis, 2014) fasc 20, cited by Giacopelli and Catelan, 'Délit et manquement d'initiés,' section 14, 'Notion d'information' (under title s 2 'Éléments constitutifs;, subtitle A, 'Une Information privilegiée: condition préalable').

[146] Crim 26 juin 1995, No 93-81.646.

[147] Giacopelli and Catelan, 'Délit et manquement d'initiés' (n 130) section 17, 'L'objet de l'information' (under title s 2 'Éléments constitutifs,' subtitle, 'Une Information privilegiée: condition préalable').

It is irrelevant whether the offence had been committed abroad, provided that at least one of the elements had been carried out.[148] Law No 2013-672 of 26 July 2013 of Separation and Regulation of Banking Activities modified the text of Article L 465-1 of the Monetary and Financial Code by expanding its criminal scope, including securities negotiated on a multilateral system of negotiation.

The offence of insider trading was carried out in two ways, either through the exploitation of privileged information, or through the communication of privileged information. The second form was committed by all those who possess information through the exercise of their profession or function and communicated it to a third person outside the normal sphere of their profession or functions. The usefulness of this last way of committing the offence of insider trading was felt in *l'affaire Péchiney* and has an objective to punish excessively talkative insiders.[149]

The French law of insider trading criminalised the attacks against the transparency of the financial markets with the purpose of ensuring its integrity. The methodology used by the French law to protect market integrity is to ensure the equality of investors regarding the information through the disclosure obligation of the possessors of inside information.[150]

C. Present Regulation of Insider Trading

According to Law No 2016-810 of 21 June 2016 reforming the repression of market abuse, the Financial and Monetary Code establishes in Article L 465-1:

> 1.-A – It is punished with 5 years of imprisonment and a hundred million Euros fine, an amount that can be increased in proportion to the advantage obtained by the crime and which should never be inferior to such profit, the action by the General Director, President, member of the Board of Directors, manager, member of the Board of Administration or member of the Oversight Board of

[148] Crim 26 Oct 1995, No 94-83.780. Bull Crim No 324 (*l'affaire Péchiney.*)

[149] Giacopelli and Catelan, 'Délit et manquement d'initiés' (n 130) at section 19 'La communication d'une information privilegiée' (under title section 2 'Éléments constitutifs,' subtitle B 'Élément materiel'). In November 1988, Pechiney SA, a state-owned French aluminium company, announced a $125 million takeover of Triangle Industries, a French packaging company. The SEC noticed the unusual facts that in a short time before the announcement between 200,000 and 300,000 shares of Triangle Industries (specifically its American National Can branch specialised in packing) had been traded at about $10 a share. After the announcement these shares rose up to $56. Since one-third of the purchases orders were made from France, the SEC warned the COB, who in its report informed that six French investors were involved in insider trading, and the government publicly disclosed the report on 31 January 1989. The investigating judge initiated criminal procedures that eventually resulted in charging nine persons, of whom one eventually, on appeal, received a sentence of one year of firm imprisonment and another a suspended one, while two others were sentenced to 18 months of imprisonment, of which 12 months were suspended.

[150] Gounot, Essai d'application de l'analyse économique du droit à la réglementation boursière des operations d'initiés, *Revue de Science Criminelle et de Driot Pénal Comparé*, 2000, 335 ff. (cited by Giacopelli and Catelan, 'Délit et manquement d'initiés' (n 130) at section 6 'Les atteintes à la trnnsparence des marchés' (under s 1 'Répression pénale des infractions d'initiés,' subtitle 'Art. 1- Délit d'initié') (n 130 above).

an issuer concerned with a privileged information, or by a person that exercises an equivalent function, by a person in possession of a privileged information concerning an issuer in which he holds a share, by a person possessing a privileged information because of his profession or function or in occasion of his participation in the commission of a crime or misdemeanor, and by any other person knowingly possessing a privileged information, to use this privileged information carrying out for himself or for others, directly or indirectly, one or more transactions, or to cancel or modify one or more orders issued before he acquired the privileged information about the financial instruments supplied by the issuer or about financial instruments involved in this privileged information.

B. – The attempt of the crime above defined is punished by the same penalties.

Article L 465-2 I of the same Monetary and Financial Code establishes that:

1.- It is punished with the penalties established in the previous article 465 1.-A the action by the persons mentioned in the same of recommending the realization of one or more transactions on financial instruments related to the privileged information or inciting the realization of transactions on the basis of such related privileged information.

Article L 465-2 II extends the criminal offence to whoever uses the recommendation or the instigation mentioned in I, knowing that it is based on privileged information.

Article L 465-2 III extends the offence to whoever communicates the recommendation or the incitement mentioned at I of the present article knowing that it is based on privileged information.

Article L 465-2 IV punishes the attempt of the offence defined in I of this article with the same penalties.

Article L 465-3 of the same Code punishes with the same penalties as in L 465-1:

I- The action committed by a person in possession of a privileged information concerning a corporate issuer in which this person exercises the functions of General Director, President, member of the Board of Directors, manager, member of the Board of Administration or member of the Oversight Board of an issuer concerned with a privileged information, or by a person that exercises an equivalent function, by a person in possession of a privileged information concerning an issuer in which he holds a share, by a person possessing a privileged information because of his profession or function or in occasion of his participation in the commission of a crime or misdemeanor, and by any other person knowingly possessing a privileged information, who communicates to a third person, unless she proves that this communication takes place within the scope of her profession or functions, including when it pertains to a market sounding carried out in accordance to sections 1 to 8 of article 11 of the EU Regulation Nr. 596/2014 of the European Parliament and the Council of April 16, 2014 about market abuse repealing the Directive 2003/6/CE of the European Parliament and the Council and the directives 2003/124/CE, 2003/125/CE and 2004/72/CE of the Commission.

II- The attempt of the offense defined in I of this article is punished with the same penalties.

The analysis of these provisions of the Monetary and Financial Code regarding insider trading should be preceded by the determination of the notion of privileged information (inside information).

As a consequence of Law No 216-819 of 31 June 2016, Article L 465-1 of the Monetary and Financial Code prescribes that the words 'privileged information' should be interpreted in the sense of paragraphs 1 to 4 of Article 7 of MAR,[151] that is, that the information should be precise, not made public and, if so, likely to have a significant effect on the prices of financial instruments. The information is deemed to be precise if it indicates a set of circumstances, where it is specific enough to enable a conclusion to be drawn as to the possible effect of those circumstances on financial instruments, and that a reasonable investor would be likely to use as part of the basis of his or her financial decisions.

These include information regarding financial instruments negotiated on a negotiation platform or for which a request for admission for negotiating on a negotiation platform has been presented. The notion of 'negotiation platform' includes now regulated markets, multilateral systems of negotiation, as well as organised systems of negotiation.[152]

At the beginning, Article L 465-1 of the Monetary and Financial Code gave no hints about the notion of privileged information. According to court decisions and scholarship it was understood that this information must be confidential, precise

[151] Art 7(1)–(4) of MAR read as follows:

1. For the purposes of this Regulation, inside information shall comprise the following types of information:
2. For the purposes of paragraph 1, information shall be deemed to be of a precise nature if it indicates a set of circumstances which exists or which may reasonably be expected to come into existence, or an event which has occurred or which may reasonably be expected to occur, where it is specific enough to enable a conclusion to be drawn as to the possible effect of that set of circumstances or event on the prices of the financial instruments or the related derivative financial instrument, the related spot commodity contracts, or the auctioned products based on the emission allowances. In this respect in the case of a protracted process that is intended to bring about, or that results in, particular circumstances or a particular event, those future circumstances or that future event, and also the intermediate steps of that process which are connected with bringing about or resulting in those future circumstances or that future event, may be deemed to be precise information.
3. An intermediate step in a protracted process shall be deemed to be inside information if, by itself, it satisfies the criteria of inside information as referred to in this Article.
4. For the purposes of paragraph 1, information which, if it were made public, would be likely to have a significant effect on the prices of financial instruments, derivative financial instruments, related spot commodity contracts, or auctioned products based on emission allowances shall mean information a reasonable investor would be likely to use as part of the basis of his or her investment decisions.

In the case of participants in the emission allowance market with aggregate emissions or rated thermal input at or below the threshold set in accordance with the second subparagraph of Article 17(2), information about their physical operations shall be deemed not to have a significant effect on the price of emission allowances, of auctioned products based thereon, or of derivative financial instruments.

[152] A Lepage, P Maistre de Chambon and R Salomon, *Droit Pénal des Affaires* (Paris, LexisNexis, 2018) 467.

and apt to influence the price of securities and to have determined the transactions in question. After 2014, Article L 465-1 referred to Article 7 of MAR, containing a definition close to the one expressed by the French Cour de Cassation (final court of appeal): the privileged information should be precise, not made public, and if made so, should be apt to have a significant effect on the price of securities. Moreover, the privileged information should be confidential, that is, secret and not known by the public. The number of persons who possess it, when these are members of a collegial body such the board of directors or the oversight board does not defeat this confidentiality. The loss of confidentiality should be interpreted in restrictive fashion, in the sense that it does only operate by the diffusion through official channels, legal publications and major newspapers, and not by vehicles of limited circulation and partial scope.[153]

According to Article 7(2) of MAR, referred to by Law 2016-819 of 21 July 2016, the privileged information should be precise, that is, it cannot be vague and consist in simple rumours.[154]

Last, according to Article 7(4) of MAR, referred to by Law 2016-819 of 21 July 2016, the information must be the determinant factor for the transaction, a requirement already present in French case law.[155] This information includes the prices of financial instruments, derivative financial instruments, related spot commodity contracts,[156] or auctioned products based on emission allowances, an information that a reasonable investor would be likely to use as part of the basis of his or her investment decision.[157]

In the case of Article L 465-1, I, A, it is enough to issue a purchase or sale order to commit the offence, independently of whether the order is executed or not.[158] Although the profit is an element to decide the sentence, it is not an element of the criminal offence.[159]

The mens rea for the commission of this crime is intent. In addition, in the case of Article L 465-2.II there must be the special intent of those who receive the inside information of knowing that the recommendations or incitements are based on privileged information.[160] This has been compared with special intent in the offence of reception of stolen goods with the knowledge that they were stolen. In the case of commission of insider trading by communication of privileged information, it is sufficient of just being aware it is illegal inside information.[161]

Parallel to the market abuse criminal offences there are corresponding administrative infringements called '*manquements*' punished by the Financial Markets

[153] ibid, 469.
[154] See n 151.
[155] ibid.
[156] See definition of 'spot commodity contracts' in n 119.
[157] See n 151.
[158] Lepage et al, *Droit Pénal des Affaire* (n 152) 473.
[159] ibid, 474.
[160] ibid, 480.
[161] ibid, 481.

Authority (Autorité des Marchés Financiers). In the case of insider trading, the corresponding administrative violation is called '*manquement d'initié*', which has the same objective elements that characterise the criminal offence. However, the administrative violation differs from the criminal offence with respect to primary insiders, who are not presumed to be insiders and the Financial Markets Authority needs to prove their knowledge of the inside information.[162] In the case of secondary insiders, that is, those who benefit from privileged information because of their profession or functions, they are subject to a simple presumption of '*manquement d'initié*'. Tertiary insiders, in turn, are very largely defined by Article 622-2, section 2 of the General Regulation of the Financial Markets Authority, as those who possess privileged information and are aware that it is so. Unlike the corresponding criminal offence, they are punished even if they act negligently.

The fines for this administrative violation can reach a €100 million or tenfold the amount of the profit obtained by the '*manquement*'.

D. Constitutionality of the Accumulation of Administrative and Criminal Sanctions

After the entry into force on 6 December 2013 of Law No 2013-1117 against fiscal fraud and serious economic and financial criminality, it was traditionally admitted that it was possible to accumulate the administrative proceedings initiated by the Monetary and Financial Authority with the criminal law proceedings launched by the Public Prosecutor of the Republic.

Since this accumulation of sanctions seemed to infringe the principle of *non bis in idem* that excludes double criminal proceedings for the same deed, the French Constitutional Council on 28 July1989, dismissed the principle of non-accumulation in the field of stock market violations, while posing the demand to respect the principle of proportionality, meaning that the global amount of the sanctions could not surpass the maximum of one of the incurred sanctions.

In this respect, the Criminal Chamber of the Cours de Cassation, in its decision No 7049 of 22 January 2014 (12-83.579) concluded that the accumulation of criminal and administrative proceedings in the field of stock market violations did not infringe Article 50 of the Charter of Fundamental Rights of the European Union (2000/C 364/01) (right not to be tried or punished twice in criminal proceedings for the same criminal offence).

After the decision of the ECtHR in the case *Grande Stevens* of 4 March 2014, the Constitutional Council reversed its position from 28 July 1989.

In the EADS (Airbus Group) insider trading case, the French Constitutional Council held that Article 8 of the French Declaration of the Rights of Man and of the Citizen precluded criminal and administrative prosecution of insider trading

[162] ibid, 520.

offences for transgressing the principle of the 'necessity of sanctions'. This made the articles of the French Monetary and Financial Code unconstitutional. The Council abrogated, effective 1 September 2016, the provisions of the Monetary and Financial Code regarding the criminal and administrative prosecution of insider trading, mandating the French legislature to bring the law on insider trading into conformity with the French Constitution.

This decision was grounded on the constitutional principle of necessity of infractions and sanctions, and declined to decide whether the principle of *non bis in idem* had constitutional value. Thus, it did not take into account the *Grande Stevens* decision of the ECtHR, holding that the Italian system of criminal and administrative prosecution of insider trading offences violated Article 4 of Protocol No 7 to the ECHR and the *non bis in idem* principle contained in such protocol.[163] The Constitutional Council, by ignoring the *Grande Stevens* decision, declined to elevate the *non bis in idem* principle to the level of a constitutional principle, but when the Paris Court of First Instance applied the Council decision of 18 March 2015 to the EADS insider trading case, it gave direct effect to *Grande Stevens*, where the substance of the decision of the ECtHR was whether Italian administrative and criminal proceeding for a market abuse offence were compatible with the principle of *non bis in idem* required by Article 4 of Protocol No 7.[164]

Following the Constitutional Council decision, the Criminal Chamber of the Cour de Cassation decided in a similar case (20 May 2015, No 13.83.489) to repeal a conviction based on Article L 465-1 preceded by the imposition by the Monetary and Financial Authority of an administrative sanction for identical facts.

The decision of the Constitutional Council, however, has to be appreciated in the light of the European reform on market abuse, especially by the 2014 Directive on criminal sanctions making it obligatory to impose such sanctions when until then it was optional.[165] Implementing this Directive, Law No 2016-819 of 21 June 2016, reforming the criminalisation system of market abuse in France, a cooperation framework between the Financial Public Prosecutor of the Republic and the Financial Markets Authority was organised, in the sense that the Public Prosecutor's criminal action can only be initiated if the Financial Markets Authority has not communicated its intent to send a notice of complaint and that this notification that sets off the administrative proceedings, can only take place if the Public Prosecutor, in their dialogue, has not communicated his intention to initiate a public action. Since this double condition may lead to a procedural paralysis, the general prosecutor at the Paris Court of Appeal, who authorises the Public Prosecutor on whether or not to initiate a public action, can settle the disagreement. It is only when he refuses the authorisation that the Financial Markets Authority can proceed to notify its complaint.

[163] AF Kirry and A Lee Wetzel, 'Evolution of French Constitutional Law and European Human Rights Law Related to the Non Bis in Idem Principle' (2015) 4 *European Human Rights Law Review* 384.
[164] ibid.
[165] Lepage et al, *Droit Pénal des Affaire* (n 152) 487.

VI. United Kingdom

The criminalisation of insider trading in the UK was preceded by a debate around Professor Henry Manne's book justifying insider dealing and proclaiming its potential beneficial aspects. According to Manne, its prohibition would adversely affect market efficiency and would prevent an effective way to compensate executives.[166] As Sarah Clarke points out, his view was a purely economic one, ignoring the viewpoint that insider dealing is 'morally reprehensible, unfair, and unethical, and, in effect, "cheating"', a viewpoint that prevailed and underpins both US and UK legislation on the subject.[167] Because it is a misuse of information, a breach of fiduciary duties, and a theft to other investors, it adversely affects the confidence in markets,[168] and this is precisely considered the major reason for controlling insider dealing.[169]

As examples of earlier condemnatory views on insider dealings, Barry AK Rider cites a 1972 leading book on the stock market expressing that a stockbroker who learned privileged information should not allow this to operate in detriment of his client.[170] Moreover, he reminds that Sir Winston Churchill considered defamatory an accusation of advantage through the use of inside information during the Marconi Scandal of 1911.[171] In this respect, Churchill also 'persuaded Lord Northcliffe not to allow the *Times* to go on the attack and FE Smith to represent Lloyd George and Sir Rufus Isaacs in their successful libel action against the French newspaper *Le Matin*'.[172]

[166] H Manne, *Insider Trading and The Stock Market* (New York, The Free Press, 1966).

[167] S Clarke, *Insider Dealing: Law and Practice* (Oxford, Oxford University Press, 2013) 25.

[168] ibid.

[169] Bazley, *Market Abuse Enforcement* n 46) 11, citing Barry Rider and Michael Ashe for this proposition.

[170] BAK Rider, 'The Control of Insider Trading – Smoke and Mirrors!' in (2000–2001) 19 *Dickinson Journal of International Law* 1, 2, citing G Cooper and RJ Cridlan, *The Law And Procedure of the Stock Exchange* (London, Sweet & Maxwell, 1972).

[171] Rider, 'The Control of Insider Trading' (n 170) 2. According to Encyclopedia.com, 'the scandal arose out of a contract for the construction of a chain of wireless stations between the English Marconi Company and the British government represented by the postmaster-general, Herbert Samuel, who was a wholly innocent party. One of the company's directors, Godfrey Isaacs, was also a director of the American Marconi Company, which had no holdings in the English company but stood to benefit indirectly from its success. In April 1912 Godfrey Isaacs offered shares in the American company to his brother Rufus Isaacs (attorney-general), Lloyd George (chancellor of the Exchequer), and Alexander Murray (Liberal Chief Whip). Lloyd George unhesitatingly bought 1,000 shares at £2 each before they went on sale to the public at a price of £3.50. In July rumors of ministerial speculation surfaced, notably in Eye Witness, a journal edited by Cecil Chesterton, which coined the phrase 'Marconi scandal'. This was taken up by the opposition and led to the appointment of a House of Commons select committee. Though this exonerated the ministers, its verdict was essentially a party political one, for Murray had purchased additional shares for Liberal Party funds and subsequently disappeared to Bogotá in South America.'

[172] A Roberts, *Churchill: Walking With Destiny* (New York, Penguin Random House, 2018) 168. On the same page this author transcribes the irate and extremely detailed negation of any possibility of an eventual indirect involvement by Churchill when the Commons Select Committee investigating the matter summoned him.

However, in the UK, the introduction of legislation on the subject ran for a number of years and up to the end of WWII, buying and selling of stocks in a company based on information known only to the company or to its directors, officers or advisors was legitimate and widespread.[173] Between the end of WWII and the late 1950s there was a perception that insider trading was unethical because of the unfairness of making personal, private profits at the expense of the shareholders. In the 1960s and the 1970s, there was a return to insider trading as being legitimate to the point that in 1973, the financial editor of the *Sunday Times* described insider dealing as the 'crime of being something in the city'. Beginning in 1973, there were attempts to pass legislation containing criminal sanctions for insider dealing but it was only in 1980 that legislation passed forbidding insider trading and the first prosecution was in 1981. The provisions of the Companies Act were revised and consolidated into the Companies Act 1985, and then revised and rebranded as the Companies Securities (Insider Dealing) Act of 1985, prohibiting directors, officers employees and various kinds of agents of the company who had access to material non-public inside information in virtue of their position within a company from dealing with the securities of a company while having that information.[174]

Moreover, these insiders were prohibited from tipping that information to others and the Act also prohibited the tippees from dealing in securities on the basis of that information. To supplement and reinforce the insider dealing ban in the UK, the legislature introduced the Financial Services Act 1986.[175] The 1985 Insider Trading Act amended by the 1986 Financial Services Act was superseded by the 1993 Criminal Justice Act, which governs today the criminal law regulation of insider dealing in the UK, while the Financial Services and Markets Act 2000 introduced a wider civil offence of market abuse, which covered 'insider dealing, disclosing insider information, and dissemination of false or misleading information'.

Part V of the 1993 Criminal Justice Act punishes the crime of insider dealing, on conviction on indictment, by a fine or imprisonment of up to seven years or both. The offence is defined as follows:

(1) An individual who has information as an insider is guilty of insider dealing if, in the circumstances mentioned in subsection (3), he deals in securities that are price-affected securities in relation to the information.

(2) An individual who has information as an insider is also guilty of insider dealing if—

(a) he encourages another person to deal in securities that are (whether or not that other knows it) price-affected securities in relation to the information,

[173] K Franklin, 'US v UK Insider Trading Laws: Who is The Top Dog?' SSRN, 21 February 2013, available at http//:://dx.doi.org (10.2139/ssrn 230856) 26.

[174] H Chitimira, 'A Historical Overview of Market Abuse Prohibition in the United Kingdom' in (2014) 3(20) *Mediterranean Journal of Social Sciences* 49, 50.

[175] ibid.

knowing or having reasonable cause to believe that the dealing would take place in the circumstances mentioned in subsection (3); or

(b) he discloses the information, otherwise than in the proper performance of the functions of his employment, office or profession, to another person.

(3) The circumstances referred to above are that the acquisition or disposal in question occurs on a regulated market, or that the person dealing relies on a professional intermediary or is himself acting as a professional intermediary.

The 1993 Criminal Justice Act continues in a number of sections to clarify the meaning of each of the terms used in the definition of the insider dealing offence. The analysis made in section 56 of 'inside information' is especially significant:

(a) it must relate to particular securities or to a particular issuer of securities or to particular issuers of securities and not to securities generally or to issuers of securities generally;
(b) it must be specific or precise;
(c) it must not been made public; and
(d) if it were made public would be likely to have a significant effect on the price of any securities.

In addition, this section indicates that securities are 'price-affected' securities in relation to inside information, and inside information is 'price-sensitive information' in relation to securities, if and only if the information would, if made public, be likely to have a significant effect on the price of the securities. Last, this section clarifies that for its purpose 'price' includes value.

It is also especially significant that section 53 establishes a series of defences based on facts such as that the individual dealing in securities or encouraging another to deal in securities:

(a) did not at the time expect that the dealing would result in a profit attributable to the fact that the information in question was price-sensitive information in relation to the securities;
(b) at the time he believed on reasonable grounds that the information had been disclosed widely enough to ensure that none of those taking part in the dealing would not be prejudiced by not having the information; and
(c) that he would have done what he did even if he had not had the information.

The MAR replaced the MAD and strengthened the market abuse regime to improve market confidence and better protect investors. Implemented via the Financial Services and Markets Act 2000 (amended through the Financial Services and Markets Act 2000 (Market Abuse) Regulations 2016 (SI 2016/689)), it makes insider dealing a civil offence, as it does with unlawful disclosure, market manipulation and attempted market manipulation.

The EU law on market abuse will be retained by the UK after Brexit. In order to address its deficiencies after the UK withdraws from the EU, Parliament enacted the Market Abuse (Amendment) (EU Exit) Regulations 2019 (SI 2019/310). In order to highlight some of the Regulations' main points, I draw here from an

Explanatory Memorandum prepared by HM Treasury and laid before Parliament by Act.

> The EU Market Abuse Regulation (MAR) applies to financial instruments admitted to trading on an EU trading venue or elsewhere where the price or value of such instruments depends or have an effect on the price or value of a financial instrument admitted to trading or traded on an EU trading venue (Explanatory Memorandum 2.4).

The Market Abuse (Amendment) (EU Exit) Regulations 2019 amend the retained EU law pertaining to market abuse so that it applies to financial instruments admitted to trading or traded on the UK as well as on EU trading venues. This is necessary to maintain the integrity and reputation of UK markets as the UK withdraws from the EU. The instrument also transfers to UK authorities the powers given by MAR to the European Commission and to the European Securities and Markets Authority (ESMA) to make supplementary legislation and technical standards. These modifications reflect a policy designed to assure that financial instruments admitted to trading or trading on UK venues continue within the scope of UK regulation after its withdrawal from the EU. This is in addition to continuing to include within the UK regulations those financial instruments admitted to trading or traded in an EU venue. This inclusion was necessary given the close relationship between UK and EU markets.

According to the Explanatory Memorandum (2.10) other key amendments include:

(1) transferring certain powers from ESMA to the FCA (Financial Conduct Authority) to enable the FCA to continue to effectively enforce the market abuse regime in the UK;
(2) transferring the power to make supplementary legislation under MAR from the Commission to HM Treasury;
(3) retaining notifications requirements for issuers who have admitted financial instruments to trading on UK trading venues; emission allowances market participants registered in the UK, and UK trading venues, to report certain information to the relevant national regulator, which will now be the FCA;
(4) removing the obligation for UK regulators to share information or to cooperate unilaterally with EU authorities without any guarantee of reciprocity;
(5) references to emission allowances markets have been retained in places as it is envisioned that UK firms will still participate in secondary market trading of emission allowances under the EU Emissions Trading Scheme (ETS) and some UK firms may continue to participate in the EU ETS through a branch in the EU, despite the UK leaving the EU in a no-deal scenario; and
(6) making technical amendments to the Commission Delegated Regulation (EU) 2016/522 in order to make it operable within the UK as piece of retained EU legislation.

In addition to these legislative changes applicable to civil sanctions, insider dealing continues to be a criminal offence under Part V of the Criminal Justice Act 1993 and market manipulation under sections 89–91 of the Financial Services Act 2012 because Directive 2014/57/EU of the European Parliament and the Council on criminal sanctions for market abuse does not bind the UK or subjects the country to its application in accordance to Protocol 21 of the Treaty on the Functioning of the European Union.[176]

VII. Italy

Arguing against those who consider that insider trading is a 'new' crime that has not been morally internalised as traditional crimes such as murder, rape, etc, Tripodi refers to ancient precedents about using confidential information for personal advantage: In the year 304 BC, Gnaeus Flavius, member of the college of Roman pontiffs, through stealing the secret book of *legis actiones* (containing the science of legal interpretation) and making it public became elected by the plebeians and eventually reached the position of *curule aedile* (responsible for public works and games, and supervisor of markets, of grain and water supplies). Another example referred to by Tripodi are the administrators of the Dutch East Indies Company, who in 1717, were accused of having sold shares exploiting their privileged knowledge of the reduction of the respective dividends. Once the news of the reduction was known the securities involved lost significant value. Last, he gives the nineteenth-century example of Nathan de Rothschild, who had an advance knowledge of the defeat of Napoleon in Waterloo and bought obligations from the British Government at a time in which other investors were precipitously selling them in fear of an Emperor's victory.[177] Tripodi traces back the modern genesis of the notion of insider trading to the US in the 1930s and its diffusion in Europe in the 1980s and 1990s.

In Italy, the regulation of insider trading began with Law 157 of 17 May 1991 as an implementation of Council Directive (89/592/ECC) of 13 November of 1989 coordinating regulations on insider dealing.[178] This law was abrogated with the entry into force of the Testo Unico Finanziario (TUF) (Single Financial Text) in 1998, which was later modified by Law 62 of 18 April 2005, implementing Directive 2003/6/CE of the European Parliament and of the Council of 28 January 2003 on insider dealing and market manipulation (market abuse),[179] increasing the punishment of imprisonment from a maximum of six years to a maximum of 12 years and doubling the amount of the fines. Moreover, Law 62 of 2005 introduced a new administrative sanctioning system, repeating the criminal law norms in the creation of identical administrative wrongdoings.

Today, the criminal sanctions against insider trading (*abuso d'informazioni privilegiate*) are contained in Article 184 of the TUF, while Article 187 *bis* of the same text contains the administrative violations.

[176] Recital 29 of the Directive.
[177] Tripodi, *Informazione Privilegiati* (n 1) xv.
[178] [1989] OJ L334/30.
[179] [2003] OJ L96/16.

Article 184 of the TUF (updated by Decree Law no 49 of 10 May 2019 (in force since 10 June 2019) defines the abuse of privileged information as follows:

1. Those who are in possession of privileged information because of their position as members of an administrative, directive or controlling organ of an issuer, of their participation in the capital of the issuer, or of their work activity or professional public functions, or of an office task, shall be punished with one to six years of imprisonment and with a fine of twenty-thousand to three-million euros (according to article 39, section 1, of the Law nr. 262 of December 28, 2005, the sanctions are doubled within the limits established for each kind of penalty by Book I, Title II, chapter II of the Penal Code) when they:
    a) Acquire, sell or perform other transactions, directly or indirectly, on their own or on behalf of third parties on financial instruments, using such privileged information.
    b) Communicate such privileged information to others outside the scope of their normal work, professional functions or office task, *or of a market sounding carried out in the sense of article 11 of the regulation (EU) No 596/2014.*[180]
    c) Recommend or induce others, on the basis of such privileged information, to perform the transactions indicated in a).
2. The same penalty established in subsection 1. applies to whomever in possession of privileged information acquired through the preparation or execution of criminal activities, carries out any of the behaviors described in subsection 1.
3. The judge can triple the fine or increase it up to ten times the value of the product or profit obtained by the offense, when such punishment appears as inadequate even if applied to its maximum.

3-*bis*. In the case of financial instruments mentioned in article 180 section 1, letter a),[181] *number 2),*[182] *2-bis)*[183] *and 2-ter,*[184] *limited to financial instruments, which price or value depends from the price or value of a financial instrument mentioned in numbers 2) and 2-bis) either have an effect on such price or value or on the one related to auctions in auction platforms authorized as a regulated market of emission quotes*, the criminal sanctions consist of fines up to a hundred and three thousand two hundred ninety one euros and arrest up to three years.

[180] The part in italics was introduced by Art 4 of the Decree Law No 107 of 10 August 2018.

[181] The part in italics was introduced by Art 4 of the Decree Law 107 of 10 August 2018. Article 180 1. a) includes under the words 'financial instruments' those admitted to negotiations or for which a request of admission has been presented, in a regulated market either Italian or of another European Union member country.

[182] Article 180 2) refers to 'financial instruments' and those admitted to negotiations or for which a request of admission has been presented in a multilateral system of negotiations either Italian or of other European Union member country.

[183] Article 180 2*bis* refers to financial instruments negotiated in an organised system of negotiations either Italian or of another European Union member country.

[184] Article 180 2ter refers to financial instruments not included in the previous articles, which price or value depends on the price or value of financial instruments mentioned therein or that have an effect on such price or value, encompassing not in an exclusive way, credit default swaps and financial contracts for differences. (A contract for differences (CFD) is an arrangement made in a future contract whereby differences in settlement are made through cash payments, rather than by the delivery of physical goods or securities (Investopedia).)

Article 184, section 4 was abrogated by Article 4 of the Decree Law No 107 of 10 August 2018.

Following the civil law teleological interpretative tradition, D'Alessandro begins his analysis of an earlier version of Article 184 inquiring into the legal interests and values protected by this criminal law provision, that is, the '*bene giuridico*', which is the Italian translation of *Rechtsgut*.[185] D'Alessandro concludes that the legal value protected by Article 184, TUF is the market as a whole, especially in its function of determining the price of financial instruments.[186]

Article 181(1), TUF, defining the notion of privileged information was abrogated by Legislative Decree No 170 of 2018, which refers to MAR, Article 7.[187]

Article 184, TUF contains a '*reato propio*', that is, a special offence that can only be committed by a specific category of offenders.[188] These are known as primary insiders and comprise members of the administration, direction or control of the issuer (corporate insiders), participants in the capital of the issuer (stockholder insiders) and those who exercise a working activity, profession or a function, including a public one, or an office task (temporary insiders). Secondary insiders, who possess the privileged information for other reasons are not affected by the criminal sanctions contained in Article 184 unless as instigators or accomplices, but are subject of administrative sanctions provided by Article 187 *bis*, TUF. Article 184, subsection 2 includes as possible perpetrators those who obtained the possession of privileged information through the preparation or execution of a criminal activity (criminal insiders) as for example those who exploit the advance knowledge of the commission of a serious crime that would significantly affect the price of financial instruments.

Summarising, according to Article 184, TUF, the crime of abuse of privileged information consists in the following actions on the part of the primary insiders in possession of the privileged information:

(a) acquire, sell, or accomplish other operations, directly or indirectly, on their own or on behalf of third parties, on financial instruments utilising such information (genuine insider trading);
(b) communicate the information to others, outside the normal performance of their work, profession, function or office task (tipping);
(c) recommend or induce others, on the base of such information, to perform any of the operations indicated in (a) (*tuyautage*).

[185] German criminal law considers the theory of *Rechtsgut* as the basic tenet of criminal law. '*Rechtsgut*' can be defined as the vital interests and values of the individual and society that are protected by criminal law. According to Jescheck and Weigend, the '*Rechstgut*' is the basis for both the structuring and the interpretation of criminal law, it gives sense and purpose to the content of its provisions and plays an essential role in its systematisation. See H-H Jescheck and T Weigend, *Lehrbuch des Strafrechts: Allgemeiner Teil* (Berlin, Duncker & Humblot, 1996) 238–46, 257.

[186] F D'Alessandro, *Regolatori del Mercato, Enforcement e Sistema Penale* (Turin, Giappichelli Editori, 2014) 113.

[187] See n 151.

[188] F Carnelutti, *Teoria Generale del Reato* (Padua, CEDAM, 1933) 135, distinguishes between those offences that can only be committed by certain qualified subjects from those that can be perpetrated by anyone but are only criminally relevant when the perpetrators are certain qualified subjects.

The abuse of privileged information is a crime of harmful action,[189] and also of abstract or presumed endangerment,[190] that is, it is not necessary to prove any result such as an effect on the functioning of the stock market, either actual or potential. The economic result is completely irrelevant, and it is only necessary to prove the normal aptitude of this type of behaviour to alter the mechanisms of price formation of financial instruments, even if in the particular case the behaviour turned out to be completely innocuous.[191]

The culpability required to commit this crime consists in the mere awareness of the informational advantage at the time the information is utilised, together with the voluntary carrying out of the objective behaviour described in Article 184. It is therefore a matter of general intent in which the desire of profit is irrelevant.[192]

The use of the expression 'utilising' (*utilizzando*) by Article 184 (a) was introduced as the result of the adjustment to the MAD, substituting this word for *avvalendosi* ('availing themselves of') contained in the 1998 version of the law. According to D'Alessandro 'the word "*utilizando*" conveys the motivational connection between the privileged information and the perpetrator's choice of action in a stronger fashion than the word "*avvalendosi*"'.[193]

These provisions deal with financial instruments admitted to operate in an Italian regulated market or in the EU market, as well as those in which at least there is a request for admission to be negotiated in one of these markets. The term 'privileged information' contained in Article 184, TUF is clarified by Article 7 of EU Regulation 596/2014, which, in sum, explains that such information relates, directly or indirectly, to issued financial instruments that are confidential, precise and price sensitive. Plantamura clarifies that such privileged information consists in corporate information but does not include market information (ie government decisions on fiscal policies, publication of a report by a rating agency, etc that regard the whole market and not a single entity or specific financial instrument). Moreover, Plantamura explains that insiders are members of the administrative, direction or control organs of the issuing entity; subjects that participate in the capital of the issuers (majority shareholders); and also individuals that have acquired the knowledge of the same information as a consequence of the exercise of a work activity, or a profession or from a function, including public functions, or from an office task in which knowledge of the

[189] GP Fletcher, *Basic Concepts of Criminal Law* (New York, Oxford University Press, 1998) 60 ff distinguishes between crimes of harmful actions completed by the mere action independently of any result, and crimes of harmful consequences, requiring a specific resulting event united to the action through a chain of causation.

[190] In criminal offences of abstract danger, as opposed to those of concrete danger, the behaviour is criminalised for its intrinsic association with the endangerment of certain legally protected interests, generally of a collective or supra individual nature, such as the integrity of the financial market, in which it is not necessary to prove any actual or concrete risk. See K Tiedemann, *Wirtschaftsstrafrecht*, 5th edn (Munich, Verlag Franz Vahlen, 2017) 84 ff.

[191] D'Alessandro, *Regolatori del Mercato* (n 186) 135.

[192] ibid.

[193] ibid, 137.

information is direct and not occasional as for example, in the case of cleaning personnel.[194]

Today, Article 184, TUF punishes with imprisonment from two to 12 years and with a fine of €20,000 to €3 million, whoever commits abuses of privileged information in the case of:

(a) *trading*, that is, purchase, sell, or other operations, directly or indirectly, for themselves or on behalf of third parties, of financial instruments, '*using*' (*utilizzando*) – as indicated above, this word has replaced the expression '*exploiting*' (*avvalendosi*) – the privileged information;
(b) *tipping*, which communicates to others the privileged information of their knowledge obtained outside the normal fulfilment of their work, profession, or trade; and
(c) '*tuyautage*', that is when on the basis of their known, privileged information, they recommend or induce others to undertake the trading operations described in (a).[195] The previous text used the expression 'advise' instead of 'recommend'.

Plantamura explains that commentators have interpreted the terminological change from 'exploiting' to 'using' as the will of the legislator to link more stringently the motivation behind the trade and the information itself. However, Plantamura believes that this change acts as a smokescreen. It is what the civil law scholars call crimes of mere danger, as opposed to crimes requiring an actual harm. In this case, it has been interpreted that the word 'using' means that the statute does not require the unfair enrichment of an insider or unfair damage to investors or to the market.

With respect to 'tipping', the present TUF definition of Article 184 requiring that the forbidden communication should be made 'outside the normal fulfilment of their work, profession, or functions', replaced the previous legal text.[196] The new text thus replaced the old expression 'without justified reason' that created a justification that shifted the burden of proof to the defence.

The most authoritative scholarship has noted that the textual change regarding 'tuyautage' from 'simple advice' to 'recommend', defined as an activity directed to third parties to effectively realise a financial operation, has limited the liability of insiders – providing a requirement that the insider actively incites an illegal activity through use of the inside information.

As in the previous text, the forms of commission of the offence – trading, tipping and tuyautage – the mens rea is represented by a general intent that requires that the insider be aware of the privileged nature of the information they use, communicate or that substantiates the recommendation.

[194] V Plantamura, 'L'*Insider Trading* e la Manipolazione del Mercato' in A Manna (ed), *Corso di Diritto Penale dell'Impresa* (Milan, CEDAM, 2010) pt VI, ch V, 670, 673.

[195] ibid, 675.

[196] Following Art 10 of EU Regulation 596/2014, which excepts from the prohibition when the communication takes place during the normal exercise of an occupation, profession or function.

Article 184 (2) introduces the category of the so-called 'criminal insiders', that is, those who obtained the knowledge of the privileged information as a result of a preparation or commission of criminal activities. According to Plantamura, examples of this would be an eco-terrorist being in possession of privileged information consisting of an imminent attack against the installations of an oil company who purchased securities from a competing oil company in the certainty that the shares would rise in value.[197] The European Community 2003 Directive on market abuse, clause 17, provides that

> as regards insider dealing, account should be taken of cases where inside information originates not from a profession or function but from criminal activities, the preparation or execution of which could have significant effect on the prices of one or more financial instruments or on price formation in the regulates market as such.[198]

Another hypothetical possibility raised by Plantamura[199] is the hacking of computer systems (Article 15 (3), TUF) through which the perpetrators acquire possession of privileged information, which could also be the basis of the crime of false social communications (Article 2621-22 of the Italian Civil Code) or market manipulations (Article 185, TUF).

Both classic insiders and criminal insiders are in fact primary insiders. The TUF also considers so-called 'secondary insiders', that is, those who, directly or indirectly, or perhaps, through a chain of persons, have become aware of the information profited immediately after the initial revelation was made by primary insiders. These insiders are included in Article 180 under the definition of 'trading'.

Under Chapter III on 'Administrative sanctions', Article 187 *bis* contains a subchapter on 'abuse and illegal communication of a privileged information' introduced by Article 4 of the Legislative Decree No 170 of 10 August 2018, establishing that:

> Except for the criminal sanctions when the offence constitutes a criminal one, whoever violates the prohibition of abuse of privileged information contained in article 14 of the European Union Regulation 596 of 2014, shall be punished with an administrative sanction of 20,000 to five million Euros.

After abrogating subparagraphs 2, 3 and 4, in subparagraph 5 the same legislative decree establishes that these penalties can be tripled or increased up to 10 times the profit obtained or the losses avoided through the illegal behaviour when, taking into account the sentencing criteria of Article 194-*bis* and the magnitude of the product or the profit from the illegal behaviour, these penalties appear to be inadequate even if applied to their maximum.

[197] Plantamura, 'L'*Insider Trading*' (n 194) 677.
[198] Directive 2003/6-EC Section 17, 28 January 2003.
[199] Plantamura, 'L'*Insider Trading*' (n 194) 677.

VIII. Germany

A. Development of Insider Trading Law in Germany

From the viewpoint of internationalisation, the German insider trading provisions are indirectly a result of the diffusion of American law, reflected in the technical adoption of the English terms. The concept of *Insiderhandel* is derived from the Anglo-American expression 'insider trading' or 'insider dealing'.[200]

According to Tiedemann, referring to the old paragraph 38 of the Securities Trading Act (WpHG),[201] the German legislator found its model in section 10(b) of the Securities Exchange Act, where insider trading is considered to be a fraud, more closely defined by rule 10(b) 5, SEC.[202] In a more direct and immediate way it is a result of the Europeanisation of insider trading, reflected in the successive EU directives.

German scholarship recognises that the phenomenon of insider trading is as old as securities themselves.[203] From the beginning of the twentieth century, however, there were attempts from about 2,000 banks to obligate themselves to regulate their staff transactions in order to avoid the dangerous possibility of insider trading.[204]

After the enactment of the section 10(b) 5 of the Securities and Exchange Act of 1934 and the following SEC Rule 10(b) 5, as well as various European legislative initiatives to criminalise insider trading in the 1970s and 1980s, the subject remained in Germany only at a non-binding level. Before 1994 there were only non-binding declarations of intent, as for example the rules of good conduct issued by the Commission of the European Economic Community in 1977 underscoring the equal treatment of all shareholders. Also, in 1967, during the preparatory discussions leading to the reform of the Stock Market Law (*Börsengesetz*), the prohibition of insider trading was discussed but finally not included in the reform.[205]

The crime of insider trading was introduced in Germany by paragraphs 12 to 14 of the Securities Trading Act in 1994.[206] These provisions, in turn were mandated

[200] A Hienzsch, *Das deutsche Insiderhandelsverbot in der Rechtswirklichkeit*, 1st edn (Baden Baden, Nomos, 2006) 18.

[201] This Act, first enacted in 1994 to implement the European Community 1989 Insider Trading Directive, initiated a new era in the legal regulation of capital markets. As Petra Wittig recalls (*Wirtchaftsstrafrect* (Munich, CH Beck, 2017) 544), this Act was revised several times under the influence of European law and became 'the permanent construction site of legislative reflections'.

[202] Tiedemann, *Wirtschaftsstrafrecht*, 5th edn (n 190) 432.

[203] R Sethe '§ 8 Insiderrecht' in H-D Assmann and R Schütze (eds), *Handbuch des Kapitalanlagerechts* (Munich, CH Beck, 2012) 453.

[204] R Sethe *Anlegerschutz im Recht der Vermögensverwaltung* (Cologne, Verlag Dr Otto Schmidt, 2005) 314, cites a communication of the Association of German Banks from 1908 regarding their obligations to self regulate.

[205] C Schröder, *Handbuch Kapitalmarktstrafrecht*, 3rd edn (Cologne, Carl Heyman's Verlag, 2015) 36, 37.

[206] BGBl I, 1994, 1749 (*Federal Law Gazette*).

by the second Financial Market Promotion Act (2. *Finanzmarktförderungesetz*), implementing the European Community Council Directive 89/592/EEC of 13 November 1989, coordinating rules on insider dealing. This insider dealing directive in Article 13 provided that 'each Member State shall determine the penalties to be applied for infringement of the measures taken pursuant to this Directive. The penalties shall be sufficient to promote compliance with those measures'.

Germany expanded the protection of investors through the enactment of a criminal law provision on insider dealing[207] within the framework of the Securities Trading Act.

From the reading of the 1989 Directive on insider trading one can interpret that the vital interest and values protected by these criminal provisions were the trust and confidence in a functional capital market as a significant area of the existing economic order.[208] As Tiedemann points out, the German insider trading law primarily protects stock markets but also allows equal access to relevant information regarding stock prices, not excluding, however, the protection of individual market participants.[209] Furthermore, these insider criminal provisions increased the attractiveness of the German financial market as a way to strengthen the competitiveness of the totality of the national economy.[210]

According to Schröder, the main emphasis of the Securities Trading Act, however, is not on the criminal law area but rather to herald a new era in the legal regulation of the capital markets that mainly concerns civil and public law.[211] It is important from a comparative legal viewpoint to emphasise that the central idea of the German insider trading provisions lie in the equal chances of accessing information.[212] These provisions guarantee equal chances to investors to promote the good functioning of the capital market. Otherwise, an unequal access to the market would lead to the desertion of investors and the consequent damage to the economy. In contrast, in the United States the central idea is the protection of fiduciary duties, leading to a more restrictive criminalisation of insider trading.[213]

Insider trading is the object of both criminal and administrative provisions. These became considerably expanded through the law about the improvement of

[207] A Hohnel, 'Wertpapierhandelsgesetz (WpHG)' in A Hohnel (ed) *Kapitalmarktstrafrecht* (Munich, CH Beck, 2013) 40.

[208] Motivations of Council Directive 89/492/EEC of 13 November 1989, [1989] OJ L334/30; see also C Schröder, 'Straf-und Buβgeldtatbestände im BörsG und WpHG' in H Achenbach and A Ransie (eds), *Handbuch der Wirtschaftsstrafrecht* (Heilderberg, CF Müller Verlag, 2012) 1169; see also K Hohn, 'Marktmissbrauch' in C Momsen and T Grützner (eds), *Wirtschaftsstrafrecht* (Munich, CH Beck, 2013) 616, affirming that the capital market despite its crises is the engine of the economy.

[209] K Tiedemann, *Wirtschaftsstrafrecht* (Special Part), 3rd edn (Munich, Verlag Franz Vahlen, 2011) 225.

[210] Hienzsch, *Das deutsche Insiderhandelsverbot* (n 200) 40.

[211] Schröder, 'Straf-und Buβgeldtatbestände' (n 208) 1169.

[212] Hohnel, 'Wertpapierhandelsgesetz' (n 207) 40.

[213] The *SEC v Texas Sulphur Co*, 401 F2nd 833 (1968) rationale of equal access to the market was considerably narrowed by the US Supreme Court in *Chiarella v US*, 445 US 222, 232 (1980) and *Dirks v SEC*, 463 US 646, 654 (1983), where the 'Supreme Court expressly reaffirmed its rejection of the equal access standard and its requirement of a breach of fiduciary duty in order for liability to be imposed'. SM Bainbridge, *Insider Trading* (New York, Foundation Press, 1999) 54.

investor's protection (*Anlegerschutzverbesserungsgesetz*) of October 2004, implementing the Market Abuse Directive 2003/6/EC of the European Parliament and Council of 28 January 2003.

The administrative provisions were included in section 39 of the Securities Trading Act, while the criminal ones were legislated in section 38. Both norms are considered to be blanket norms.[214] The criminal norm, that is, the definition of the offence was contained in paragraph 38 of the Securities Trading Act, which incorporated by reference paragraph 14 of the Securities Trading Act's description of the perpetrator's action. On a second stage it also incorporated by reference paragraphs 2, 12, and 13 of the Securities Trading Act: paragraph 2 contained the definitions of the different terms used within the scope of the statute, including securities and other financial instruments; paragraph 12 specified the securities that were relevant for insider trading provisions; and paragraph 13 defined the notion of 'inside information'.[215]

Paragraph 14 of the Securities Trading Act included the substance of the legal prohibition of insider trading, incriminating the following behaviour: making use of inside information to acquire or dispose of insider securities for the defendant's own account or for the account of a third party; disclosing or making available inside information to a third party without the authority to do so; or recommending, on the basis of inside information, that a third party acquired or disposed of insider securities,[216] or otherwise inducing a third party to do so.

Paragraph 38 of the Securities Trading Act defined the criminal offence of insider trading, specifying its perpetrators and their respective penalties, and incorporating by reference the prohibitions contained in paragraph 14. According to paragraph 38(1), the offence could be committed by any person. Paragraph 38(1) No 2 referred to those persons whom scholars have classified as primary insiders. These primary insiders were members of the executive bodies (eg board of directors or supervisory board of a joint stock corporation), shareholders and professionals (eg accountants or lawyers) who while providing their services acquired the inside information. The mere belonging to one of these positions within the corporation

[214] The doctrine of blanket criminal laws (*Blankettstrafgesetze, leyes penales en blanco, leggi penali in bianco, lois cadres*) basically consists of a special case of legislative drafting techniques that entail the incorporation by reference of a norm existing elsewhere in the legal system to complete a criminal provision. See ch 3, section V.B, 'Second Critique of *Vilar*', nn 140 to 148.

[215] Schröder, 'Straf-und Buβgeldtatbestände' (n 208) 1170; Hohn, 'Marktmissbrauch' (n 208) 622.

[216] According to para 12 of the Securities Trading Act insider securities are financial instruments:

(1) admitted to trading on a German stock exchange or included in the regulated market (*regulierter Markt*) or the regulated unofficial market (*Freiverkehr*);
(2) admitted to trading on an organised market in another member state of the European Union or signatory to the Agreement on the European Economic Area and
(3) the prices of which depend directly or indirectly on financial instruments within the meaning of nos 1 or 2.

Securities shall be deemed admitted to trading on an organised market or included on the regulated market or the regulated unofficial market if the application for such admission or inclusion has been made or publicly announced.

organs made the person a primary insider. This did not exclude the possibility of other persons becoming primary insiders when they work with inside information as part of their profession (paragraph 38(1)(2)(c) of the Securities Trading Act).[217] Primary insiders committed their criminal offence not only by using the inside information to purchase and sell securities, but also by communicating or recommending others to trade with the inside information. Inside information was defined in paragraph 13 of the Securities and Trading Act[218] and paragraph 15 prescribed obligations regarding this type of information.[219]

The inside information had to be apt to considerably influence the stock prices once the information became public. Moreover, the information had to be precise and concrete to constitute an adequate basis to assess the future stock prices. Rumours about stocks were not enough unless they contained clear statements of facts. According to Section 13 of the Securities Trading Act insider information could also consist of value judgments, estimates, prognoses, plans and intentions, when there was a sufficient but not a necessarily overwhelming possibility that these would happen or be carried out in the future.[220] Tiedemann gives as example the decision of the Federal High Court in which a member of the board of directors sold securities with the knowledge of a decline of revenues and profits before these were made public in accordance with § 15 Securities Trading Act.[221]

It was debated in Germany whether the own intentions of the operator could be considered as insider information and used as such. Tiedemann gives the example of an analyst who after purchasing a certain type of equities for himself later recommends those equities to his clients in order to lift the prices. While a widespread scholarly opinion denies its criminality on the basis that no one can be his own insider, some German courts have considered these operators as punishable primary insiders.[222]

[217] Hohn, 'Marktmissbrauch' (n 208) 650 ff.

[218] According to para 13 of the Securities Trading Act, inside information was:

(1) any concrete information about circumstances which are not public knowledge relating to one or more issuers of insider securities, or to the insider securities themselves, which, if it became publicly known, would likely have a significant effect on the stock exchange or market price of the insider security. Such likelihood is deemed to exist if a reasonable investor would take the information into account for investment decisions. The references to circumstances which are not public knowledge also applies to cases in which they may reasonably be expected to come into existence in the future. Specifically, inside information refers to information about circumstances which are not public knowledge within the meaning of (1), related to orders by third parties for the purchase or sale of financial instruments or (2) related to derivatives within the meaning of section 2 (2) no 2 relating to commodities and which market participants would expect to receive in accordance with the accepted practice of the markets in question.

(2) A valuation based solely on information about publicly known circumstances is not inside information, even if it could have a significant effect on the price of insider securities.

[219] According to para 15 of the Securities Trading Act, inside information should be published and reported to the Federal Financial Supervisory Authority (BaFin [*Bundesanstalt für Finanzdienstleistungsaufsicht*]) to prevent insider trading liability.

[220] Tiedemann, *Wirtschaftsstrafrecht*, (Special Part) (n 209) 226.

[221] BGH JZ 2010, p 367.

[222] Tiedemann, *Wirtschaftsstrafrecht*, (Special Part) (n 209) 226.

In this context, the 2003 Directive on insider trading is decisive. This Directive demanded that the perpetrator should have had the aim to obtain a profit through a behaviour apt to considerably influence the prices. The extent of this potential was measured through the subjective representation of a reasonable investor. In the past there was an objective measure to decide these cases – a change of price of at least five per cent was necessary. In both cases the issue is to avoid trifling offences.[223]

The administrative offences related to insider trading were contained in paragraph 39(2) 1 and 4 of the Securities and Exchange Act. According to these provisions, in connection with paragraph 14(1) 2 and 3 of the same statute, the administrative offence of insider trading was committed by those who communicated, made available, recommended or induced to acquire or sell insider securities.[224] The actual behaviour was the same in the case of administrative offences as in criminal ones. The difference lied in the mens rea: the criminal offences required intent, while for the administrative ones, negligence was enough.

Paragraph 39(2) 3 and 4 of the Securities Trading Act imposed administrative sanctions on secondary insiders even when committed intentionally. Persons not possessing the characteristics described in paragraph 38(1) a-d of the Securities Exchange Act, as for example a taxi driver, did not fit within the definition of primary insider and were only subject to administrative sanctions. It was therefore of primary importance to determine whether the perpetrator was a primary or secondary insider.

In the case of the President of the Board of Directors, who as a primary insider, passes on insider information he was liable for criminal punishment under paragraph 38(1) 2. In contrast, secondary insiders, whose work was unrelated to the relevant inside information, such as taxi drivers who overheard such information, they could only be liable for an administrative offence in case of passing on the information or inducing others to exploit it.

When the primary insiders purchased or disposed of securities on the basis of their inside information, they were criminally liable under paragraph 38(1) 1 of the Securities Trading Act in conjunction with paragraph 14(1) 1 of the same statute.

Primary insiders as tippers committed the criminal offence defined in paragraph 38(1) 2 of the Securities Trading Act when they intentionally communicated or made available inside information or when they recommended to dispose or purchase the relevant securities on the basis of such information. When primary insiders made the same communications or recommendations with gross negligence, they were liable for an administrative offence under paragraph 39(2) 3 and 4 of the Securities and Trading Act. Secondary insiders, in contrast, who communicated or recommended the relevant information, were liable for an administrative offence whether they perpetrated the same actions intentionally or negligently.

[223] ibid, 227.

[224] See para 39, 'Provisions concerning administrative fines' in *Bundesanstalt für Finanzdienstleistungsaufsicht* (BaFin): Securities Trading Act (WpHG), 9 September 1998 (*Federal Law Gazette* I, 2708).

Tippees who purchased or disposed of securities on the basis of the relevant inside information were criminally liable under paragraph 38(1) 1 of the Securities and Trading Act in conjunction with paragraph 14(1) 1.

According to paragraph 38(1) 2 in conjunction with paragraph 39(2) 3 or 4 of the same statute, primary insiders committed an administrative offence when they acted negligently (*leichtfertig*).

Paragraph 39(2) 3, 4 referred to those whom scholars have classified as secondary insiders. Secondary insiders were persons other than the primary insiders who obtained the inside information indifferently from whom or where they received it. Tippees were included in the category of secondary insiders. When these insiders wilfully or negligently disclosed or made available the inside information, or recommended to a third party to acquire or to dispose of insider securities, they committed an administrative offence and became liable to an administrative sanction (*Ordnungswidrigkeit*).[225] While secondary insiders who communicated or recommended the relevant information could only commit an administrative violation, the tippees who purchased or sold a security on the basis of the information received committed a criminal offence under paragraph 38 I (1) and 14 I Securities Trading Act.[226] This meant that the middleman committed an administrative violation but the one who received the information (tippee) committed a (paragraph 38(1)(1)) crime, notwithstanding whether the person who gives the information was a primary or secondary insider that is, it was indifferent whether original tippers were primary or secondary insiders. On the other hand, tippers who would have been normally punishable as instigators or accomplices were only liable according the provision of the Securities Trading Act for an administrative offence.[227] The tippers were therefore not punishable as accessories (paragraph 27 of the German Penal Code) or as instigators (paragraph 26 of the German Penal Code). In this way the legislator maintained an important difference between primary and secondary insiders in the sense that the latter could only commit an administrative offence when they communicated or recommended using the relevant inside information. Otherwise both would have been criminally punished as instigators or accessories.

Even if the tippee did not use the inside information, the primary insider intentional tipper was still criminally liable because the reason of the prohibition was to avoid expanding the circle of insiders in order not to endanger the equal chances of the market participants, thus maintaining a level playing field. Tipping included not only the transmission of the inside information but also making it available to others, including not only to determined persons but also uncertain recipients.

[225] Hohnel, 'Wertpapierhandelsgesetz' (n 209) 45; Tiedemann, *Wirtschaftsstrafrecht* (Special Part) (n 209) 225.

[226] Hohnel, 'Wertpapierhandelsgesetz' (n 207) 45.

[227] ibid, 45.

The expression 'circumstances' contained in the definition of inside information of paragraph 13 of the Securities Trading Act[228] encompassed value judgments and prognoses. The prohibition to acquire or dispose of securities was infringed by a simple order to buy or sell.[229] In 2004, the Law on Improvement of the Protection of Investors (*Anlegerschutzverbesserungsgesetz* – AnSVG) modified paragraph 14(1) of the Securities Trading Act, replacing the word 'exploit' (*ausnutzen*) of the inside information by the mere 'use' (*verwenden*).[230] Although the use of the information consisted in the mere undertaking of a transaction, it still required the difficult proof that such an undertaking was intentional. Moreover, the prevailing scholarship demanded a causal relationship between the knowledge of the inside information and the undertaking of the transaction.[231] The perpetrator should have been aware of such a causal relation and acted thereupon. The intent included the obtaining of a special benefit from the transaction based on the insider information.[232] For example, paragraph 14(1) 1 of the Securities Trading Act was not transgressed when both parties of a transaction disposed of the same inside information given that from the beginning there was no special profit in using this information. According to the *Spector Photo Group* decision, there is a rebuttable presumption that the primary insiders are using their inside information in the transaction.[233] The European Court of Justice assumed that the possession of an inside information implied that the holders through a securities transaction used such information.[234] This decision has been criticised on the basis that general presumptions have no place in criminal law. With respect

[228] According to para 13 of the Securities Trading Act inside information is:

(1) any specific information about circumstances that are not public knowledge relating to one or more issuers of insider securities, or to the insider securities themselves, which, if it became publicly known, would likely have a significant effect on the stock exchange or market price of the insider security. Such likelihood is deemed to exist if a reasonable investor would take the information into account for investment decisions. The term circumstances within the meaning of sentence 1 also apply to cases that may reasonably be expected to come into existence in the future. Specifically, inside information refers to information about circumstances which are not public knowledge within the meaning of sentence 1, which

a. is related to orders by third parties for the purchase or sale of financial instruments or
b. is related to derivatives within the meaning of section 2 (2) no 2 relating to commodities and which market participants would expect to receive in accordance with the accepted practice of the markets in question.

(2) A valuation based solely on information about publicly known circumstances is not inside information, even if it could have a significant effect on the price of insider securities.

[229] Hohn, 'Marktmissbrauch' (n 208) 645.

[230] The old provision was imposed by Art 2 (1) of the Insider Directive of 1989, replaced by the Market Abuse Directive of 2003. See also Hohn, ibid, 645.

[231] ibid, 646.

[232] Hohn, 'Marktmissbrauch' (n 208) 647.

[233] On 23 December 2009, the European Court of Justice (Third Chamber) decided Case C-45/08 *Spector Photo Group NV and Chris Van Raemdonck v Commissie voor het Bank-, Financie-en Assurantiewezen (CBFA)* interpreting the meaning of Art 2(1) of Directive 2003/6 in the sense that whenever an insider makes a transaction with a related financial instrument, he is presumed to have 'used' inside information.

[234] *Spector Photo Group NV* (n 232) recital 1.

to such criticism, Hohn points out that the viewpoint of the European Court of Justice is similar to German law in the sense that both aim at the deprivation of unjustified profits from the insider traders because these infringe the informational equal chances of market participants.[235] This interpretation coincided with Article 2 I from the Market Abuse Directive.

Insider trading can be committed through gross negligence, but the punishment should not exceed one year in prison or a criminal fine,[236] as opposed to the intentional commission of the offence, which carried a penalty of imprisonment for a term not exceeding five years or to a criminal fine.[237] According to paragraph 38(1) 1 of the Securities and Trading Act, both provisions related to the purchase or disposition of securities. Primary insiders could not commit insider trading with gross negligence, since in such cases they only committed an administrative offence.

B. Effectiveness of Insider Trading Provisions

According to Andreas Hohnel, the practical significance of the insider trading provisions regulating both criminal and administrative offences is extremely slight. He mentions that in 2011 only two persons were convicted of insider dealing, in one case with a minor punishment without trial. In the same year, four procedures were terminated with the payment of a fine.[238]

André Hienzsch carried out an intensive research on the practical application of German insider trading law, questioning the effectiveness of the criminalisation of insider trading.[239] His research tried to determine to what extent the relatively new German legislation of insider trading was successfully implemented. First, Hienzsch determined that the goal of the German insider trading legislation was to enhance the attractiveness of the German financial market and the use of the insider trading prohibition to reinforce the competitiveness of the German economy. By maintaining the effective functioning of the German capital market, the insider trading prohibition removed an obstacle preventing the satisfaction of the financial needs of the economy. The loss of investors' confidence would lead to an aversion of the public from the German capital market and to resort instead to foreign capital markets, facilitated by the internationalisation of financial markets. He insists that to protect the German capital market, it is necessary to assure the confidence and trust of investors through increased transparency and information. Hienzsch's research goals were: (a) to show in detail the implementation of the prohibition of insider trading and what are the difficulties in the various stages

[235] Hohn, 'Marktmissbrauch' (n 208) 647.
[236] Securities Trading Act, para 38 (4).
[237] ibid, para 38(1).
[238] Hohnel, 'Wertpapierhandelsgesetz' (n 207) 40. According to s 153 of the Criminal Procedure Act (StPO), the prosecutor can put an end to the oral trial with the payment of a fine.
[239] Hienzsch, *Das deutsche Insiderhandelsverbot* (n 200).

of prosecution of insider transactions; and (b) whether the insider trading prohibition has protected or reinforced the trust of potential or actual investors in the German capital market. His conclusions were that the legislative prohibition of insider trading in Germany has until now hardly succeeded in promoting the trust of investors. These poor results are attributed by Hienzsch on the one hand by problems related to the enforcement of the insider regulations, and on the other, the circumstance that the prohibition of insider trading is in itself not sufficient to influence the trust in the capital market. The difficulties in the enforcement lie both in the, until now, serious insufficiencies of the prosecutor's dealing with insider trading cases and also insufficiencies from the Federal Financial Supervisory Authority (BaFin).

C. Recent Reforms

As deemed by Recital 3 of Directive 2014/57/EU of the European Parliament and of the Council of 16 April 2014 on criminal sanctions for market abuse (MAD II), the existing legislation was insufficient to prevent market abuse and fight it, and that 'the Member States sanctioning regimes were in general weak and heterogeneous'. The High-Level Group on Financial Supervision in the EU (the 'de Larosière Group') considered that supervisory authorities must be equipped with sufficient powers to act and that there should be equal, strong and deterrent sanctions regimes against all financial crimes, sanctions which should be enforced effectively in order to preserve market integrity. For that purpose, the Directive demanded the criminalisation of serious market abuse offences (Recitals 8 and 10) and also the punishment of instigation, complicity and attempt regarding market abusive behaviours (Article 6). Moreover, on 3 July 2016, the MAR came into force. Since Germany is a member of the European Union, this Regulation applied immediately in German law after 3 July 2016, changing parts of the German Securities Trading Act.

The MAR has a broader scope than both the Market Abuse Directive of 2003 and the German Securities Trading Act. The new regulation encompasses not only the officially regulated market but also the unregulated one (Article 2). The definition of insider information of Article 7 of MAR, basically incorporates the definition of paragraph 13 of the German Securities Trading Act: it should be:

> of a precise nature, which has not been made public, relating, directly or indirectly, to one or more issuers or to one or more financial instruments, and which, if it were made public, would be likely to have a significant effect on the prices of those financial instruments or on the price of related derivative financial instruments.

Also, MAR determines in Article 7 (2) when an information should be considered 'precise', that is, when:

> it indicates a set of circumstances which exists or which may reasonably be expected to come into existence, or an event which has occurred or which may reasonably be

> expected to occur, where it is specific enough to enable a conclusion to be drawn as to the possible effect of that set of circumstances or event on the prices of the financial instruments or of the related derivative financial instruments, the related spot commodity contracts, or the auctioned products based on the emission allowances. In this respect, in the case of a protracted process that is intended to bring about, or that results in, particular circumstances or a particular event, those future circumstances or that future event, and also the intermediate steps of that process which are connected with bringing about or resulting in those future circumstances or that future event, may be deemed to be precise information.

It is new that the notion of insider information is extended to the so-called intermediate steps, when they satisfy the criteria of inside information contained in the Regulation (Article 7 (3)).

Article 7 (3) is a codification of the European Court of Justice decision in the case *Geltl/Daimler*.[240] Following a general meeting on 17 May 2005, the Chairman of Daimler's Board of Management discussed his intention to resign with the Chairman of the Supervisory Board. Between June and July of 2005 other Daimler officials were informed of the resignation plans. The decision of early departure of the Chairman took place on 27 July 2005 subject to the Supervisory Board approval the next day. The decision was announced and sent to the Federal Office for the Supervision of Financial Services and published on 28 July 2005. Following the announcement, Daimler's share price rose sharply. Mr Geltl and other investors, who had sold Daimler shares before the announcement, initiated legal action against Daimler seeking compensation for what they considered to be a late ad-hoc announcement. The lower Court referred the case to the Stuttgart Higher Regional Court to rule on a number of questions. In April of 2009 this Court decided that it could not be proven that on 27 May 2005, or subsequently, there was inside information to the effect that the Chairman would resign unilaterally, whether or not Daimler's Supervisory Board approved. For the Stuttgart Higher Regional Court the decisive price-relevant event was the Supervisory Board's decision of 28 July 2005. Such a decision had become sufficiently likely during the meeting of 27 July 2005, and therefore, there was insider information only as from that date.

On appeal, the trial court, that is, the referring court, observed that the Stuttgart Higher Regional Court did not consider whether the individual steps leading up to the decision of 28 July 2005 were such as to influence Daimler's share price. Because there was another interpretation from a different regional higher court, the case went to the Federal Court of Justice (*Bundesgerichtshof*). The Federal Court of Justice decided to stay the proceedings and to refer a number of questions to the Stuttgart Higher Regional Court for a preliminary ruling. The answer to those questions can be summarised as follows: in the event that a protracted

[240] (ECLI; EU;C;2012;397) in Case C-19/11 for a preliminary ruling under Art 267, TFEU from the Bundesgerichtshof (Germany), made by decision of 22 November 2010, received at the Court on 14 January 2011, in the proceedings *Markus Geltl v Daimler AG*.

process intended to bring about a particular circumstance or to generate a particular event, not only may that future circumstance or future event be regarded as precise information, but also may be regarded as such the intermediate steps of the process bringing about that future circumstance or event, that is, 'a set of circumstances which exists or may reasonably be expected to come into existence or an event which has occurred or may reasonably be expected to do so'.

Article 7(3) of MAR has reflected this decision as follows: 'An intermediate step in a protracted process shall be deemed to be inside information if, by itself, it satisfies the criteria of inside information as referred to in this Article.'

Intermediate steps are qualified as insider information when there is a realistic possibility that the insider relevant event occurs.[241] It is not necessary to take into consideration the extent of the effects of the prices or to introduce the US 'probability/magnitude-test'.[242] Furthermore, for information to qualify as precise it is necessary to take into account the 2015 decision of the European Court of Justice in the *Lafonta* case[243] interpreting Article 1 of the 2003/6/EC Market Abuse Directive notion of precise information as part of the definition of inside information. The Court decided that for information to be regarded as being of precise nature, 'it need not be possible to infer from that information, with a sufficient degree of probability, that, once it's made public, its potential effect on the prices of the financial instruments concerned will be in a particular direction'. Otherwise stated, the foreseeability for the change of the price of the share was not an element to be taken into account to determine its qualification as inside information.

According to Recital 15 of MAR, 'Ex post information can be used to check the presumption that ex ante information was price sensitive, but should not be used to take action against persons who drew reasonable conclusions from ex ante information available to them.'

On 25 June 2017, the German legislator modified the German law on insider trading through the Second Financial Market Revision Act ('2. *Finanzmarktnovellierungsgesetz*'). Accordingly, since 3 January 2018 the insider trading provision contained in Section 38(3) of the Securities Trading Act became

[241] Recital 16 of the Regulation EU 596/2014 (MAR) expresses: 'Where inside information concerns a process, which occurs in stages, each stage of the process as well as the overall process could constitute inside information. An intermediate step in a protracted process may in itself constitute a set of circumstances or an event which exists or where there is a realistic prospect that they will come into existence or occur, on the basis of an overall assessment of the factors existing at the relevant time. However, that notion should not be interpreted as meaning that the magnitude of the effect of that set of circumstances or that event on the prices of the financial instruments concerned must be taken into consideration. An intermediate step should be deemed to be inside information if it, by itself, meets the criteria laid down in this Regulation for inside information.'

[242] The Second Circuit Court of Appeal in *SEC v Texas Gulf Sulphur Co* (n 12) decided that only material information was included in the duty to disclose or abstain for insider trading and whether information about an event is 'material' depends on the probability the event will occur balanced with the magnitude of the event.

[243] Case C-628/13, *Jean-Bernard Lafonta v Autorité de Marches Financiers* (ECJ, 11 March 2015).

paragraph 119 (3). This constitutes a blanket provision.[244] The real prohibitory norm (the filling norm) is contained in Article 14 of MAR.[245]

Paragraph 119, subparagraph (3) punishes with imprisonment of up to five years or a fine, the infringement of its prohibitory provisions, in connection with Article 14 of MAR: performance of insider deals, prohibition of recommendations and of incitement to carry out insider deals; and prohibition to disclose insider information.

Articles 7, 8 and 10 of MAR, respectively, define the concepts of 'insider information', 'insider dealing' and 'unlawful disclosure' used by Article 14 of MAR. Attempts at the commission of the forbidden forms of insider trading are punished by paragraph 119, section 4.

The criminalisation of insider trading protects the functionality of the capital market and the confidence of investors in the price formation. Investors, however, are only indirectly protected.[246]

This provision covers both primary and secondary insiders. This distinction cannot be found in paragraph 119, section 3 of the Securities Trading Act or in Article 14 of MAR. Hellmann points out that according to Article 8, paragraph 4 of MAR,[247] also applicable to the unlawful disclosure of inside information through express reference of Article 10, paragraph 1, subsection 2,[248] the rules about insider trading expressly remain valid for both primary insiders and secondary

[244] The doctrine of blanket criminal laws (*Blankettstrafgesetze, leyes penales en blanco, leggi penali in bianco, lois cadres*) basically consists of a special case of legislative drafting techniques that entail the incorporation by reference of a norm existing elsewhere in the legal system to complete a criminal provision. See under ch 3, section V.B, 'Second Critique of *Vilar*', nn 140 to 145.

[245] U Hellmann, *Wirtschaftsstrafrecht*, 5th edn (Stuttgart, Kohlhammer, 2018) 12. Art 14 of MAR contains the prohibition to engage or attempt to engage in insider dealing as well as to recommend another person to engage in insider dealing or induce another person to engage in insider dealing. The same provision also prohibits unlawfully disclosing inside information.

[246] Hellmann, *Wirtschaftsstrafrecht* (n 245) 13.

[247] Art 8, para 4 of MAR provides:

4. This Article [8] applies to any person who possesses inside information as a result of:
   (a) being a member of the administrative, management or supervisory bodies of the issuer or emission allowance market participant;
   (b) having a holding in the capital of the issuer or emission allowance market participant;
   (c) having access to the information through the exercise of an employment, profession or duties; or
   (d) being involved in criminal activities

[248] Art 10 on 'Unlawful Disclosure of Inside Information' provides:

(1) For the purposes of this Regulation, unlawful disclosure of inside information arises where a person possesses inside information and discloses that information to any other person, except where the disclosure is made in the normal exercise of an employment, a profession or duties. This paragraph applies to any natural or legal person in the situations or circumstances referred to in Article 8(4).

(2) For the purposes of this Regulation the onward disclosure of recommendations or inducements referred to in Article 8(2) amounts to unlawful disclosure of inside information under this Article where the person disclosing the recommendation or inducement knows or ought to know that it was based on inside information.

insiders, though certainly without using these terms.[249] Furthermore, Hellmann labels the four categories of primary insiders enumerated by Article 8, paragraph 4, of MAR,[250] as 'determined by status' (subparagraph a), 'for participation reasons' (subparagraph b), 'for occupational reasons' (subparagraph c), and as a result of primary insiders involved in criminal offences (subparagraph d). Secondary insiders are, according to the same Article 8 paragraph 4 *in fine* of MAR, 'all persons who in whatever way dispose of the inside information under circumstances other than those referred in the first subparagraph where that person knows or ought to know that it is inside information'. This distinction shows that primary insiders who infringe the prohibition against communication and recommendation regarding inside information commit criminal offences, while secondary insiders are only liable for regulatory offences only punished by fines.

The distinction between primary and secondary insiders is important because while the infringements against the prohibition of communicating and recommending based on the inside information constitute criminal offences in the case of primary insiders, when committed by secondary insiders they are only punished with fines. Secondary insiders can only be criminally punished when they actually perform insider deals.[251]

Primary insiders for status reasons are according to Article 8, section 4, subsection 1, letter a of MAR, are those who dispose of the inside information because of their position in the company, such as members of the Board of Directors, Supervisory Board or managers.

Primary insiders for participation reasons according to Article 8, section 4, subsection 1, letter b of MAR are those who obtained the inside information because of their participation as shareholders in the capital of the issuer.

Primary insiders for reasons of their occupation in the company, according to Article 8 section 4, subparagraph 1, letter c of MAR are those who have access to the relevant inside information because of their work, exercise of a profession or performance of any task strictly in accordance to the purpose of their occupation, such as lawyers, accountants and business consultants. If they obtain the information by chance they are considered as secondary insiders.

Also persons who obtain their inside information because of their participation in criminal activities are primary insiders in two situations: first, when the preparation or execution of the criminal offence reveals the possession of inside information as a means to prepare or plan its commission or attempted commission, and second, when the crime is a means to obtain the inside information, that is, the goal of the criminal offences includes the obtainment of the inside information. Who, otherwise, obtains the inside information by chance on occasion of the perpetration is a secondary insider.[252]

[249] Hellmann, *Wirtschaftsstrafrecht* (n 245) 14.
[250] Reproduced in n 247.
[251] Hellmann, *Wirtschaftsstrafrecht* (n 245).
[252] ibid, 17.

The insider trading provisions contained in paragraph 119, section 3 of the Securities Trading Act demand intent as mens rea, including *dolus eventualis*.[253] Negligent infringements of this provision are punished with administrative offences (*Ordnungswidrigkriten*).[254]

[253] ibid, 22. Perpetrators act with *dolus eventualis* when having represented themselves the result described in the definition of the offence as the possible consequence of their behaviour, they accept this possibility in case it would hypothetically happen. The attitude of the perpetrator is indifference regarding the occurrence of the prohibited result. The criminal result is ratified ex ante and the perpetrator does not believe in the possibility of avoiding the result.

[254] ibid.

5

The Internationalised Repression of Stock Market Manipulation

I. Introduction

Dramatic changes in the trading of securities in world markets, such as high frequency trading and the multiplication of trading platforms have offered the possibility of trading almost instantly a large variety of products in markets around the world. Together with the benefits of global markets, these have also facilitated unfair and illegal trading practices that demand an adequate global legal response, including at the criminal law level.

The criminalisation of fraudulent stock market manipulation has been internationalised both at the European and global level. The latest development at the European level is represented by the 2014 market abuse regulation and by the directive of the same year on criminal sanctions. At the global level, the International Organization of Securities Commission (IOSCO)[1] published a report on 'Investigating and Prosecuting Market Manipulation',[2] pointing out the need of an internationally concerted action to detect, investigate and prosecute market manipulation.

The deliberate distortion of the process of price formation of securities seems to be as old as the stock markets themselves. Talis Putniņš cites Joseph de la Vega's 1688 description of the Amsterdam Stock Exchange[3] to bring home the fact that market manipulation is as old as trading in organised stock exchanges.[4] Furthermore, he exemplifies the possibility of astronomic amounts funding manipulation with a 2004 case, in which Citigroup netted a €18.2 million profit

[1] The IOSCO is the international body that brings together the world's securities regulators and is recognised as the global standard setter for the securities sector. IOSCO develops, implements and promotes adherence to internationally recognised standards for securities regulation. It works intensively with the G20 and the Financial Stability Board (FSB) on the global regulatory reform agenda.

[2] IOSCO, 'Investigating and Prosecuting Market Manipulation' (2000) 1.

[3] TJ Putniņš, 'Market Manipulation: A Survey' [2011] *Journal of Economic Surveys* available at https://ssrn.com/abstract=1805642, 2.

[4] Joseph de la Vega wrote the oldest account about stock market speculation and trading in his book, *Confusion de Confusiones: Dialogo Curioso Entre un Filosofo Agudo, un Mercader Discreto y un Accionista Erudito* (Amsterdam, 1688).

'from manipulation that involved placing €12.9 billion worth of sell orders in 200 different government bonds within 18 seconds and later repurchasing them'.[5]

Putniņš points out that there is no generally accepted definition of market manipulation. Despite prohibiting it by means of a number of provisions, the 1934 Securities Exchange Act does not attempt to precisely define manipulation.[6] Article 12 of the 2014 EU market abuse regulation clearly describes the various actions that constitute market manipulation, but abstains to define it generically.

The criminalisation of this type of fraudulent activity has been generally traced back to the UK. Indeed, in the case *The King v De Berenger and others*, the King's Bench confirmed on 20 August 1814 Lord Ellenborough's decision that to conspire to increment by false rumours the price of public government funds was an indictable offence.[7]

On 21 July 1814, Charles Random De Berenger, Sir Thomas Cochrane, otherwise called Lord Cochrane, and others were convicted upon an indictment of conspiracy. The defendants had conspired together by spreading false rumours in different places that Napoleon had been defeated in order to cause the rise of public funds, to the detriment of all those who might had purchased the securities on that particular day.[8] The culprits were sentenced to various fines and to be 'set in and upon the pillory opposite to the Royal Exchange in the City of London for one hour and then committed to the custody of the Marshal of Marshalsea and be imprisoned until the fines be paid'.[9]

Fraudulent stock market manipulation was later criminalised by other legislations, such as Germany and under the general repression of frauds in France. But it is only when globalisation facilitated and generalised the phenomenon of securities manipulation across borders that collective rule making became imperative to effectively counteract this phenomenon, including the introduction of criminal norms to protect the vital economic interests depending on the integrity of financial markets.

Manipulation of stock markets or of market prices were already criminalised in Germany at the end of the nineteenth century in paragraph 88 (old version) of the Stock Market Act (BörsG). These provisions were seldom applied, however. It was only 'the sustained impulse of European Law and the introduction of comprehensive market supervision made criminal law enforcement officials fully conscious of the availability and significance of such European norms regulating a fair price formation and transparency'.[10] Paragraph 88 (old version) of the Stock Market

[5] Putniņš, 'Market Manipulation: A Survey' (n 3) 3.

[6] ibid, 957.

[7] See H Cecil, *A Matter Of Speculation: The Case of Lord Cochrane* (London, Hutchinson Co, 1965; reprint by Gaunt, Inc, 1996) esp 97–156.

[8] WB Gurney, *The Trial Of Charles Random De Berenger, Lord Cochrane And Others* (London, J Butterworth and Son, and Gale, Curtis and Fenner, 1814) 588.

[9] ibid, 600.

[10] C Schröder, *Handbuch Kapitalmarktstrafrecht*, 3rd edn (Cologne, Carl Heyman'sVerlag, 2015) 125.

Act (BörsG) was ultimately abrogated and the rules prohibiting market manipulation were transferred to Section 20(a) of the Securities Exchange Act, and most recently, to Section 119 of the reformed Securities Exchange Act.

In France, the crime of market manipulation was introduced in the French Criminal Code in 1926, repealed in 1986, and reintroduced after the stock market crash of 1987 into the Monetary and Financial Code. After successive reforms, this low-ranking criminal offence regained importance after the successive European Market Abuse Directives of 2003, 2014 and the European Market Abuse Regulation.

It is important to focus on the role of the US statutory and judicial response to market manipulation, given its momentous role in the internationalisation process.

II. Market Manipulation in the United States

In the US, manipulations are not only punished by the Securities Exchange Act as a form of securities fraud, but also criminalised by other laws. The Commodities Exchange Act punishes manipulations and the Energy Policy Act of 2005, amending the Federal Power Act and the Natural Gas Act, grants authority and directs the Federal Energy Regulatory Commission (FERC) to promulgate rules prohibiting manipulation in the electricity and natural gas markets.[11] Another area where manipulation is outlawed is in the field of benchmarks, that is, standards or points of reference to compare and evaluate, including interbank lending rates and currencies.[12]

The Securities Exchange Commission (SEC) Rule 10b-5 addresses market manipulation, while Section 9 of the Securities Exchange Act addresses manipulation of securities prices. Because Section 9 requires a mens rea that is very difficult to prove (specific intent of inducing the purchase or sale of a security by others or creating a false or misleading appearance of market activity), prosecutors prefer to initiate manipulation proceedings under Rule 10b-5.[13] Technical progress and internationalisation of securities markets have favoured the development of new schemes of market manipulation, such as new forms of trade execution and market platforms and derivatives that exclude from legal prohibition new forms of market manipulation.

It is necessary to distinguish between legitimate open market manipulations, which are not illegal, from illegal transactions. With modern expansion of the

[11] MK Multer, 'Open-Market Manipulation under SEC Rule 10b-5 and its Analogues: Inappropriate Distinctions, Judicial Disagreement and Case Study: Ferc's Anti-Manipulation Rule' (2011) 39(2) *Securities Regulation Law Journal* 97, 100.

[12] See section V.B, 'Benchmark Manipulation'.

[13] Multer, 'Open-Market Manipulation' (n 11) 106.

types and availability of derivatives, it is possible to carry out legally successful and lucrative manipulations. Courts in general have expressed reticence to impose liability for acts that are not inherently illegal.[14]

Illegal manipulations are expressly prohibited under Section 9(a)(1) of the Securities Exchange Act; these prohibitions include wash sales, matched orders, and fictitious trading carried out with the purpose of inducing the purchase or sale of such security by others or the purpose of creating a false or misleading appearance of market activity.

The Securities Exchange Act of 1934 addresses primordially the issue of speculation in the securities market.[15] Speculation is regulated but not prohibited. Section 10(b) makes unlawful, among other behaviours, the use or employment, in connection with the purchase or sale of any security registered on a national securities exchange or any security not so registered, or any securities-based swap agreement, any *manipulative* or deceptive device or contrivance in contravention of such rules and regulations as the Commission may prescribe as necessary or appropriate in the public interest or for the protection of investors. Accordingly, the SEC promulgated Rule 10b-5, entitled 'Employment of *Manipulative* and Deceptive Devices'. However, the text of the rule does not contain the words 'manipulative' or 'manipulate'. The rule essentially prohibits a series of behaviours operating as a 'fraud'. In *Ernst & Ernst v Hochfelder*, the Supreme Court decided that 'manipulation' is a term of art when used in connection with securities markets, connoting 'intentional or willful conduct designed to deceive or defraud investors by controlling or artificially affecting the price of securities'.[16] The significance of this case is to exclude negligent behaviours from the prohibition. Again, in *Santa Fe v Green*, the Supreme Court connected the notion of 'manipulation' to deceptive practices such as wash sales, matched orders or rigged prices intended to mislead investors.[17] Federal courts reinforced the idea that market manipulation under Rule 10b-5 requires some inherently deceptive conduct.[18]

Fernando Londoño Martínez systemises the differences between the Anglo-Saxon and the continental European approaches to illegal stock market manipulations.[19] Countries belonging to the common law system specially concentrate on: (i) the description of both the phenomenon of market manipulation and of the legal system in which it inserts itself; (ii) the description of the manifold casuistry that may be included under the respective title; and (iii) the identification of the consequences that such insertion would imply for the regulated context.

[14] ibid.
[15] HR Rep No 73-1383, 2d Sess.
[16] See *Ernst & Ernst v Hochfelder*, 425 US 185m 199, 96 S Ct 1375 (1976).
[17] *Santa Fe Industries, Inc v Green*, 430 US 462, 476, 97 S Ct 1292, 1302 (1997).
[18] Multer, 'Open-Market Manipulation' (n 11) 108.
[19] F Londoño Martínez, 'Ilícito de Manipulación Bursátil: Fenómeno y lesividad. Aspectos de Política Sancionatoria' (2013) 8 *Politica Criminal*, available at http://ssrn.com/abstract=2531802, 66.

On the other hand, the countries belonging to the European Continental tradition[20] would devote much time to: (i) conceptualise the values and interests protected ('*Rechtsgut*', '*bien juridico*')[21] by the rules that prohibit market manipulations; and (ii) the explanation and critical interpretation, as well as the systematisation of the concepts used by the legislator to define the texts where this matter is legislated, leaving little room to discuss the consequences.[22] The first approach thrusts us into the unpredictable world of the 'special', while the second keeps us at the abstract level of the 'general'.[23]

Both systems share at least certain common features such as the flexibility and openness of the formulas used to define this type of manipulative behaviour. These formulas refer either to the aptness of the behaviour to alter market prices, and to drive them to an artificial or abnormal level (result-oriented approach), or to the use of certain deceptive means related to the notion of fraud (instrumental approach).

Drawing from a comparative analysis of a number of laws (European Market Abuse Directive, Italian, British, German, US and Chilean capital market legislations), Londoño establishes a typology of market manipulations. He distinguishes trade-based manipulations, from information-based and action-based manipulations. Trade-based manipulations are carried out through either real or sham negotiations, intervening directly in the market dynamics of supply and demand. Information-based manipulations are executed by diffusing false information operating indirectly on supply and demand, and action-based manipulations are performed through deceitful behaviour taking place outside of the market context, such as closing the establishments of a company listed in the market, to re-open it shortly after. The elimination of manipulative activities affecting the US' securities markets was one of the most important goals sought to be attained with the 1934 Securities and Exchange Act (SEA).[24]

The specific provisions regulating this matter are Section 9(a), 15 USC Section 78i(a) (proscribing manipulation of securities prices); Section 10(b), 15 USC Section 78j(b) (proscribing manipulative deceptive practices and devices); Section 14(c), 15 USC Section 78n(e), (proscribing manipulative acts or practices

[20] The expression 'civil law' is used to demarcate those systems of law derived from Roman law, including private and public law, and that are mainly located in Western Europe and Latin America, but can be also found in numerous other parts of the world. Among other sources, see HJ Berman and WR Greiner, *The Nature And Functions of Law* (New York, Foundation Press, 1980) 571–72.

[21] German criminal law considers the theory of *Rechtsgut* as the basic tenet of criminal law. '*Rechtsgut*' can be defined as the vital interests and values of the individual and society that are protected by criminal law. According to Jescheck and Weigend, the 'Rechstgut' is the basis for both the structuring and the interpretation of criminal law, it gives sense and purpose to the content of its provisions and plays an essential role in its systematisation. See H-H Jescheck and T Weigend, *Lehrbuch des Strafrechts: Allgemeiner Teil* (Berlin, Dunker & Humblot, 1996) 238–46, 257.

[22] Londoño Martínez, 'Ilícito de Manipulación Bursátil' (n 19) 66.

[23] ibid, 67.

[24] LD Lowenfels and AR Bromberg, 'Securities Market Manipulation: an Examination and Analysis of Dominating and Control, Frontrunning and Parking' (1991) 55 *Albany Law Review* 293, 294.

with respect to proxies); and Section 15(c)(l), 15 USC Section 780o(c)(l) (proscribing manipulative acts or practices with respect of registration of broker-dealers). The 1933 Securities Act contains 15 USC Section 77q(a)-(b), proscribing fraudulent or deceptive interstate transactions in securities.

III. Traditional Forms of Market Manipulation

In May 2000, IOSCO published a Report on *Investigating and Prosecuting Market Manipulation*,[25] claiming that market manipulation harms the integrity of securities and derivative markets by distorting prices and undermining public confidence in securities and derivatives. Twelve years later, IOSCO published an *Addendum to IOSCO Report on Investigating and Prosecuting Market Manipulation*. The IOSCO Report describes the following examples of methods of manipulation:

(1) Painting the tape: 'engaging in a series of transactions that are publicly displayed to give the impression of activity or price movement in a security' (IOSCO Report 5). It is also called 'window dressing', meaning 'ramping' by institutional investors to allow valuation at desired prices.[26]
(2) Wash sales: 'improper transactions in which there is no genuine change in the actual ownership of the security or derivative contract' (IOSCO Report 5). These manipulations often use 'painting the tape.' They aim at creating a misleading appearance of active trading in the security.[27]
(3) Improper matched orders: 'transactions where both buy and sell orders are entered at the same time, with the same price and quantity by different but colluding parties' (IOSCO Report 5). These manipulations often use 'painting the tape:' A matched order involves associated parties entering an order for the purchase/sale of shares with the knowledge that other associates will enter similar or corresponding orders.[28]
(4) Advancing the bid: 'increasing the bid for a security or derivative to increase its price' (IOSCO Report 5).
(5) Pumping and dumping: 'this form of manipulations involves the manipulator using devices to drive up the stock that he or she owns, then "dumping or selling the shares at an artificially high price' (IOSCO Report 6). It may attain the forms of 'hype and dump' or 'slur and dump', which respectively mean 'talking up the price of stock using false or exaggerated reports, rumors, broker

[25] *Investigating and Prosecuting Market Manipulation*, Report of the Technical Committee of IOSCO, May 2000, available at www.iosco.org/library/pubdocs/pdf/IOSCOPD103.pdf.

[26] V Goldwasser, 'Stock Market Manipulation and Short Selling' (Centre for Corporate Law and Securities Regulation and CCH Australia Limited, 1999) 162, defines 'ramping' or 'marking the close' as the term applied to transactions resulting in a quick movement in the share price just before the close of the trading.

[27] ibid, 161.

[28] ibid.

recommendations, etc' to raise the price of stocks and subsequently dump them; or talking down the price of stocks to buy them after at lower prices.[29]

(6) Marking the close: 'consists in buying or selling securities or derivative contracts at the close of the market in an effort to alter the closing price of the security contract' (IOSCO Report 6). This form of manipulation is also called "ramping up the close." A quick movement just before the end of trading aims at misleading the market giving the impression of high demand for the stock while dropping the bid or selling them the following morning.'[30]

(7) 'Cornering': securing such control of the bid or demand side of both the derivative and underlying asset that leads to a dominant position in order to manipulate the price of the derivative and/or the asset. In the 'corner' the manipulator acquires all the supplies of a commodity to reach a dominant position allowing dictating prices for future purchasers.[31]

In the 'squeeze' the manipulator acquires a substantial portion of the available supplies of a particular commodity, but not all, enabling the manipulator to squeeze the prices higher.[32] The manipulator generally 'takes advantage of a shortage in an asset by controlling the demand-side and exploiting market congestion during such shortages in such a way as to create artificial prices'(IOSCO Report 6). A 'short squeeze' involves 'purchasing significant amount of stock, that is "cornering" the market, in order to force short sellers to purchase shares to cover their short positions at successively higher prices, thereby increasing the price'.[33]

Markham mentions 'cross trades' in which the floor brokers become buyers with respect to selling orders of customers and vice versa. They appear as a double order and sale between two brokers, that is, a strictly fictitious trade.[34]

In sum, Tom CW Lin, in his article on new market manipulation, examined in section IV of this chapter, enumerates as traditional forms of market manipulation, a number of transactions described above by the IOSCO report, such as cornering and squeezing; front running, in which brokers execute on their own account after receiving – but before processing – large purchase or sell orders from their clients; wash trading; and pumping-and-dumping. Although benchmark manipulation is especially relevant today, Lin questionably includes it among the traditional forms as a manipulation of standards or metrics to 'distort affiliated financial instruments or products in their favor to the detriment of honest participants in the marketplace'.[35]

[29] ibid, 162.

[30] ibid.

[31] JW Markham, *Law Enforcement And The History Of Financial Market Manipulation* (Armonk, NY, ME Sharpe, Inc, 2014) 3.

[32] ibid.

[33] Goldwasser, 'Stock Market Manipulation and Short Selling' (n 26) 162.

[34] Markham, *Law Enforcement* (n 31) 89.

[35] TCW Lin, 'The New Market Manipulation' (2017) 66 *Emory Law Journal* 1263, 1281–86.

IV. New Forms

The transformation of securities markets in recent years – multiplication of markets, multiplicity of venues, direct access trading and high-frequency trading – has made market manipulation far more elusive to regulators.[36]

Tom CW Lin describes new forms of market manipulation, 'in which millions of dollars can vanish in seconds, rogue actors can halt the trading of billion-dollar companies, and trillion-dollars financial markets can be distorted with a simple click or few lines of code'.[37] He exemplifies with the Flash Crash of 2010 and with the publication of Michael Lewis's book *Flash Boys*.

During the trading session of 6 May 2010, the US stock market experienced 30 minutes of extreme decline and volatility in which approximately $1 trillion disappeared before the market rebounded and most of the losses were recovered. Nearly five years after the crash, Navinder Singh Sarao was arrested for market manipulation that contributed to the crash.[38] In November of 2016 he pleaded guilty to one count of wire fraud and one count of 'spoofing'. The proceedings against him started in 2015, when the Department of Justice and the Commodity Futures Trading Commission revealed that Navinder Singh Sarao had flooded the Chicago Mercantile Exchange with an enormous amount of sell orders for E-mini S&P 500 stocks.[39] Through 'spoofing', he submitted the sell orders and then entered orders to buy the same contracts at artificially depressed prices.[40] The other event that brought the new forms of market manipulation to the forefront is Michael Lewis's *Flash Boys*, a story about high-frequency trading on Wall Street.

Lin uses the Flash Crash and *Flash Boys* as 'flashpoints in recent history about a larger sea change occurring in financial markets'.[41] He explains how the rise of artificial intelligence, automation and other technological advances have led to the fact that autonomous high-speed machines running on algorithmic programs have transformed the nature of the financial industry. Most notably, he mentions how recently, start-up companies exclusively use algorithmic programs to manage the assets of investors, completely abandoning the traditional model of financial advisors.[42]

The author underscores both the virtues and vices of the heavy reliance on technology in the new financial reality. On the bright side it has accelerated execution speed, decreased transactional costs, increased liquidity and diminished price spreads, facilitating the expansion of capital markets and lowering the cost

[36] J Austin, 'Protecting Market Integrity in an Era of Fragmentation and Cross-Border Trading' (2014) 46:1 *Ottawa Law Review* 25, 27–29.

[37] Lin, 'The New Market Manipulation' (n 35) 1253.

[38] ibid, 1262.

[39] KN Johnson, 'Regulating Innovation: High Frequency Trading in Dark Pools' (2017) 42:4 *The Journal of Corporation Law* 833, 836.

[40] ibid.

[41] Lin, 'The New Market Manipulation' (n 35) 1270.

[42] ibid, 1272.

of capital for businesses.[43] On the negative side, Lin cites the risks connected to speed, connectivity and complexity, including increasing the likelihood of malicious acts.[44] Example of the new forms of malfeasance and manipulation are the rogue trader Jerome Kerviel who in 2008, while exceeding his powers, brought about the devastating loss of $7.2 billion to Societé Génerale, one of the most prominent of European banks. Also, in 2011 Kweku Adoboli caused the Swiss investment bank UBS a loss of $2 billion through unauthorised trades.[45]

In addition to the traditional forms of manipulation, Li mentions those using the new financial technology to carry out both old and new financial schemes, which he denominates 'cybernetic market manipulation'.[46] He lists as its more common methods: pinging and spoofing, electronic front running and mass misinformation.

With 'pinging', a profuse amount of small orders are offered and withdrawn by computerised platforms[47] in fractions of a second to provoke good-faith investors to reveal their price and volume preferences so that the pinging party may take advantage in future operations.

'Spoofing' is a form of high-speed trading in which the operator 'engages in a series of orders to give the impression of activity or price movement in a security but the orders are withdrawn before they are executed'.[48] With spoofing the orders placed in computerised platforms are meant not to be executed but to manipulate good-faith market participants in the marketplace. Both pinging and spoofing are made possible by 'high speed supercomputers running on smart algorithms' capable of a rapid submission and cancellation of voluminous orders.[49]

'Layering' occurs in high frequency trading when 'as the price of a security moves up a trader takes out the posted asking prices for the security furthering inflating the price'.[50]

Electronic front running allows brokers using high-tech computers to catch sight of order flows in one venue 'to jump ahead of those flows to their advantage at another trading venue'.[51]

Mass misinformation is another form of cybernetic market manipulation in which false information aimed at deceiving investors can distort the market in unprecedented speed and volume.[52]

[43] ibid, 1273.
[44] ibid.
[45] ibid, 1274.
[46] ibid, 1288.
[47] A computer platform is a system that consists of a hardware device and an operating system that an application, program or process runs upon. So, in order to have a functional device, it needs hardware and an operating system together to make a usable computer platform for a program to run on.
[48] Austin, 'Protecting Market Integrity' (n 36) 25, 39.
[49] Lin, 'The New Market Manipulation' (n 35) 1289.
[50] Austin, 'Protecting Market Integrity' (n 36) 25, 39.
[51] Lin, 'The New Market Manipulation' (n 35) 1290.
[52] ibid, 1292.

As Kristin N Johnson points out, new technological advances in financial markets, algorithmic and high-frequency trading have been followed by 'a number of important shifts in financial markets intermediation'.[53]

Conventional trading has been increasingly displaced by alternative trading systems, which include a small group of platforms known as 'dark pools' that allow a large number of securities to be traded without disclosure of the trading counterparties or of the identity of the intermediaries, a disclosure that is normally required by national regulations of exchanges.

'Dark pools' are anonymous trading platforms, related to high-frequency trading. Orders are not visible to the public but only revealed to other dark pool participants.[54] The use of these alternative trading systems has grown exponentially, 'eclipsing conventional trading venues' market share, and redefining the balance of power in the financial market ecosystem'.[55]

Diego Leis points out that high-speed trading 'offers new possibilities for manipulating the market either through new techniques or by applying existing strategies in a more sophisticated, undetectable way'.[56]

V. Benchmark Manipulation

A. Significance: LIBOR and its Replacement

A benchmark is a standard against which the performance of a security, mutual fund or investment manager can be measured.[57] An example of benchmark manipulation was the LIBOR (London interbank offered rate) 2012 manipulation scandal. The LIBOR served to decide the value of the interest rates in other transactions that amounted to trillions of dollars, as well as to gauge the degree of confidence banks have in each other's financial systems. LIBOR and EURIBOR (Euro Interbank Offered Rate) are benchmark reference rates that indicate the interest rate that banks charge when lending to each other. They are fundamental to the operation of both UK and international financial markets, including markets in interest rate derivatives contracts.

The BBC[58] explains how a group of leading banks submit interest rates every day for which they are willing to lend to other banks. The LIBOR is calculated by an average of the submissions for three months. It was alleged that traders at Barclays

[53] Johnson, 'Regulating Innovation' (n 39) 833.

[54] Markham, *Law Enforcement* (n 31) 323.

[55] Johnson, 'Regulating Innovation' (n 39) 833.

[56] D Leis, 'High Frequency Trading: Market Manipulation and Systemic Risk from an EU Perspective' (29 February 2012) available at htpps://ssrn.com/abstract=2108344, 79.

[57] www.investopedia.comm/terms/b/benchmark.

[58] *BBC News*, 'Libor: What is it and why does it matter' (3 August 2015) available at www.bbc.com/news/business-19199683.

Bank, JP Morgan, Swiss bank UBS, Royal Bank of Canada and Deutsche Bank had submitted false figures.[59] The banks were heavily fined and in August 2015 former city trader Tom Hayes was convicted of conspiracy to defraud through manipulating LIBOR. His 14-year prison sentence was reduced to 11 years.[60] As a result of the scandal, LIBOR was revised, and its oversight passed from the British Bankers Association to the Intercontinental Exchange (ICE).[61]

LIBOR is derived from a daily survey of large banks that estimate the cost of borrowing from one another on an unsecured basis. Because this type of borrowing has become rare the estimate 'was becoming more of a theoretical exercise'.[62] Moreover, LIBOR rates were potentially susceptible to manipulation because they were based on 'expert judgment' rather than on actual transactions.

LIBOR will be last published in 2021, and the United States Federal Reserve Bank's Alternate Reference Rates Committees (ARRC) has named SOFR (the Secured Overnight Financial Rate) as its successor. SOFR is based on the Treasury repurchase market (repo), that is, treasuries loaned or borrowed overnight. SOFR uses data from overnight Treasury repurchase activity to calculate a rate. This index has been published since the beginning of April 2018, while at first the New York Federal Reserve Bank admitted to having included some incorrect trades in the reference rate over its first two weeks. However, the comparative data for LIBOR and SOFR during four months was encouraging.[63] Fannie Mae issued $6 billion in securities tied to SOFR in July of 2018 and Barclays became the first bank to issue commercial paper tied to the rate in August of the same year. The SOFR language will come in new contract documents, and there are amendments to existing loan facilities on a case-by-case basis. This language could include references to SOFR or not, but it is likely to include the potential for a 'spread adjustment' to account for the daily basis point difference between LIBOR and SOFR as banks do not want to make less money on loans just because a new index came about that happens to be lower than LIBOR. In addition, the contracts will likely include 'triggers' – specific events that will cause a replacement reference rate (read: SOFR) to be imposed. Swap and cap markets for SOFR-based derivatives are coming along shortly as well so borrowers can hedge their floating rate exposure just like they do today with LIBOR. The over-the-counter (OTC) derivatives market has evolved from varying floating rate indices over time, and the SOFR conversion will be no different. But so far, despite fits and starts, the fear of the unknown, and less than two quarters of market activity, the LIBOR to SOFR change would seem to be for the better. Informed advisory services and sound legal advice are warranted during these periods of change, to be sure.

[59] ibid.

[60] ibid.

[61] According to Investopedia. the ICE has been at the forefront of the commodities exchange market since its foundation in May 2000 in Atlanta, Georgia, to facilitate the electronic exchange of energy commodities, including commodities derivatives and futures.

[62] B Klein, 'Goodbye LIBOR, Hello SOFR', post in *Forbes New York Business Council Post* (19 April 2018).

[63] 'LIBOR replaced by SOFR – So far. So good?' *Derivative Logic Advisors* (23 August 2018).

The manipulation of currencies, on its side, can be exemplified by the Forex scandal, involving banks that colluded to manipulate exchange rates. Certain currency dealers had been front-running client orders and rigging the foreign exchange benchmark WM/Reuters rates by colluding with counterparts and pushing through trades during the 60-second window when the benchmark rates are set.

Andrew Verstein points out that markets today focus on benchmarks of prices that summarise market prices and since benchmarks are derived from a small slice of the markets, they are easier to manipulate than the underlying market prices.[64]

Further, Verstein argues, 'manipulation scholarship and law both reflect an outdated view of markets'.[65] Today, benchmark manipulation has increasingly become the only viable form of market manipulation. Trade-based manipulation is self-deterring given the daunting economic challenges of manipulative trading. For example, tampering with the benchmark price of oil is equivalent to moving the whole worldwide supply of oil.[66] Manipulative trading in large markets is extremely costly and risky. To affect the market price of certain assets would require an outlay of billions of dollars, to cover transaction, transportation, storage and insurance costs, and still the results may be uncertain.[67]

In contrast with the monumental costs and difficulties of moving the real price of the asset, tampering with the benchmark is 'far easier and can have an equivalent impact to actually moving the real price of the asset'.[68]

B. EU Benchmarks Regulation

At the regional level, the internationalisation of benchmarks regulation culminates with Regulation (EU) 2016/1011 of the European Parliament and of the Council on indices used as benchmarks in financial instruments and financial contracts or to measure the performance on investment funds and amending Directives 2008/48/EC and 2014/17/EU and Regulation (EU) No 596/2014. This Regulation entered into force on 30 June 2016, while most of its provisions came into effect on 1 January 2018. The text includes transitional arrangements for existing EU and third-country benchmark administrators allowing these administrators to apply for authorisation any time before 1 January 2020. On 26 February 2019, the European Council and the Parliament amended the European Benchmark Regulation to extend the transitional provisions for critical[69] and third-country

[64] A Verstein, 'Benchmark Manipulation' (2015) 56 *Boston College Law Review* 215.
[65] ibid, 217.
[66] ibid.
[67] ibid, 221, 222 and 223.
[68] ibid, 225.
[69] As explained below, critical benchmarks are those where the value of contracts underlying the benchmark are at least €500 billion, or when a benchmark has been recognised as critical by a Member State (Art 20).

benchmarks[70] for a further two years to comply and undertake the requirements in the Regulation.

The Regulation introduces a common framework and consistent approach to preserve the accuracy and integrity of indices used as benchmarks across the EU to avoid serious cases of manipulation such as LIBOR and EURIBOR. Such failures 'can undermine market confidence, cause losses to consumers and investors, and distort the real economy'.[71]

Article 3 defines an index as a figure that is publicly available and is regularly determined entirely or partially, either by the application of a formula or by any other method of calculation or by an assessment on the basis of the value of one or more underlying assets or prices, including estimated prices, actual or estimated interest rates, quotes and committed quotes, or other values or surveys.

An index becomes a benchmark when it is used to determine the amount payable under a financial instrument or a financial contract or the value of a financial instrument or when it is used to measure the performance of an investment fund with the purpose of tracking the return of such index or of defining the asset allocation of a portfolio or of calculating the performance fees (Article 3(3)).

The Regulation contains six types of benchmarks: (1) 'critical benchmarks', which are used directly or indirectly among a combination of benchmarks as a reference for financial instruments or financial contracts or for measuring the performance of investment funds having a total average value of at least €500 billion, on the basis of all the range of maturities or tenors of the benchmark where applicable or when the benchmark is based on submissions by contributors the majority of which are located in one Member State and is recognised as being critical in that Member State through an elaborate procedure that includes the intervention of the European Securities Market Authority (ESMA) (Article 20); (2) 'significant benchmarks', where the benchmark is used directly or indirectly within a combination of benchmarks as a reference for financial instruments or financial contracts or for measuring the performance of investment funds having a total average value of at least €50 billion, on the basis of all the range of maturities or tenors of the benchmark where applicable over the period of six months or where there are no or very few market-led substitutes and where there would be an impact on financial stability if the benchmark ceased to be produced (Article 24(1)(a) and (b)); (3) 'Non-significant benchmarks', which do not fulfil the conditions laid down for critical benchmarks or for significant benchmarks (Article 3(1)(27)); (4) 'commodity benchmarks', where the underlying assets are commodities as defined

[70] As explained below, benchmarks produced by third-country administrators can be added to the ESMA list of benchmarks either where an equivalence decision has been adopted by the European Commission (Art 30), or when such administrators have been recognised by a Member State (Art 32), or when an administrator or any supervised entity located in the Union complying with the requirements set in Arts 33 and 34 apply to the competent authority to endorse a benchmark or a family of benchmarks provided in a third country for their use in the Union if the list of conditions set in Art 33 are met.

[71] Recital (1).

by Article 3(1)(23), that is, within the meaning of Article 2(1) of Commission Regulation (EC) No 1287/2006, 'any goods of a fungible nature that are capable of being delivered, including metals and their ores and alloys, agricultural products, and energy such as electricity'; (5) 'regulated data benchmarks', determined by the application of a formula from input data[72] provided entirely and directly from a series of regulated venues or from net asset values of investment funds (Article 3 1[14]); (6) 'interest rate benchmarks', determined on the basis of the rate at which banks may lend to, or borrow from, other banks, or agents other than banks, in the money market (Article 3 1[22]).

Article 34(1) of Chapter 1, Title VI provides that every natural or legal person located in the Union that intends to act as an administrator shall apply to the competent authority designated under Article 40[73] of the Member State in which that person is located in order to receive:

(a) authorisation if it provides or intends to provide indices which are used or intended to be used as benchmarks within the meaning of the Regulation.
(b) registration if it is a supervised entity, other than an administrator who provides or intents to provide indices which are used or intended to be used as benchmarks within the meaning of the Regulation, on condition that the provision of a benchmark is not prevented by the sectoral discipline applying to the supervised entity and that none of the indices provided would qualify as a critical benchmark
(c) registration if it provides or intends to provide only indices which would qualify as non-significant benchmarks.

The 2016 EU Regulation thoroughly covers every aspect of the creation, administration and use of benchmarks by its Member Countries.

Article 14(1) imposes on administrators the duty to establish adequate systems and effective controls to ensure the integrity of input data[74] in order to be able to identify and report to the competent authority any conduct that may involve manipulation or attempted manipulation of a benchmark under the EU Market Abuse Regulation (MAR). Furthermore, Article 14(2) mandates administrators to monitor input data and contributors[75] in order to be able to notify the competent authority and provide all relevant information where administrators suspect that, in relation to a benchmark, any conduct has taken place that may involve manipulation or attempted manipulation of a benchmark under MAR, including collusion to do so; and Article 14(3) also imposes on administrators the duty to

[72] 'Input data' means the data in respect of the value of one or more underlying assets, or prices, including estimated prices, quotes, committed quotes or other values, used by an administrator to determine a benchmark (Art 3(1)(14)).

[73] Art 40 imposes on each Member State the duty to designate a competent authority responsible to carry out the duties under the Regulation and to inform the Commission and the ESMA thereof.

[74] See n 72.

[75] 'Contributor' means a natural or legal person contributing input data (Art 3(1)(9)).

have procedures in place for their managers, employees and other natural persons whose services are placed at their disposal or under their control to report internally any infringement of the Regulation.

Among the powers of competent authorities, Article 41 enumerates a series of supervisory and investigatory powers, such as access to documents; demands of information; request information, in relation to commodity benchmarks, from contributors on related spot markets[76] according, where applicable, to standardised formats and reports on transactions and direct access to traders' systems; enter premises; require recordings of telephone conversations and electronic communications; and on-site inspections. In addition, competent authorities are empowered to request to freeze assets, request the temporary cessation and impose temporary prohibitions of certain activities; and publicity measures related to ensure that the public is correctly informed about the vicissitudes of a benchmark.

Besides all the investigatory and supervisory powers developed in detail by Article 41 and the right of Member States to provide for criminal sanctions, Article 42(1) imposes on Member States, in conformity with national law, the duty to provide for competent authorities to have the power to impose appropriate administrative sanctions and other administrative measures for infringements to a series of provisions of the Regulation enumerated by article numbers in Article 42(1)(a) and for failure to cooperate or comply in an investigation or with an inspection or request covered by Article 41. These administrative sanctions and other administrative measures must be effective, proportionate and dissuasive (Article 42(1)(b)).

Article 42(2) establishes the duty of Member States, in conformity with their national laws, to confer with competent authorities in case of the above-mentioned infringements, the power to impose at least the following administrative sanctions and other administrative measures:

(a) to order to cease and to desist from repeating the infringing behaviour;
(b) to order to disgorge the profits gained or losses avoided through the infringement;
(c) to issue a public warning indicating the administrator or entity responsible for the infringement, as well as the nature of such infringement;
(d) withdrawal or suspension of the administrator or of his registration;
(e) temporary ban prohibiting any natural person, who is held responsible for such infringement, from exercising management functions in administrators or supervised contributors;
(f) the imposition of maximum administrative pecuniary sanctions of at least three times the amount of the profits gained or losses avoided because of the infringement where those can be determined;

[76] Spot markets differ from futures markets in that delivery takes place immediately. For example, if one wishes to purchase Company XYZ shares and own them immediately, one would go to the cash market on which the shares are traded (the New York Stock Exchange, for example). If one wanted to buy gold on the spot market, one could go to a coin dealer and exchange cash for gold (https//investinganswers.com, dictionary, spot markets).

(g) in respect of natural persons, to impose a maximum administrative pecuniary sanctions of at least –
   (i) €500,000 for infringement of a number of provisions identified by the number of articles where they are contained in the Regulation, or in the Member States where the currency is not the euro, the corresponding value in the national currency on 30 June 2016, or
   (ii) to impose €100,000 for infringements of Article 11(1)(d)[77] or Article 11(4)[78] or in the Member States whose official currency is not the Euro, is the corresponding value in their currency on 30 June 2016;

(h) in respect of legal persons, to impose a maximum administrative pecuniary sanctions of at least –
   (i) €1,000,000 for infringement of a number of provisions identified by the number of articles where they are contained in the Regulation, or in the Member States where the currency is not the euro, the corresponding value in the national currency on 30 June 2016 or 10 per cent of its annual turnover according to the available accounts approved by the management body, whichever is higher, or
   (ii) to impose €250,000 for infringements of Article 11(1)(d)[79] or Article 11(4)[80] requirement of an input data governing the provision of a benchmark or in the Member States whose official currency is not the Euro, is the corresponding value in their currency on 30 June 2016 or 2 per cent of its annual turnover according to the available accounts approved by the management body, whichever is higher.

For the purposes of point (h)(i) and (ii) where the legal person is a parent undertaking or subsidiary of a parent undertaking which has to prepare consolidated financial accounts in accordance with Directive 2013/34/EU on the annual financial statements, consolidated financial statements and related reports of certain types of undertakings, the relevant total annual turnover shall be the total annual

[77] Omission of the administrators to obtain, where appropriate, the input data from a reliable and representative panel or sample of contributors so as to ensure that the resulting benchmark is reliable and representative of the market or economic reality that the benchmark is intended to measure, where the benchmark is based on input data from contributors.

[78] Omission of the administrators to either change the input data, the contributors or the methodology, in a reasonable time, in order to ensure that the input data does represent the market or economic reality or else cease to provide that benchmark, whenever the administrators consider that the input data does not represent the market or economic reality the benchmark is intended to measure.

[79] Omission of the administrators to obtain, where appropriate, the input data from a reliable and representative panel or sample of contributors so as to ensure that the resulting benchmark is reliable and representative of the market or economic reality that the benchmark is intended to measure, where the benchmark is based on input data from contributors.

[80] Omission of the administrators to either change the input data, the contributors or the methodology, in a reasonable time, in order to ensure that the input data does represent the market or economic reality or else cease to provide that benchmark, whenever the administrators consider that the input data does not represent the market or economic reality the benchmark is intended to measure.

turnover or the corresponding type of income in accordance with Council Directive 86/635/EEC on the annual consolidated accounts of banks and other financial institutions and Council Directive 01/674/EEC on the annual consolidated accounts of insurance undertakings, for insurance companies according to the last available consolidated accounts approved by the management body of the ultimate parent undertaking, or if the person is an association, 10 per cent of the aggregate turnovers of its members.

VI. Swiss Criminal Law: Internationalisation of the Market Price Manipulation Prohibition through the Diffusion of the American Model

The criminalisation of market manipulation in Switzerland closely followed the criminalisation of insider trading; originally called *Lex Americana* because of the pressure exercised by the US to obtain its enactment.[81] Indeed, Article 161 of the Swiss criminal code was followed on 3 March 1996 by Article 161*bis*, introducing a specific criminal provision for market manipulation, in force since 1 February 1997.

Wohlers points out that 'here is also central the effort of the Swiss legislator to ensure the relevant legal cooperation, especially in accordance with the United States'.[82]

The listlessness of the Swiss legislator was reflected in the restrictive way these provisions were enacted.[83] Both provisions were transferred on 1 May 2013 from the Criminal Code to the Stock Market Act (*Börsengesetz*). Thomas Jutzi notes that the enactment of this Act was expressly oriented towards international standards, especially with regard to US capital market law, not always voluntarily but under direct or indirect pressure of the US, following the prominent examples of the introduction of the insider trading prohibition and the market manipulation prohibitions.[84]

Responding to the demands of the G20 and of the Financial Stability Board,[85] both provisions became respectively Article 154 and Article 155 of the Financial Structuring Act 2016.

[81] See ch 4, section III, 'Switzerland', esp nn 50 to 56.

[82] W Wohlers, '§ 14 Finanz-und Kapitalmarktstrafrecht' in G Ackermann and G Heine (eds), *Wirtschaftsstrafrecht in der Schweiz* (Bern, Stämpfli, 2013) 363.

[83] M Pieth, *Wirtschaftsstrafrecht* (Basel, Helbing Lichtenhahn, 2016) 121.

[84] T Jutzi, *Unternehmenspublizität: Grundlinien Eine Rechtlichen Dogmatik zur Offenlegung von Unternehmensbezogenen Informationen* [*Enterprise Transparency and Disclosure: Outline of a Legal Dogmatic about Enterprise-Related Information*] (Bern, Stämpfli Verlag, 2017) 1047, 1048.

[85] International body composed of 68 member institutions, comprising ministries of finance, central banks, and supervisory and regulatory authorities from 25 jurisdictions as well as international organisations, standard-setting bodies, and six Regional Consultative Groups reaching out to 65 other jurisdictions around the world, that monitors and makes recommendations about the global financial system.

Article 155 of the Swiss Financial Market Infrastructure Act (FinfraG) contains two forms of commission of the crime of market price manipulation: diffusion of false or misleading information (Section 1a) and the double-sided purchase and sale of securities that are made directly or indirectly on account of the same person or persons connected with them for the same purpose (Section 1b).

Section 1a encompasses with the expressions 'false' and 'misleading' two different ways of inducing false representations, to considerably influencing the price of securities.[86] Moreover, 'false' addresses direct lies. To 'diffuse' presupposes the existence of a group of persons capable of influencing the play of supply and demand. In addition, diffusion may mean that the false or misleading information has attained the knowledge of powerful financiers.[87] As a result of this diffusion the securities at play appear overvalued or undervalued so that investors are led to buy or sell.

Section 1b deals with sham transactions in which the same person or a connected person stands at both sides of the transaction, as in the case of wash sales or of matched orders respectively. Deviating from European law and from the law of neighbouring countries, real transactions of manipulative nature, that is genuine transactions that simulate trading, continue to be interpreted as excluded from this provision.[88] Examples are 'front running'[89] and 'scalping'.[90]

Some of these genuine but manipulative courses of action were apprehended by traditional business-related criminal law definitions, such as fraud by deceit (*Betrug*) in cases of churning[91] or of price manipulation, or by the offence of deceitful management (*ungetreuen Geschäftsbesorgug*) in certain cases of front running.[92]

Some of these genuine but manipulative behaviours fall under the existing supervisory offences of Articles 142 and 143 of the Financial Market Infrastructure Act. According to Article 143, section 1, letter b of the Act, a person behaves inadmissibly when he or she 'carries out either transactions of acquisition or disposal

[86] Pieth, *Wirtschaftstrafrecht* (n 83) 125.

[87] ibid.

[88] ibid.

[89] Front running is a trading strategy when a broker enters into an equity trade with foreknowledge of a block transaction, which will influence the price of the equity, resulting in an economic gain for the broker. It also occurs when a broker buys shares for their account ahead of a firm's strong buy recommendation to clients. Front running is also known as tailgating (www.investopedia.com/terms/s/front-running).

[90] 'Scalping' is 'the activity of buying small quantities of shares, bonds, etc and then selling them quickly in order to make a small profit' (*Cambridge English Dictionary Online*). Scalping is geared toward attaining small profits on minor price changes. Traders who implement this strategy place anywhere from 10 to 200 trades in a single day with the belief that small moves in stock price are easier to catch than large ones; traders who implement this strategy are called scalpers. Many small profits can easily compound into large gains if a strict exit strategy is used to prevent large losses (www.investopedia.com/terms/s/scalping).

[91] 'Churning' is 'the illegal practice by stockbrokers of buying and selling a client's investments more often than necessary, in order to make more money in commissions' (*Cambridge English Dictionary Online*).

[92] Pieth, *Wirtschaftstrafrecht* (n 83) 126.

orders, which he or she knows or should have known give false or misleading signals regarding the supply, demand or price of securities admitted to trading on a trading venue in Switzerland'. The supervisory offences renounce to the elements related to the subjective side of the offence's definition, they are directed toward prevention, and are primarily aimed at opposing parties, such as banks, securities traders, insurers and investment funds and similar institutions. Article 143, section 2 of the Financial Market Infrastructure Act entrusts the Federal Council to issue provisions regarding admissible conduct, in particular in connection with: (a) securities transactions for price stabilisation purposes; and (b) buyback programmes for a company's own securities. These demands are enforced through the Stock Market Regulation (BEHV) and the Financial Market Infrastructure Regulation (FINMA). Mark Pieth considers these developments the opposite of speculation: time-limited price stabilisation during the initial placement of securities and under certain circumstances the repurchase of equity securities.[93]

While for the mens rea of the insider trading offence it is enough to act with *dolus eventualis*,[94] direct intent is required in the case of manipulation through the giving of false or misleading information. Next, it is necessary to have specific intent to considerably influence the price of stock and bonds admitted in a Swiss trading centre. Finally, the offence requires perpetrators to have an ulterior intent to pursue a pecuniary advantage for themselves or for others.

VII. European Regulation of the Market Manipulation Prohibition

According to Article 12 of the new EU Regulation on Market Abuse (No 596/2014) (MAR), market manipulation, forbidden by Article 15 in both its complete and attempted forms, comprises the following activities:

(a) Entering into a transaction, placing an order to trade or any other behaviour which:

(i) gives or is likely to give, false or misleading signals as to the supply of, demand for, or price of, a financial instrument, a related spot commodity contract,[95] or an auctioned product based on emission allowances;[96] or

[93] ibid.

[94] Perpetrators act with *dolus eventualis* when having represented themselves the result described in the definition of the offence as the possible consequence of their behaviour, they accept this possibility in case it would hypothetically happen. The attitude of the perpetrator is indifference regarding the occurrence of the prohibited result: The criminal result is ratified ex ante and the perpetrator does not believe in the possibility of avoiding the result.

[95] According to Investopedia, 'A spot commodity is a commodity up for immediate trade, as opposed to a commodity under contract for trade at a future date. A commodity is a necessary good, which is used in commerce that is interchangeable with other commodities of the same type. Spot commodities are traded on the spot market with an expectation of delivery at settlement. In contrast, commodities traded on the futures market have a delivery set at a future date.'

[96] The European Union Emission Trading Scheme trades primarily in EU allowances. Emissions trading is a market-based approach to control pollution. In an emission trading system the government sets

(ii) secures, or is likely to secure, the price of one or several financial instruments, a related spot commodity contract or an auctioned product based on emission allowances at an abnormal or artificial level.

None of these behaviours constitutes market manipulation when they have been carried out for legitimate reasons and conform to accepted market practices as described in detail in Article 13.

(b) Entering into a transaction, placing an order to trade, or any other activity or behaviour which affects or is likely to affect the price of one or several financial instruments, a related spot commodity contract or an auctioned product based on emission allowances, which employs a fictitious device or any other form of deception or contrivance.

(c) Disseminating information through the media, or by other means, which gives, or is likely to give, false or misleading signals as to the supply of, demand for, or price of, a financial instrument, a related spot commodity contract or an auctioned product based on emission allowances or secures or is likely to secure the price of the same at an abnormal or artificial level, including the dissemination of rumors, where the person who made the dissemination knew or ought to have known, that the information was false or misleading.

(d) Transmitting false or misleading information or providing false or misleading inputs in relation to a benchmark where the person who made the transmission or provided the input knew or ought to have known that it was false or misleading or any behaviour which manipulates the calculation of a benchmark.

In Article 12(2) the Regulation enumerates in a non-exhaustive way, a series of behaviours that it qualifies as market manipulation:

(a) the conduct of a person or persons acting in collaboration, to secure a dominant position over the supply of or demand for a financial instrument, a related spot

an overall limit on emissions and issue allowances or authorisations equal to each participant pollution baseline calculated on each participant's historical emissions in a way that to comply the pollution emitted should equal the pollution allowances. Participants that pollute less can sell their allowances to those who need to increase their pollution levels. To avoid the risk that polluters who receive their allowances for free may maintain their pollution levels to receive more allowances in the future, the allowances are auctioned. Commission Regulation EU No 1031/2010 governs the timing, administration and other aspects of auctioning of greenhouse gas emission allowances. Aside from the prohibition of insider trading in Arts 38 and 39 (see n 118 in ch 4), this Regulation prohibits market manipulation in Art 41. According to Art 37, market manipulation consists in bids or transactions or orders in the secondary markets, which give or are likely to give, false or misleading signals as to demand for or price of the auctioned products, or which secure, by a person, or persons acting in collaboration, an auction clearing price for the auctioned products at an abnormal or artificial level. Transactions or orders in the secondary markets are excluded from the aforementioned definition of market manipulation when the person who made the bid, or transactions or orders in the secondary markets, establishes that the reasons for so dealing are legitimate. Market manipulation can also consist in bids which employs fictitious devices or any other form of deception or contrivance, as well as dissemination of information through the media, including the internet, or by any other means, which gives, or is likely to give, false or misleading signals as to the auctioned products, including the dissemination of rumours as to the auctioned products and false or misleading news, where the person who made the dissemination knew, or ought to have known, that the information was false or misleading. With respect to journalists when they act in their professional capacity such dissemination of information is to be assessed, taking into account the rules governing their profession, unless these persons derive, directly or indirectly, an advantage or profits from the dissemination of the information in question.

commodity contract or an auctioned product based on emission allowances which has or is likely to have the effect of fixing directly or indirectly, purchase or sale prices or creates, or is likely to create, other unfair trading conditions;

(b) the buying or selling of financial instruments at the opening or closing of the market, which has or is likely to have the effect of misleading investors acting on the basis of the prices displayed, including the opening or the closing prices;

(c) the placing of orders to a trading venue, including any cancellation or modification thereof, by any available means of trading, including by electronic means, such as algorithms and high-frequency trading strategies, and has one of the effects referred to in paragraph (1)(a) or (b), by –

  (i) disrupting or delaying the functioning of the trading system of the trading venue or being likely to do so,

  (ii) making it more difficult for other persons to identify genuine orders on the trading system of the trading venue or being likely to do so, including entering orders which result in the overloading or destabilisation of the order book, or

  (iii) creating or being likely to create a false or misleading signal about the supply of, or the demand for, or price of, a financial instrument in particular by entering orders to initiate or exacerbate a trend;

(d) the taking advantage or occasional or regular access to the traditional or electronic media by voicing an opinion about a financial instrument, a related spot commodity contract or an auctioned product based on emission allowances (or indirectly about their issuer) while having previously taken positions on those financial instruments, contracts or products and profiting subsequently from the impact of the opinion voiced on the price of that instrument, related spot commodity contract or an auctioned product based on emission allowances, without having simultaneously disclosed that conflict of interest to the public in a proper and effective way;

(e) the buying or selling on the secondary market of emission allowances or related derivatives prior to the auction pursuant to Commission Regulation (EU) No 1031/2010 (of 12 November 2010 on the timing, administration and other aspects of auctioning of greenhouse emission allowances) with the effect of fixing the auction clearing price for the auctioned products at an abnormal or artificial level or misleading bidders bidding in the auction.

On the same day in which the European Parliament and the Council issued MAR repealing the 2003 Market Abuse Directive to complete, update, simplify, strengthen and make more uniform the Union's legal framework to protect market integrity, the same EU organs issued the Directive 2014/57/EU to reinforce such protection with criminal sanctions.

The new Directive for criminal sanctions against market abuse also followed the recommendations contained in the 2009 Report of the High-Level Group on Financial Supervision in the EU chaired by Jacques de Larosière leaning towards strong and deterrent sanction regimes against financial crimes.[97]

[97] Directive 2014/57/EU of the European Parliament and the Council of 16 April 2014 of criminal sanctions for Market Abuse, Recital (3).

This Directive was required to remedy the failure of some Member States to provide for criminal sanctions for some forms of serious breaches of national law, undermining the uniformity of conditions of operations in the internal market and predisposing persons to commit market abuses in those countries where criminal sanctions are absent. The new Directive requires minimum rules with regards to the definition of criminal offences committed by natural persons, liability of legal persons and the relevant sanctions.[98]

Regarding market manipulation, the 2014 Directive on Criminal Sanctions for Market Abuse underscores that it has the potential to cause widespread damage to the lives of millions of people. Moreover, it points out that the LIBOR benchmark manipulation scandal demonstrated that these cases impact severely on market confidence, cause significant losses on investors and distort the real economy.[99]

Member States are directed to criminalise market manipulation at least in serious cases and when committed intentionally.[100] It comprises the following:

(a) entering into a transaction, placing an order to trade or other activity which –
   (i) gives false or misleading signals as to the supply or, demand for, or price of, any financial instrument or a related spot commodity contract, or
   (ii) secures the price of one or more financial instruments or a related spot commodity contract at an abnormal artificial level; unless the reasons for so doing or the person who entered into the transaction or issued the orders to trade are legitimate and those transactions or orders to trade are in conformity with accepted market practices on the trading venue concerned;

(b) entering into a transaction, placing an order to trade, or any other activity or behaviour which affects the price of one or several financial instruments or related spot commodity contract which employs a fictitious device or any form of deception or contrivance;

(c) disseminating information through the media, including the Internet; or by any other means, which gives false or other misleading signals as to the supply of, demand for, or price of a financial instrument or a related spot commodity contract at an abnormal or artificial level, when the persons who made the dissemination derive for themselves or for another person an advantage or profit from the dissemination of the information in question; or

(d) transmitting false or misleading information or providing false or misleading signals inputs or any other behaviour which manipulates the calculation of a benchmark.

[98] ibid, Recital (7).
[99] ibid.
[100] ibid, Art 5.

VIII. Developments in Some EU Member States Towards Adjusting to European Regulation

A. France

i. Legislative Developments

In French law speculation is not prohibited in itself but only in case of market price manipulation, that is, when it constitutes a scheme to reduce speculative risk.[101]

The crime of market manipulation was introduced in the French Criminal Code in 1926,[102] repealed in 1986 and reintroduced after the stock market crash of 1987 into the Monetary and Financial Code. After successive reforms, this low-ranking criminal offence regained importance as a consequence of the European Market Abuse Directive of 2003.[103] The corresponding administrative violation (*manquement au bon établissement des cours*) had more frequent application, however.[104]

Law No 816-819 of 21 June 2016, reforming the system of market abuse, distinguishes three forms of market manipulation:

(1) Trading-based market manipulations contained in Article L 465-3-1 of the Monetary and Financial Code that punishes with the penalties prescribed in Article L 465-1 A,[105] whoever carries out a transaction, places an order or engages in a behaviour that gives or is able to give misleading indications about an offer, a demand, or the price of a financial instrument or that fixes or is able of fixing the price of a financial instrument at an abnormal or artificial level.

According to subparagraph B of the same article, this provision is not applicable when such placement or behaviour are based on legitimate motives and are an admitted market practice in the sense of paragraph 9 of Article 3 of the 2014 European Regulation on market abuse. According to paragraph 9 'accepted market practice' means a specific market practice that is accepted by a competent authority in accordance with Article 13, which in turn details all the criteria used by a competent authority to admit certain market practices. Part II of

[101] A Lepage, P Maistre de Chambon and R Salomon, *Droit Pénal des Affaires* (Paris, LexisNexis, 2018) 500.

[102] Art 139.

[103] Directive 2003/6/EC of the European Parliament and of the Council of 28 January 2003 on insider dealing and market manipulation (MAD).

[104] Lepage, Maistre de Chambon and Salomon, *Droit Pénal des Affaires* (n 101) 500.

[105] Art L 465 1, subpara 1 A, punishes behaviours related to insider trading with 'five years of imprisonment and a fine of a hundred million Euros, amount that can be increased to ten times the profit obtained by the commission of the crime, excluding the possibility of a fine lower than such profit'.

the same Article 465-3-1 punishes with the same penalties prescribed in the first part, '[w]hoever carries out a transaction, places an order, or engages in a behaviour that affects the price of a financial instrument using fictitious procedures or any other form of deception or artifice'.

The last paragraph of the same provision punishes with the same penalties the attempt at committing the above-defined behaviours.

The offence is committed by the placement of the order irrespective of the attainment of the desired result. It is, therefore, not necessary to establish a causal nexus between the action and its effect on the market,[106] this is, what in American legal literature is called a crime of harmful actions as opposed to a crime of harmful results.[107] The Paris Court of Appeal decided that the success of the manipulative scheme is not necessary for the commission of the offence but only the possibility of success.[108] The obtainment of a profit is not an element of the crime. The manipulation could have well been intended to obtain a replacement in the board of directors.[109]

The impact on the market, however, has an important evidentiary value, as well as relevance at the sentencing stage.

(2) According to Article L 465-3-2, market manipulation resulting from the diffusion of false or misleading information is punished with the same penalties referred to by the previous article, and is defined in the following terms:

> whoever diffuses by any means, information that gives false or misleading indications about the situation or prospects of an issuer or about the offer, demand or price of a financial instrument or that fixes or is able of fixing the price of a financial instrument at an abnormal or artificial level.

When the financial manoeuvres consist in false information, the offence of market manipulation can cumulate with the general offence of diffusion of false information on the public, even when the latter can also be committed outside the market area.[110] This instance of market manipulation includes the practice of 'scalping' when the internet or discussion groups are used to prop up manoeuvres to bring up or down the price of securities artificially.[111] As Jerry W Markham clarifies, scalping in the securities industry involves an actor who publishes market-moving information about a security and trades in front of that publication, knowing that it will have market effect.[112]

Attempts to commit this crime are punished with the same penalties.

[106] Lepage, Maistre de Chambon and Salomon, *Droit Pénal des Affaires* (n 101) 504.
[107] GP Fletcher, *Basic Concepts of Criminal Law* (New York, Oxford, Oxford University Press, 1998) 60–61.
[108] Decision of the Paris Court of Appeal of 30 November 2004, cited by Lepage, Maistre de Chambon and Salomon, *Droit Pénal des Affaires* (n 101) 504.
[109] ibid.
[110] ibid.
[111] ibid.
[112] Markham, *Law Enforcement* (n 31) 252.

This criminal offence concerns issuers of securities admitted to trade on a regulated market, that is, in France, on the Paris subsidiary of Euronext,[113] but was extended to securities traded in an organised multilateral system of negotiations, whether organised or not, and to securities subject to a request for admission for trading either in a regulated market or in a multilateral system of negotiations.[114] Because the information requires a certain level of quantitative significance, a mere rumour is not sufficient to satisfy the definition of the offence.[115] Moreover, the information should have the potential to influence market prices and be untruthful or deceptive at the time the diffusion takes place.[116]

This offence has to be committed actively and mere omissions of the duty to inform do not reach the criminal level.[117] It is not necessary for the production of a tangible result and the judge does not need the evidence of a trade on the security or variations of its price. The law requires, however, that the information be real, as for example when contained in communications to the general assembly, in prospectuses, in bulletins, press interviews, press conferences and in meetings with financial analysts.[118] The only condition is that the information is widespread to the public, and this may be fulfilled with a single addressee.[119]

As in the previous form of market manipulation, the penalty for physical persons is the same as the one reserved for insider trading. For moral persons, Law No 2016-1691 of 9 December 2016, as in other stock market-related offences, allows for an increase of the penalty up to 15 per cent of the turnover of the company.[120]

The mens rea of this intentional offence consists in the knowledge that one deceives the market.[121]

(3) Article 465-3-3 of the Monetary and Financial Code punishes with the same penalties prescribed for the previous two articles: (a) 'whoever provides or transmits false or deceptive data or information used to calculate a benchmark or information capable to distort the price of a financial instrument or of assets to which such reference benchmark is connected'; (b) whoever engages in 'any behaviour leading to the manipulation of such benchmark index calculation'. A benchmark index is constituted:

> by any rate, index or name made available to the public that is determined periodically or regularly by application of a formula or on the basis of the value of one or more assets or underlying prices, including estimated prices, interest rates

[113] Euronext is the largest stock Exchange in Continental Europe with its registered office in Amsterdam and other markets operating in Brussels, London, Lisbon, Dublin and Paris.
[114] Lepage, Maistre de Chambon and Salomon, *Droit Pénal des Affaires* (n 101) 490.
[115] ibid, 491.
[116] ibid, 492.
[117] ibid.
[118] ibid, 493.
[119] ibid.
[120] ibid, 496.
[121] ibid, 494.

or other values, real or estimated, or data from surveys in reference to which the amount to pay for a financial instrument or the price of such financial instrument are determined.

The attempt to commit the offences defined in (a) and (b) is punished with the same penalties provided for such offences.

ii. Constitutionality of the Accumulation of Criminal and Administrative Sanctions Dealing with Market Manipulation

Law 2013-1117 of 6 December 2013 on fight against tax fraud and serious economic and financial crime authorised the accumulation of administrative procedures initiated by the Financial Market Authority and the criminal procedures initiated by the financial public prosecutor. The Constitutional Council (*Conseil Constitutionnel*) had allowed it in 1989, demanding that the global amount of both sanctions did not exceed the maximum of one of the penalties.[122]

In 2015, the Constitutional Council changed its position by declaring the unconstitutionality of Article L 465-1 of the Monetary and Financial Code for violation of the principle of necessity of sanctions contained in Article 8 of the French Declaration of the Rights of Man and of the Citizens.[123]

By making criminal sanctions against market abuse obligatory, the 2014 Directive on criminal sanctions on market abuse[124] eliminates the possibility of reducing the state reaction to merely administrative sanctions.

On the other hand, a reduction of the state reaction to exclusive criminal sanctions would annul the expert action of the Financial Market Authority.[125] To overcome this dilemma, Law 2016-819 of 21 June 2016, reforming the market abuse sanctioning system, organised a concerted action between the judiciary and the administrative authority: the public prosecutor can only proceed when the Financial Market Authority has not manifested its intent through a notice of complaint (*notification de grief*) and this notice of complaint launching the administrative proceedings can only take place when the public prosecutor has no intention to set off the public action.[126] When both the Monetary and Financial Authority and the public prosecutor intend to initiate their respective actions, paralysis is avoided by empowering the general prosecutor sitting by the Paris Court of Appeal to settle the matter by authorising or not the public financial prosecutor to initiate the public action. If the prosecutor does not authorise, the Monetary and Financial Authority can proceed with the notification of the complaint.[127]

[122] Decision of the Constitutional Council of 28 July 1989, nr 89-260.

[123] Conseil Constitutionnel 18 March 2015, nr 2014-453, 454.

[124] Directive 2014/57/EU of the European Parliament and of the Council of 16 April 2014 on criminal sanctions for market abuse (market abuse directive).

[125] Lepage, Maistre de Chambon and Salomon, *Droit Pénal des Affaires* (n 101) 460.

[126] This procedure is specified by Decree No 2016-1121 of 1 August 2016 (Financial and Monetary Code, Arts R 465-1 to R 461-4.

[127] Monetary and Financial Code, Art L 465-3-6 IV.

B. United Kingdom

Aside from the *Berenger* case, discussed in section I, historical examples of market abuse range from the collapse of the South Sea Company[128] to the Guinness affair in the 1980s,[129] involving the manipulation of the London stock market to inflate the price of Guinness shares with the purpose of assisting the Guinness takeover bid for the Distillers Company Limited, a leading Scottish drinks and pharmaceutical company. As the result of the action of the Serious Fraud Office, four perpetrators of the manipulation paid large fines and served prison sentences.[130]

According to the Financial Services and Market Act 2000, the following manipulative behaviours constitute market abuse:

(1) Behaviours effecting transactions or orders to trade (otherwise than for legitimate reasons and in conformity with accepted market practices on the relevant market), which –

 (a) give, or are likely to give, a false or misleading impression as to the supply of, or demand for, or as to the price of, one or more qualifying investments, or

 (b) secure the price of one or more such investments at an abnormal or artificial level;

(2) Behaviours effecting transactions or orders to trade which employ fictitious devices or any other form of deception or contrivance;

(3) Dissemination of information by any means which gives, or is likely to give, a false or misleading impression as to a qualifying investment by a person who knew or could reasonably be expected to have known that the information was false or misleading.

(4) Behaviour not falling within previous subsections –

 (a) likely to give a regular user of the market a false or misleading impression as to the supply of, demand for or price or value of, qualifying investments, or

 (b) that would be, or would be likely to be, regarded by a regular user of the market as behaviour that would distort, or would be likely to distort, the market in such an investment, and the behaviour is likely to be regarded by a regular user of the market as a failure on the part of the person concerned to observe the standard of behaviour reasonably expected of a person in his position in relation to the market.

[128] The South Sea Company was founded in 1711 as a joint-stock company (corporation with transferable shares) to relieve the government of its burdensome unsecured public debt. The £9 million worth of unfounded government securities were to be exchanged compulsorily for shares at par of the South Sea Company. By an Act of Parliament this company obtained the monopoly of England's trade with Spanish colonies in the West Indies and South America. In addition to this monopoly, the company was guaranteed by state an annual payment from the Exchequer of 6% on the debt taken over. See J Carswell, *The South Sea Bubble* (Stanford, CA, Stanford University Press, 1960) 54.

[129] SR Bazley, *Market Abuse Enforcement: Practice And Procedure* (London, Bloomsbury Professional, 2013) 4.

[130] ibid 8.

Today, the UK's criminal law on market manipulation is contained in Part 7 of the 2012 Financial Services Act, named 'Offences Relating to Financial Services'. This Part includes Sections 89–91, entitled respectively: 'Misleading Statements', 'Misleading Impressions' and 'Misleading Statements etc in Relation to Benchmarks'.

Under Section 89 'Misleading Statements' regarding the financial situation, this section includes:

(1) Subsection (2), applies to a person (P) who:

  (a) makes a statement which P knows to be false or misleading in a material respect,
  (b) makes a statement which is false or misleading in a material respect, being reckless as to whether it is, or
  (c) dishonestly conceals any material facts whether in connection with a statement made by P or otherwise.

(2) P commits an offence if P makes the statement or conceals the facts with the intention of inducing, or is reckless as to whether making it or concealing them may induce, another person (whether or not the person to whom the statement is made):

  (a) to enter into or offer to enter into, or to refrain from entering or offering to enter into, a relevant agreement, or
  (b) to exercise, or refrain from exercising, any rights conferred by a relevant investment.

(3) In proceedings for an offence under subsection (2) brought against a person to whom that subsection applies as a result of paragraph (a) of subsection (1), it is a defence for the person charged (D) to show that the statement was made in conformity with:

  (a) price stabilising rules,
  (b) control of information rules, or
  (c) the relevant provisions of article 5 (exemption for buy-back programmes and stabilisation) of the market abuse regulation.

(4) Subsections (1) and (2) do not apply unless—

  (a) the statement is made in or from, or the facts are concealed in or from, the United Kingdom or arrangements are made in or from the United Kingdom for the statement to be made or the facts to be concealed,
  (b) the person on whom the inducement is intended to or may have effect is in the United Kingdom, or
  (c) the agreement is or would be entered into or the rights are or would be exercised in the United Kingdom.

The second offence relating to financial services is Section 90, 'Misleading Impressions':

(1) A person (P) who does any act or engages in any course of conduct which creates a false or misleading impression as to the market in or the price or value of any relevant investments commits an offence if:

  (a) P intends to create the impression, and
  (b) the case falls within subsection (2) or (3) (or both).

(2) The case falls within this subsection if P intends, by creating the impression, to induce another person to acquire, dispose of, subscribe for or underwrite the investments or to refrain from doing so or to exercise or refrain from exercising any rights conferred by the investments.
(3) The case falls within this subsection if:

  (a) P knows that the impression is false or misleading or is reckless as to whether it is, and
  (b) P intends by creating the impression to produce any of the results in subsection (4) or is aware that creating the impression is likely to produce any of the results in that subsection.

(4) Those results are:

  (a) the making of a gain for P or another, or
  (b) the causing of loss to another person or the exposing of another person to the risk of loss.

(5) References in subsection (4) to gain or loss are to be read in accordance with subsections (6) to (8).
(6) 'Gain' and 'loss':

  (a) extend only to gain or loss in money or other property of any kind;
  (b) include such gain or loss whether temporary or permanent.

(7) 'Gain' includes a gain by keeping what one has, as well as a gain by getting what one does not have.
(8) 'Loss' includes a loss by not getting what one might get, as well as a loss by parting with what one has.
(9) In proceedings brought against any person (D) for an offence under subsection (1) it is a defence for D to show:

  (a) to the extent that the offence results from subsection (2), that D reasonably believed that D's conduct would not create an impression that was false or misleading as to the matters mentioned in subsection (1),
  (b) that D acted or engaged in the conduct:

    (i) for the purpose of stabilising the price of investments, and
    (ii) in conformity with price stabilising rules,

  (c) that D acted or engaged in the conduct in conformity with control of information rules, or
  (d) that D acted or engaged in the conduct in conformity with the relevant provisions of article 5 (exemption for buy back programs and stabilisation) of the market abuse regulation.

(10) This section does not apply unless:

  (a) the act is done, or the course of conduct is engaged in, in the United Kingdom, or
  (b) the false or misleading impression is created there.

(11) See section 137Q(3) of FSMA 2000 regarding the power of the FCA (Financial Conduct Authority) to make rules for the purposes of subsection 9 (d).

The third offence related to financial services is Section 91, 'Misleading statements etc in relation to benchmarks':

(1) A person (A) who makes to another person ('B') a false or misleading statement commits an offence if:

  (a) A makes the statement in the course of arrangements for the setting of a relevant benchmark,
  (b) A intends that the statement should be used by B for the purpose of the setting of a relevant benchmark, and
  (c) A knows that the statement is false or misleading or is reckless as to whether it is.

(2) A person (C) who does any act or engages in any course of conduct which creates a false or misleading impression as to the price or value of any investment or as to the interest rate appropriate to any transaction commits an offence if:

  (a) C intends to create the impression,
  (b) the impression may affect the setting of a relevant benchmark,
  (c) C knows that the impression is false or misleading or is reckless as to whether it is, and
  (d) C knows that the impression may affect the setting of a relevant benchmark.

(3) In proceedings for an offence under subsection (1), it is a defence for the person charged (D) to show that the statement was made in conformity with:

  (a) omitted (3.7.2016) by virtue of the Financial Services and Markets Act 2000 (Market Abuse) Regulations 2016 (SI 2016/680), regs 1, 15 (4)(a)(1).
  (b) control of information rules, or
  (c) the relevant provisions of article 5 (exemption for buy-back programmes and stabilisation) of the market abuse regulation.

(4) In proceedings brought against any person (D) for an offence under subsection (2) it is a defence for D to show:

  (a) that D acted or engaged in the conduct

    (i) for the purpose of stabilising the price of investments, and
    (ii) in conformity with price stabilising rules;

  (b) that D acted or engaged in the conduct in conformity with control of information rules; or
  (c) that D acted or engaged in the conduct in conformity with the relevant provisions of article 5 (exemption for buy-back programmes and stabilisation) of the market abuse regulation.

(5) Subsection (1) does not apply unless the statement is made in or from the United Kingdom or to a person in the United Kingdom.

(6) Subsection (2) does not apply unless—

  (a) the act is done, or the course of conduct is engaged in, in the United Kingdom, or
  (b) the false or misleading impression is created there.

(7) See section 137Q(3) of FSMA 2000 regarding the power of the FCA (Financial Conduct Authority) to make rules for the purposes of subsection 4 (c).

Section 92 of the Financial Services Act 2012 contains the following penalties:

(1) A person guilty of an offence under this Part is liable:

(a) on summary conviction, to imprisonment for a term not exceeding the applicable maximum term or a fine not exceeding the statutory maximum, or both;

(b) on conviction on indictment, to imprisonment for a term not exceeding 7 years or a fine, or both.

(2) For the purpose of subsection (1)(a) 'the applicable maximum term' is:

(a) in England and Wales, 12 months (or 6 months, if the offence was committed before the commencement of section 154(1) of the Criminal Justice Act 2003);

(b) in Scotland, 12 months;

(c) in Northern Ireland, 6 months.

In addition, section 93 of the Financial Services Act 2012 contains the following rules of interpretation:

(1) This section has effect for the interpretation of this Part.

(2) 'Investment' includes any asset, right or interest.

(3) 'Relevant agreement' means an agreement—

(a) the entering into or performance of which by either party constitutes an activity of a kind specified in an order made by the Treasury, and

(b) which relates to a relevant investment.

(4) 'Relevant benchmark' means a benchmark of a kind specified in an order made by the Treasury.

(5) 'Relevant investment' means an investment of a kind specified in an order made by the Treasury.

(6) Schedule 2 to FSMA 2000 (except paragraphs 25 and 26) applies for the purposes of subsections (3) and (5) with references to section 22 of that Act being read as references to each of those subsections.

(7) Nothing in Schedule 2 to FSMA 2000, as applied by subsection (6), limits the power conferred by subsection (3) or (5).

(8) 'Price stabilising rules' and 'control of information rules' have the same meaning as in FSMA 2000.

(8A) "Market abuse regulation" means Regulation (EU) No 596/2014 of the European Parliament and of the Council of 16 April 2014 on market abuse (market abuse regulation) and repealing Directive 2003/6/EC of the European Parliament an of the Council and Commission: Directives 2003/124/EC, 2003/125/EC ad 2004/72/EC.

(8B) References to article 5 of the market abuse regulation include any directly applicable EU Regulation made under that article.

(9) In this section 'benchmark' has the meaning given in section 22(6) of FSMA 2000.[131]

[131] Financial Services and Markets Act 2000, s 22(6) 'Benchmark' means an index, rate or price, that: (a) is determined from time to time by reference to the state of the market; (b) is made available to the public either free of charge or on payment; and (c) is used for reference for purposes that include one or

The withdrawal of the UK from the European Union (Brexit) does not affect the British criminal provisions on market manipulation because the Directive 2014/57/EU of the European Parliament and the Council on Market Abuse does not bind the UK or subject the country to its application in accordance to Protocol 21 of the Treaty on the Functioning of the European Union (Recital 29 of the Directive). On the other hand, the impact of the withdrawal on civil sanctions for market abuse is dealt with in Chapter 4, section VI.

C. Italy

i. Legislative Developments

Market manipulation has very solid roots in the Italian legal system. It represents a species under the general notion of *agiotaggio*, which can be translated as 'market rigging' or 'market manipulation'.

Until the legislative Decree No 61/2002 of reform of Italian corporation law, various forms of *aggiotaggio* coexisted in Italian law. The Italian penal code defined *aggiotaggio* in Article 501 as the fraudulent increase or decline of prices in public markets or in the stock market, while Article 501*bis* punished certain speculative manoeuvres on merchandises. There were also provisions about manipulation of securities, banks, and financial services.

With the legislative Decree 61/2002, the Italian legislator tried to systemise all the legal aspects of *aggiotaggio* in Article 2637 of the Civil Code,[132] entitled 'Aggiotaggio':

> Whoever spreads false news or engages in simulated operations or other contrivances concretely apt to cause a sensible alteration of the price of financial instruments not quoted and for which there is norequest for admission to negotiations in a regulated market, or to affect in a significant way the public trust on the stability of banks or banking groups assets, shall be punished with imprisonment of one to five years.

This provision was intended to identify the elements of the crime in a more precise way, attuned to the constitutional principle of legality and avoid the interpretative uncertainty that prevailed at the time of coexistence of various forms of *aggiotaggio*. According to scholarly critiques this simplification was only apparent and different interpretations of the various categories of this offence re-emerged. Three years later, under the influence of the 2003 MAD, Law No 62/2005 replaced the previous regime of *aggiotaggio* with chapter V of the Testo Unico Finanziario (Single Financial Text (TUF)).

more of the following: (i) determining the interests payable or other sums due under loan agreements or under other contracts relating to investments; (ii) determining the price at which investments may be bought or sold or the value of investments; (iii) measuring the performance of investments.

[132] L Lipari, *Gli Abusi di Mercato* (Rome, Aracne Editrice, 2017) 101.

Today, three criminal provisions coexist in the Italian legal system under the general umbrella of *aggiotaggio*: Article 501 of the Penal Code, Article 2367 of the Civil Code and Article 185, TUF. Article 185, TUF, under the label of 'market manipulation' punishes with imprisonment of one to six years and fines of €20,000 to €1 million 'whoever spreads false news, engages in simulated operations or other contrivances concretely apt to cause a sensible alteration of the price of financial instruments'. The second section of this article allows the judge to increase the fine up to triple or the larger amount of 10 times the profit obtained through the crime when the normal sanctions appear as inadequate even if applied to their maximum because of the harmfulness of the crime, the degree of culpability of the offender or the magnitude of the product or of the profit obtained by the crime. The only difference between Article 3467 of the Civil Code and Article 185, TUF is that the latter refers to securities quoted or requested to be quoted in regulated stock exchange markets, while the former refers to financial instruments withdrawn from regulated markets, or that are not quoted by them.

Sciumbata underscores that between Article 2637 of the Civil Code and Article 185, TUF there is a profound difference even when their written text is almost identical. This diverse significance lies on their different systematic location.[133] Article 2637 remains isolated within the context of the Civil Code scarcely supported by other provisions. In this respect, Sciumbata points out that it would have been better to insert it within the context of a modern penal code.[134] Article 185, TUF is, instead, supported by the definitions, institutions and norms with which it is connected within the context of the Single Financial Text.[135] In sum, Article 2367 has been confined to market manipulation of securities not negotiated in regulated markets, thus reducing the scope of its application and transforming it in a subsidiary provision with regard to Article 185, TUF.[136]

In addition, Article 187-*ter* TUF contains heavy administrative sanctions that punish with fines of €20,000 to €5 million whoever spreads through means of communication such as internet, or others, false or misleading information, rumours or news that provide or are apt to provide false information about financial instruments.[137]

Article 185, TUF punishes both the spreading of false news, classified as 'informative manipulation', as well as carrying out simulated transactions or other contrivances, classified as 'transactional manipulation', with reference to securities that are admitted for negotiations or for which a request for admission had been presented in an Italian regulated market or in the market of any Member State of the EU, as well as those securities authorised or for which a request for admission had been presented in any Italian system of multilateral negotiations.

133 G Sciumbata, *I Reati Societari* (Milan, Giuffre, 2008) 138.
134 ibid.
135 ibid.
136 ibid.
137 F D'Alessandro, *Regolatori del Mercato, Enforcement e Sistema Penale* (Turin, Giappichelli Editori, 2014) 170.

With the exception of the above-described characteristics, whatever is explained regarding Article 185, TUF is also applicable to Article 2637 of the Italian Civil Code.[138] In both criminal provisions the vital interest or value protected (*bene giuridico*) is the regular functioning of markets by deterring through a penal sanction any fraudulent influence on the process of price formation.

The qualifications of the perpetrators within the corporation such as administrators, general directors, and liquidators are relevant at the sentencing level to decide for the application of the aggravated second section of Article 185, TUF, insofar as they weigh as a personal factor that helps to determine the degree of culpability of the perpetrator.[139]

The commission of the offence through the spreading of false news (informative manipulation) consists in diffusing the false information by any technical means to an indeterminate number of addressees, and must be suitable to significantly alter the price of the security.[140] Diffusion means communication of any kind, written or oral, using any means, and directed to an indeterminate number of persons. If directed to a restricted circle of persons it may fall under Article 185, TUF's residual hypothesis of 'other contrivances'.[141]

Given that the news must be objectively false, the legislator chose to exclude rumours from the notion of false news in according to the constitutional requirement of legal certainty as a basis for criminal sanctions.[142]

The false information may concern the issuer (corporate information), as well as the securities themselves (market information).[143]

An informative manipulation supposes an actual causal relationship between the public diffusion of the false information and the securities' price variations.[144] Therefore, the information must be capable to potentially alter the price of the securities.[145]

After defining informative manipulation, Article 185, TUF refers to the execution of simulated transactions, as well as to other contrivances, that constitute transactional or action-based manipulations.

With respect to these forms of manipulations, D'Alessandro[146] provides the examples of wash trades,[147] painting the tape[148] and improper matched orders.[149]

[138] ibid, 171.
[139] ibid, 174.
[140] ibid, 174, 175.
[141] Lipari, *Gli Abusi di Mercato* (n 132) 109.
[142] D'Alessandro, *Regulatori del Mercato* (n 137) 175; as well as Lipari, *Gli Abusi di Mercato* (n 132) 111.
[143] Lipari *Gli Abusi di Mercato* (n 132)110.
[144] ibid, 113.
[145] ibid, 114.
[146] D'Alessandro, *Regulatori del Mercato* (n 137) 181.
[147] 'The investor sells and buys a financial instrument or vice versa to give the misleading impression of trading activity (D'Alessandro, *Regulatori del Mercato* (n 137) 181). This form of manipulation is forbidden in the US since the enactment of the Commodities Exchange Act of 1936.
[148] Investors sell and buy securities among themselves to create a false impression of market activity and thus mislead other investors about the price of a security (D'Alessandro, *Regulatori del Mercato* (n 137) 181).
[149] Illegal buying and selling orders of the same security at the same time by colluding investors to mislead others about the activity of the market (D'Alessandro, *Regulatori del Mercato* (n 137) 181).

Miedico, in turn, points out that the legal expression 'with other contrivances of article 185 TUF should be interpreted in a restrictive way, overcoming the apparent indeterminacy of the expression by always demanding a deceptive attitude'.[150] He insists, citing court decisions and scholarly opinions, that the wrongfulness of the behaviour is based in its inherent stiltedness rather than in its objectives, that is, that the result aimed by the conduct should not be the only element to take into account when deciding about its illegality.[151]

The expression 'other contrivances' covers all the forms of transactional manipulation, also called 'trade-based manipulation' and 'action-based manipulation'. This legal expression covers concerted sales or acquisitions of securities that provide false or misleading indications about the offer, demand and price of financial instruments, including fixing their price at an abnormal or artificial level. On another occasion the simulated operations of a stockbroker gradually lowering prices caused a trend downwards reaching a knock in level, which gave the option to the issuer to repurchase its own stock.[152]

Another interesting example of *aggiotaggio* is the case decided by the Court of Milan on 21 December 2016. The operation consisted in the issuing of an enormous volume of selling orders at the lowest price allowed by the market at the time, made with the purpose of eliminating all the purchase proposals present in the market. In a second phase, simultaneous proposals of sale and acquisition were issued at a price much lower than the one recently registered for analogous quantities. This second phase took place between different intermediaries that acted in execution of an order of the same principal. This was accompanied by the lack of activation of the 'cross orders', which would have precluded that the transaction had any weight in the determination of both the price of reference and the official price of the securities. The following determination of the price of the securities took place in the final phase of an operation that forecasted enormous number of sale proposals issued a few seconds before the market closed. Such transactions, reconstructed in the Court's decision, aimed at reducing the official price of the title in order to diminish the extraordinary financial costs and therefore obtain a more handsome yearly profit.[153]

The Committee of European Securities Regulators (CESR) mentions hypotheses of wash trades, painting the tape and improper matched orders,[154] as well as placing orders without intention to execute them, marking the close, creating the floor in a price pattern, pump and dump and trash and cash operations.

According to Article 185, TUF the manipulative behaviour must be apt to cause a sensitive price alteration. The reference to price sensitivity excludes the criminal

[150] M Miedico, 'La Disciplina Penalistica deglu Abusi di Mercati' in A Alessandri (ed), *Reati In Materia Economica* (Turin, Giappichelli Editore, 2017) 319, 339.

[151] ibid.

[152] ibid, 341.

[153] D'Alessandro, *Regulatori del Mercato* (n 137) 141.

[154] The Committee of Europeans Securities Regulators, CESR/04-505, 12.

relevance of marginal alterations. The extension of the provision of *aggiotaggio* was originally restrained subjectively by the requirement of a specific intent.[155] Now only a general intent is required. On the other hand, the behaviour must be considered as a whole; and rigorously evaluated to determine its simulative or deceitful nature.[156]

ii. The Two-Track Sanctioning System and the Principle Non Bis in Idem

In 2005 the legislator flanked an administrative sanction alongside every criminal one.

Italian scholarship believed that criminal and administrative sanctions for abuse of privileged information and for market manipulation could function contemporaneously, except in cases exclusively reserved to administrative sanctions.

Italian scholars have tried to distinguish administrative and criminal sanctions by looking at the elements of the offence. In the case of abuse of privileged information both offences are objectively identical and diverge only partially at the mens rea level, while in the case of market manipulation both offences also diverge at the objective level. The criminal offence refers to behaviours typically fraudulent and contrived that are specifically apt to appreciably alter the price of financial instruments, while administrative offences carry out an earlier protection, when the capacity to harm is still absent. In sum, the commission of an illegal transgression to the norms regulating market abuse may bring about a criminal offence plus an administrative one. The administrative violation can result from the application of decree-law 231 of 2001[157] or may be derived from the criminal offence. This interpretation was very much criticised by scholars,[158] and in 2014 the European Court of Human Rights in the case *Grande Stevens v Italy* decided that the double track system of administrative and criminal sanctions for market abuse was incompatible with the European Convention on Human Rights and its Protocols. Indeed, the Court established that the procedural and substantive norms regulating market abuse infringed Article 6 of the European Convention on Human Rights regarding equal process[159] and Article 4 of Protocol 7 to the Convention prohibiting double jeopardy (*non bis in idem*).[160]

[155] Miedico, *La Disciplina Penalistica* (n 150) 346.

[156] ibid.

[157] Legislative Decree No 231 of 6 June 2001 provided for a direct liability of legal entities, companies and associations for certain crimes committed by their representatives.

[158] Miedico, *La Disciplina Penalistica* (n 150) 353.

[159] *Grande Stevens v Italy* App no 18640/10 (Final Judgment) (Merits) (ECR, 7 July 2014), holding unanimously that there has been a violation of Art 6 of the European Convention of Human Rights.

[160] ibid, holding unanimously that the respondent state must ensure that the still pending procedures opened against the applicants in violation of Art 4 of Protocol 7 to the European Convention of Human Rights are closed as rapidly as possible.

D. Germany

Initially, the old German Commercial Code of 1884 included a provision on market manipulation without much practical significance. While manipulation of the stock market or of market prices were already criminalised in Germany at the end of the nineteenth century in paragraph 88 (old version) of the Stock Market Act (BörsG), these provisions were seldom applied. It was only 'the sustained impulse of European law and the introduction of comprehensive market supervision that made criminal law enforcement officials fully conscious of the availability and significance of such European norms regulating a fair price formation and market transparency'.[161] Paragraph 88 (old version) of BörsG were ultimately abrogated and the rules prohibiting market manipulation were transferred to paragraph 20(a) of the Securities Trading Act (WpHG). These provisions improved and replaced paragraphs 88 and 89 from BörsG.

The prohibition of market price manipulation in paragraph 20(a) of WpHG was included at the time in which a downfall in the Stock Market and cases of market manipulation had threatened the reliance of the public in the stock market.[162] This market manipulation prohibition was introduced in July 2002 by the Fourth Financial Market Promotion Act as paragraph 38, subparagraph 2, in combination with paragraph 20(a) of WpHG. The new provisions protected the integrity of the stock market as a central element of the German economy. Next, on 24 October 2004, the Act to Improve Investor Protection (*Anlegerschutzverbesserungsgesetz*) implemented Directive 2003/6/EC of the European Parliament and the Council against insider trading and market manipulation (market abuse).

Thus, paragraph 20(a) of WpHG's scope of protection guaranteed the proper and regular formation of stock market prices. A regular formation of prices promoted investors' confidence in the efficient functioning of the stock market.[163]

Paragraph 20(a) prohibited two forms of market manipulation: manipulation based on the diffusion of false or misleading information and manipulation based on trading behaviour. Subparagraph 1, number 1 prohibited not only the diffusion of false or misleading information but also the wrongful concealment of circumstances of obligatory disclosure that were of considerable importance for the appraisal of a security when the diffusion or the concealment were apt to influence the stock market or the market price.

The objective of this prohibition was to protect investors through criminal sanctions. The price formation according to pre-existing rules contributed to the trust of investors in the correct functioning of stock markets. A price formation in conformity to those rules also protects property values in other states of the European economic area and the normal functioning of securities markets

[161] Schröder, *Handbuch Kapitalmarktstrafrecht* (n 10) 125.
[162] ibid, 126.
[163] A Hohnel (ed), *Kapitalmarktstrafrecht* (Munich, CH Beck, 2013) 17.

in such places. The German Minister of Finances issued in 2004 an Ordinance for concretisation of the prohibition of market manipulation (*Verordnung zur Konkretisierung des Verbotes der Marktmanipulation* (MaKonV)). The MaKonV affirmed the conditions for the offence contained in paragraph 20(a) of WpHG and supported in this way the broad prohibition of this section, taking into account the criminal law basic principle of legal certainty.[164] The prohibition of price manipulation coincided to a great extent with the prohibition of insider dealing in both its legislative aim and protected values. This closeness of both offences was underscored by their common treatment in the 2003 MAD. The area of tension between the prohibition of paragraph 20(a)(1) and the allowed behaviour of paragraph 20(a)(2), reflected the difficulty of regulating criminal law provisions in stock exchanges and markets. Paragraph 20(a)(3) contained an exclusion of market manipulation on cases of self-trading with stock, when the company buys its own stock on European law-based measures to stabilise prices.

The vital legal value protected by paragraph 20(a) was the capital market and its functioning, as well as the reliability and truth of the price formation in stock markets.[165] Commentators who argued that the notion of a capital market was not well defined and not formulated in detail criticised this conclusion.[166] The art of legislating consists in including as many as possible facts encompassed by a few concepts, thus satisfying the constitutional principle of certainty (Article 103(2) of the Basic Law). This effort was reflected in paragraph 20(a) in the field of capital market criminal law. Because the capital market was changing rapidly, paragraph 20(a) regulated this area in a very comprehensive way. This is shown in the various forms of behaviour contained in the definition of the offence:[167] 'to make deceptive statements', 'to conceal circumstances', 'to undertake transactions', 'to give orders' and finally 'to undertake other deceptive actions'.

Paragraph 38(2) of WpHG, on the other hand, constrained the criminalised behaviour by demanding an actual result: influencing the price of the financial instruments at stake,[168] as opposed to the administrative fine contained in paragraph 39, which only required the aptitude to do so.

The Europeanisation of the provisions regarding market manipulation continued through the First and Second Financial Market Revision Acts. The German legislator implemented the 2014 EU Market Abuse Directive on Criminal Sanctions through the First Financial Market Revision Act with the repeal of paragraph 20(a) and the new referral to Article 15 of MAR, the adding of qualifications and the criminalisation of attempts. Through the Second Financial Market Revision Act the legislator added less serious offences to the Securities Trading Act and on

[164] ibid, 18.
[165] ibid.
[166] ibid.
[167] See n 162.
[168] K Tiedemann and M Engelhart, *Wirtschaftsstrafrecht* (Munich, Franz Vahlen, 2017) 430.

3 July 2018 the numeration of WpHG was changed and the object of the crime was extended from securities to include also commodities.[169]

Today, the provision against market manipulation is a multilevel blanket criminal law norm.[170] Paragraph 119, subparagraph 1 of the reformed WpHG[171] refers to the fine-penalties provision of paragraph 120, subparagraph 15, No 2 of WpHG, which in turn refers to the prohibition contained in Article 15 of MAR, the actual prohibitory norm.[172]

Hellmann refers to this chain of referrals as a 'true legislative master performance' because paragraph 119, section 1(1) of WpHG clearly expresses:

> Whoever perpetrates intentionally the action described in § 120, section 2, No 3 (market manipulation in connection with article 15 of MAR) or Section 15, No 2 (market manipulation infringing article 15 of MAR) and thereby influences the domestic stock markets or the price of financial instruments (…), shall be punished with imprisonment up to five years or fines.

As Hellmann points out,[173] the referral to Article 15 of MAR is devoid of content because this article only contains the prohibition and it is necessary to bring in Article 12[174] to define the prohibited manipulative behaviour. Moreover, he considers dubious whether this legislative technique is compatible with the constitutional principle of certainty.[175]

Hellmann analyses Article 12 of MAR through the prism of three basic forms of market manipulation: information-based manipulation (diffusion of false or misleading information that represent a financial incentive for investors);

[169] U Hellmann, *Wirtschaftsstrafrecht*, 5th edn (Stuttgart, Kohlhammer, 2018) 29.

[170] The notion of blanket criminal norms is basically a legislative drafting technique that entails the incorporation by reference of a norm existing elsewhere in the legal system to complete a criminal provision. In later developments this doctrine included the incorporation by reference of norms existing within the same statute. The subject of blanket criminal norms is developed in detail in ch 3, section V.B, specifically in the text corresponding to nn 140 to 146.

[171] Paragraph 119 punishes with imprisonment of up to 5 years or a fine to whoever perpetrates intentionally the action described in para 120, s 2, 3 (market manipulation in connection with Art 15 of MAR) or s 15, 2 (market manipulation infringing Art 15 of MAR) and thereby influences: (1) The domestic stock market or market price of a financial instrument, in connection with a spot contract in the sense of para 2, s 5 (fungible assets that can be delivered, including metals, ore, and alloys, farm products, energy as electrical one); and means of payments in the sense of para 51 of the Stock Market Law; (2) market price of a financial instrument, or of a connected merchandise-spot-contract in an organised commercial market or in a multilateral or organised commercial system in another Member State, or in another country party to the treaty on the European economic space; (3) the price of a merchandise in the sense of para 2, s 5 or means of payments in the sense of para 51 of the Stock Market Law or on the stock market of another Member State comparable with the domestic stock market, or on another country party to the treaty on the European economic space; or (4) the calculation of a reference value domestically or in other Member State or in another state party to the treaty on the European economic space.

[172] 'A person shall not engage in or attempt to engage in market manipulation.'

[173] Hellmann, *Wirtschaftsstrafrecht* (n 169) 30.

[174] Art 12 of Regulation (EU) No 596/2014 of MAR describes the different forms of market manipulation analysed by Hellmann in the following paragraphs.

[175] Hellmann, *Wirtschaftsstrafrecht*) (n 169) 30.

trade-based manipulation (mere trading action directly influencing the price of a financial instrument) and action-based manipulation (actions indirectly influencing the value of a financial instrument).[176]

Article 12, section 1 contains four forms of manipulations: under (a), trade-based manipulations ('entering into a transaction, placing an order to trade or any other behaviour which: (i) gives, or is likely to give, false or misleading signals as to the supply of, demand for, or price of, a financial instrument, a related spot commodity contract[177] or an auctioned program based on emission allowances;[178] or (ii) secures, or is likely to secure, the price of one or several financial instruments, a related spot commodity contract, or an auctioned product based on emission allowances at an abnormal or artificial level'); under (b), trade-based and information-based manipulations ('entering into a transaction, placing an order to trade or any other activity or behavior which affects or is likely to affect the price of one or several financial instruments, a related spot commodity contract or an auctioned product based on emission allowances, which employs a fictitious device or any form of deception or contrivance'); under (c) information based manipulations ('disseminating information through the media, including the internet, or by any other means, which gives, or is likely to give, false or misleading signals as to the supply of, demand for, or price of, a financial instrument, a related spot commodity contract or an auctioned product based on emission allowances or secures, or is likely to secure, the price of one or several financial instruments, a related spot commodity contract or an auctioned product based on emission allowances at an abnormal or artificial level, including the dissemination of rumours, where the person who made the dissemination knew, or ought to have known, that the information was false or misleading'; and under (d), again information-based manipulations, 'transmitting false or misleading information or providing false or misleading inputs in relation to a benchmark where the person who made the transmission or provided the input knew or ought to have known that it was false or misleading, or any other behaviour which manipulates the calculation of a benchmark').

Article 12, section 2 of MAR contains a binding but not conclusive catalogue of applications, which are generally regarded as constituting autonomous prohibitions, rather than mere examples of section 1 of the same article.[179] The list begins with the conduct of a person or persons acting in collaboration, to secure a dominant position over the supply and demand of a financial instrument, 'which has or is likely to have, the effect of fixing, directly or indirectly, purchase or sale prices or

[176] ibid.

[177] According to Investopedia, 'A spot commodity is a commodity up for immediate trade, as opposed to a commodity under contract for trade at a future date. A commodity is a necessary good, which is used in commerce that is interchangeable with other commodities of the same type. Spot commodities are traded on the spot market with an expectation of delivery at settlement. In contrast, commodities traded on the futures market have a delivery set at a future date.'

[178] See n 96.

[179] Hellmann, *Wirtschaftsstrafrecht* (n 169) 31.

creates, or is likely to create, other unfair trading conditions', and continues with other forms such as 'scalping' and others that may not only not be mere specifications of Article 12, section 1, but constitute a barrier to its application.[180]

Paragraph 119 of the Securities Trading Act also punishes the attempt at market manipulation, as for example when the intended effect on market prices do not actually take place.[181]

Paragraph 119 criminalises market manipulations influencing:

(1) domestic stock markets or the price of a financial instrument, a related commodity spot contract, a merchandise or a foreign means of payment;
(2) the price of a financial instrument or a related commodity spot contract in an organised market, in a multilateral or organised trading system in another member state or in another state party to the treaty on the European economic area;
(3) the price of a merchandise in the sense of paragraph 2, section 5 (fungible economic assets that can be sent, including metals, ore, and alloys, agricultural products and energy such as electricity) or a foreign means of payment in a market comparable with a domestic one in another member state or in another state party to the treaty on the European economic area; and
(4) the calculation of the reference value in domestic territory or in another member state or in another state party to the treaty on the European economic area.[182]

The penalties of paragraph 119 are increased from one to 10 years of imprisonment or fines according to section 5(1) when the crime is committed by a professional criminal or a member of a gang and, according to section 5(2) when it is committed by capital market professionals acting in exercise of their functions within a domestic supervising financial office, a securities service company, a stock market, or an operator of a trading place.

Paragraph 119, section 6 foresees for less serious cases of infringements to section 5(2) a penalty of imprisonment from six months to five years.

[180] ibid.
[181] ibid.
[182] The European Economic Area agreement ((EEA) was concluded in 1992 between the European Union member countries and three of the European Free Trade Association (EFTA) countries: Iceland, Lichtenstein and Norway (Switzerland refused to join). See Eu-Lex, 21994A0103 (74), [1994] OJ L1/3.

Conclusions

The progressive globalisation of financial markets has dramatically expanded the turf for fraudsters and tricksters to the extent of imperilling the integrity of such markets and compromising the confidence of investors, thus affecting the economy as a whole. The urgent need to counteract this phenomenon generated the expansion of an internationalised securities fraud-related criminal law.

As a result, in the past two decades, a remarkable transformation has taken place around the world in the legal treatment of financial crimes. While long being sidelined as incidental legal violations, financial crimes have been increasingly spotlighted as dangerous legal breaches.

As this book has shown, securities fraud-related criminal law has diachronic and synchronic dimensions. The diachronic dimension is represented by the gradual convergence through time of the norms criminalising insider trading and market manipulation. The synchronic dimension is reflected by the present structure of European law and that of its Member States, largely harmonised with the current US courts' evolving interpretation of the 1930s pioneering statutes.

The two main forms of market abuse, insider trading and market manipulation, bear different histories. Despite its present association with insider trading under the label of market abuse, market manipulation has a different historical development. Besides isolated examples[1] and the role of insider trading in the debacle of the South Sea Company,[2] the modern genesis of the notion of insider trading as a criminal offence began only with the late 1960s US Supreme Court's interpretation of the 1930s American statutes.

While the deliberate distortion of securities' price formation seems to be as old as the stock markets themselves, as Joseph de la Vega accounted in 1688,[3] the criminalisation of market manipulation, in contrast to insider trading, has been generally traced back to the 1814 UK decision in *The King v de Berenger and others* case.[4] In recent years, both insider trading and market manipulation have taken

[1] AF Tripodi, *Informazione Privilegiati e Statuto Penale del Mercato Finanziario* (Padua, Casa Editrice Dott. Antonio Milani, 2012) xv, offers the following examples: Gnaeus Flavius, stealing and publicising the secret book of the *legis actionis* to gain political advantages; the administrators of the Dutch East Indies Company selling their shares on the advanced knowledge of dividends reduction; and Nathan de Rostschild's purchases with the advance knowledge of Napoleon's defeat in Waterloo.

[2] R Dale, *The First Crash: Lessons From The South Sea Bubble* (Princeton, NJ, Princeton University Press, 2004) 97 and 179.

[3] TJ Putniņš, 'Market Manipulation: A Survey' *Journal of Economic Surveys* (8 April 2011) available at https://ssrn.com/abstract=1805642, 2.

[4] WB Gurney, *The Trial of Charles Random De Berenger, Lord Cochrane And Others* (London, J Butterworth and Son, and Gale, Curtis and Fenner, 1814) 588.

a more dramatic turn because of globalised high-speed trading and the advent of benchmark manipulation.

Increasing global awareness of the vital nature of financial markets' integrity and the need to maintain a level playing field for participants in world financial markets brought about a resurgence of criminal sanctions for market abuse.

As Mireille Delmas-Marty has pointed out, in response to globalisation the world market utilised criminal law to address serious imbalances (namely those caused by economic advantages obtained through insider trading or market manipulation) in countries competing in the world market. Delmas-Marty contends that in contrast with the traditional attitude that dismisses business-related crimes,[5] world trade now requires the use of criminal law to guarantee equality among competitors.[6]

The need for criminal sanctions to deter and punish market abuse is made explicit by Recital (6) of the 2014 EU Directive of the European Council and the Parliament, as it declares that the norms protecting against market abuse be strengthened by the availability of criminal sanctions which demonstrate a stronger disapproval compared to administrative penalties. Establishing criminal offences for at least serious forms of market abuse sets clear boundaries for types of behaviour that are considered particularly unacceptable and send a message to the public and to potential offenders that competent authorities take such behaviour very seriously.

This book's analysis thus demonstrates the necessity for criminal sanctions for securities fraud and documents how this repression has internationalised in multiple ways, including the extraterritorial application of national law; diffusion of the American legal model; European Directives and Regulations; legislative convergence; and, at the global level, informal international cooperation of securities supervisory national authorities coordinated by the International Organization of Securities Commissions (IOSCO).

A clear example of internationalisation through the diffusion of the American model is the case of Switzerland. Although this type of internationalisation operated in other countries in various degrees, it constituted the motor of both Switzerland's insider trading and market manipulation criminal law provisions: the incorporation of a provision criminalising insider trading in the Swiss Penal Code was closely followed by another addressing market manipulation. These developments originated under pressure from the US to comply with the dual criminality requirement for extradition. Swiss legislation, however, later took an autonomous direction, culminating in the 2016 Financial Market Infrastructure Act.

[5] On the traditional underestimation of financial crimes as non-stigmatising professional risk-taking, see E Rotman, 'La Criminalidad Financiera en el Siglo XIX' in *Revista de Derecho Penal y Criminolgia* (April–June 1969) 231.

[6] M Delmas-Marty, 'Aplanir le terrain de jeu' in 'Les Figures de l'Internationalisation en Droit Pénal des Affaires' (2005) 4 *Revue de Science Criminelle et de Droit Pénal Comparé* 735.

While also influenced by the American model, British, French, Italian and German laws on insider trading and market manipulation followed statutory and case law distinct trajectories, strongly shaped and harmonised by European law, culminating in the EU 2014 Regulation, which established a common regulatory framework on insider dealing, unlawful disclosure of inside information, and market manipulation. It also established measures to prevent market abuse in order to ensure the integrity of financial markets in the Union and to enhance investor protection and confidence in those markets.

Reinforcing the EU 2014 Regulation with criminal sanctions, the EU Directive issued on the same day, required all Member States (except for the UK and Denmark for reservations included in the EU treaties) to introduce criminal sanctions for at least serious market abuse offences to ensure effective implementation of the Union policy on fighting market abuse.

BIBLIOGRAPHY

Alexander, RCH, *Insider Dealing and Money Laundering in the EU: Law and Regulation* (Burlington, VT, Ashgate Publishing Company, 2007)
Anagnostopoulos, I, 'Vom nationalen Strafrecht zum Strafrecht der Nationen' in I Anagnostopoulos (ed), *Internationalisierung Des Strafrechts* (Baden-Baden, Nomos, 2003) 7
Ancel, M, 'Preface' in E Aftalion, *Derecho Penal Económico* (Buenos Aires, Abeledo-Perrot, 1959)
Austin, J, *The Province of Jurisprudence Determined* (London, John Murray, 1832)
Austin, J, 'IOSCO's Multilateral Memorandum of Understanding Concerning Consultation and Cooperation and the Exchange of Information – a Model for International Regulatory Convergence' (2012) 23(4) *Criminal Law Forum* 393
——, 'Protecting Market Integrity in an Era of Fragmentation and Cross-Border Trading' (2014) 46:1 *Ottawa Law Review* 25
——, 'The Power and Influence of IOSCO in Regulating and Enforcing Securities Regulations' (2015) 15 *Asper Review of International Business & Trade Law* 1
Bacastow, DJ, 'Due Process and Criminal Penalties under Rule 10b-5: the Unconstitutionality and Inefficiency of Criminal Prosecutions for Insider Trading' (1982) 73 *Journal of Criminal Law & Criminology* 96
Bainbridge, SM, *Insider Trading* (New York, Foundation Press, 1999)
——, 'An Overview of Insider Trading Law and Policy: an Introduction' in SM Bainbridge (ed), *The Research Handbook on Insider Trading* (Northampton, MA, Elgar Publishing, 2013)
——, *Insider Trading Law and Policy* (St Paul, MI, West Academic, Foundation Press, 2014)
Battacharya, U and Daouk, H, 'The World Price of Insider Trading' (2002) LVII(1) *The Journal of Finance* 75
Bazley, SR, *Market Abuse Enforcement: Practice and Procedure* (London, Bloomsbury Professional, 2013)
Beling, E, *Die Strafrechtliche Bedeutung der Exterritorialität* (Breslau, Scheletter'sche Buchhandlung, 1896)
Bell, A, *Forum Shopping and Venue in International Litigation* (New York, Oxford University Press, 2007) 20
Bentham, J, *Traité de Législation Civile et Pénale*, vol I (Paris, E Dumont, 1820)
Berman, HJ, *Law and Revolution: The Formation of the Western Legal Tradition* (Cambridge, MA, and London, Harvard University Press, 1983)
—— and Greiner, WR, *The Nature and Functions of Law* (New York, Foundation Press, 1980)
Binding, K, *Die* Normen *und ihre Übertretung: eine Untersuchung über die rechtmässige Handlung und die Arten des Delikts* 4th edn (Munich, Scientia Verlag Aalen (ed), 1922, rep 1965)
Boister, N, 'Transnational Criminal Law?' (2003) 14(5) *European Journal of International Law* 953
Born, GB, *International Civil Litigation in the United States* (Deventer, Netherlands and Boston, MA, Wolters Kluwer, 1996)
Brace, CL, *The Dangerous Classes of New York* (New York, Wynkoop & Hallenbeck, 1872)
Brummer, C, 'Why Soft Law Dominates International Finance and not Trade' (2010) 13 *Journal of International Economic Law* 623
——, *Soft Law and the Global Financial System: Rule Making in the 21st Century* (New York, Cambridge University Press, 2012)
Bruppacher, B, 'Schweiz als Eldorado für Insider-Deals' in *20 Minuten*, retrieved from www.20min.ch/finance/news/story/29474512

Buell, SW, 'What is Securities Frauds?' (2011) 61(3) *Duke Law Journal* 511
Callies, G-P and Maurer, A, 'Transnationales Recht-eine Einleitung' in G-P Calliess (ed), *Transnationalen Recht: Stand und Perspektiven* (Tübingen, Mohr Siebeck, 2014) 36
Carnelutti, F, *Teoria Generale del Reato* (Padua, CEDAM, 1933)
Carswell, J, *The South Sea Bubble* (Stanford, CA, Stanford University Press, 1960)
Cecil, H, *A Matter Of Speculation: The Case of Lord Cochrane* (London, Hutchinson Co, 1965; reprint by Gaunt, Inc, 1996)
Cedras, J, 'L'Hypothèse de l'américanisation du droit pénal français' in *L'Américanisation du Droit*, vol 45 (Paris, Dalloz, 2001) 149
Chafee, EC, 'Finishing the Race to the Bottom: an Argument for the Harmonization and Centralization of International Securities Law' (2012) 40 *Seton Hall Law Review* 1581
Chan Mora, G and Llobet Rodriguez, J, 'Francisco Castillo Gonzalez y el Derecho Penal Costarricense' (2013) 5 *Revista Digital de la Maestría en Ciencias Penales de la Universidad de Costa Rica* 11
Chehtman, A, *The Philosophical Foundations of Extraterritorial Punishment* (New York, Oxford University Press, 2010)
Cherif Bassiouni, M, *International Extradition: United States Law and Practice* (New York, Oxford University Press, 2007)
—— and Wise, EM, *Aut Dedere aut Judicare: The Duty to Extradite or Prosecute in International Law* (Leiden, Martinus Nijhoff, 1995)
Chitimira, H, 'A Historical Overview of Market Abuse Prohibition in the United Kingdom' in (2014) 3(20) *Mediterranean Journal of Social Sciences* 49
Clarke, S, *Insider Dealing: Law and Practice* (Oxford, Oxford University Press, 2013)
Clopton, ZD, 'Replacing the Presumption Against Extraterritoriality' (2014) 98 *Boston University Law Review* 1
Coffee, JC, Jr, 'Extraterritorial Financial Regulation: Why E.T. Can't Come Home' (2014) 99 *Cornell Law Review* 1259
Consulich, F, *La Giustzia e il Mercato: Miti e Realtà di una Tutela Penale dell' Investimento Mobiliare* (Milan, Dott A Giuffrè, 2010)
Conte, P, 'Marchés d'instruments financiers – Activité des marchés d'instruments', *Juris-classeur Droit Pénal des Affaires* (Paris, Lexis-Nexis, 2014)
Conway III, GT, 'Extraterritoriality after Dodd-Frank' *The Harvard Law School Forum on Corporate Governance and Financial Regulation* (5 August 2010) available at http://corpgov.law.harvard.edu/2010/08/05/extraterritoriality-after-dodd-frank/
Cooper, G and Cridlan, RJ, *The Law And Procedure of the Stock Exchange* (London, Sweet & Maxwell, 1972)
Cotterrell, R, 'What is Transnational Law?' (2012) 37(2) *Law & Social Inquiry* 500
Currie, RJ, *International & Transnational Criminal* Law (Toronto, Irwin Law Inc, 2010)
Cury Urzúa, E, *Derecho Penal, Parte General*, vol 1, 2nd edn (Santiago, Editorial Juridica de Chile, 1992)
Dale, R, *The First Crash: Lessons From The South Sea Bubble* (Princeton, NJ, Princeton University Press, 2004)
D'Alessandro, F, *Regolatori del Mercato, Enforcement e Sistema Penale* (Turin, Giappichelli Editori, 2014)
de la Bruyère, J, *Les Caractères* (Paris, Ed Garnier, 1960)
de la Vega, J, *Confusion de Confusiones: Dialogo Curioso Entre un Filosofo Agudo, un Mercader Discreto y un Accionista Erudito* (Amsterdam, 1688)
Delmas-Marty, M, 'Aplanir le terrain de jeu' in 'Les Figures de l'Internationalisation en Droit Pénal des Affaires' (2005) 4 *Revue de Science Criminelle et de Droit Pénal Comparé* 735
——, *Les Forces Imaginantes du Droit*, vol 2: *Le Pluralisme Ordonné* (Paris, Seuil, 2006) 255
——, 'Introduction: Objectifs et Méthodes' in M Delmas-Marty, M Pieth and U Sieber (eds), *Les Chemins de l'Harmonisation Pénale/Harmonizing Criminal Law* (Paris, Société de législation comparée, 2008) 29
——, 'Introduction' in M Delmas-Marty and S Breyer (eds), *Regards Croisés sur l'Internationalisation du Droit: France_États-Unis* (Paris, Société de Législation Comparé, 2009) 15

——, Pieth, M and Sieber, U (eds), *Les Chemins de l'Harmonisation Pénale/Harmonizing Criminal Law* (Paris, Société de Legislation Comparée, 2008)
Dervan, LD, 'Evaluating Corporate Criminal Liability: the DOJ's Internal Mutual Culpability Standard for Corporate Criminal Liability' (2011) 41 *Stetson Law Review* 7
di Martino, A, *La Frontiera e il Diritto Penale: Natura e Contesto delle Norme di 'Diritto Penale Transnazionale'* (Turin, G Giappichelli Editore, 2006)
Dodge, WS, 'Extraterritoriality and Conflict-of-Laws Theory: An Argument for Judicial Unilateralism' (1998) 39 *Harvard International Law Journal* 101
——, 'Understanding the Presumption Against Extraterritoriality' (1998) 16 *Berkeley Journal of International Law* 85
Doty, JR, 'The Role of the Securities and Exchange Commission in an Internationalized Marketplace' (1992) 60 *Fordham Law Review* 77
Dressler, J, *Understanding Criminal Law*, 5th edn (New York, LexisNexis, 2009)
Dubber, MD, 'The Promise of German Criminal Law: A Science of Crime and Punishment' (2005) 6 *German Law Journal* 1049
——, 'Criminal Law in Comparative Context' (2006) 56 *Journal of Legal Education* 433
Duke, SB, 'Legality in the Second Circuit' (1983) 49 *Brooklyn Law Review* 911
Dupuy, PM, *Droit International Public*, 6th edn (Paris, Dalloz, 2002)
Eicher, S, 'Introduction: What Corruption is and Why it Matters' in S Eicher (ed), *Corruption in International Business: The Challenge of Cultural and Legal Diversity* (Burlington, VT, Gower, 2009) 12
—— (ed), *Corruption in International Business: The Challenge of Cultural and Legal Diversity* (Burlington, VT, Gower, 2009)
Engle, E, 'Insider Trading in US and EU Law: A Comparison' (2010) 26 *European Business Law Review* 490
Eskridge, WN, Jr, 'Dynamic Statutory Interpretation' (1987) 135 *University of Pennsylvania Law Review* 1479
Ezrachi, A and Kindl, J, 'Cartels as Criminal? The Long Road from Unilateral Enforcement to International Consensus' in C Beaton-Wells and A Ezrachi (eds), *Criminalising Cartels: Critical Studies of an International Regulatory Movement* (Haywards Heath, Bloomsbury Professional, 2011) 419
Fallon, RH, Manning, JF, Melzer, DJ and Shapiro, DL, *Hart and Wechsler, The Federal Courts and the Federal System* (New York, Foundation Press, 2009)
Faure, MG and Leger, C, 'The Directive on Criminal Sanctions for Market Abuse: A Move Towards Harmonizing Insider Trading Criminal Law' (2015) 9 *Brooklyn Journal of Corporate, Financial & Commercial Law* 387
Fletcher, GP, *Basic Concepts of Criminal Law* (New York, Oxford University Press, 1998)
——, *The Grammar of Criminal Law: American, Comparative, and International*, vol 1: *Foundations* (New York, Oxford University Press, 2007)
Folsom, RH, *Principles of European Union Law*, 2nd edn (The Concise Hornbook Series, Saint Paul, MN, West Academic Press, 2009)
Forstmoser, P, 'Die neue Schweizerische Strafnorm gegen *Insider*-Geschäfte' (1989) *Zeitschrift für Unternehmens- und Gesellschaftsrecht* 124
Foster, S, 'Should Courts Give Stare Decisis Effect to Statutory Interpretation Methodology?' (2008) 96 *Georgetown Law Journal* 1863
Foucault, M, *Discipline and Punish: The Birth of the Prison* (New York, Vintage Books, 1979)
Fox, MB, Glosten, LR and Rauterberg, GV, 'The New Stock Market: Sense and Nonsense' (2015) 65(2) *Duke Law Journal* 1
Frank, R, *Über den Aufbau des Schuldbegriffs* (Giessen, Alfred Töpelmann, 1907)
Franklin, K, 'US v UK Insider Trading Laws: Who is The Top Dog?' SSRN, 21 February 2013, available at http//://dx.doi.org(10.2139/ssrn 230856)
Friedrichs, DO, 'White-Collar Crime in a Postmodern, Globalized World' in HN Pontell and G Geis (eds), *International Handbook on White Collar and Corporate Crime* (Boston, MA, Springer Verlag, 2007) 176

Friese, S et al, *US Regulation of Hedge Funds* (Chicago, IL, American Bar Association Publishing, 2013)
Gallant, KS, 'What Exactly is "Extraterritorial Application" of a Statute?' *Jurist Forum* (28 May 2013) available at http://ssrn.com/abstract=2271267
Gersen, JE and Posner, EA, 'Soft Law', *University of Chicago Public Law and Legal Theory Working Paper Series* (2008) available at http:/ssrn.com/abstracts=1113537
Gevurtz, FA, 'The Globalization of Insider Trading' (2002) 15 *Transnational Law* 63
Giacopelli, M and Catelan, N, 'Délit et manquement d'initiés' in *Répertoire de Droit Pénal et de Procedure Pénale* (initiated in 1970) (Paris, Dalloz, May 2015)
Gillis, RJ, *Navigational Servitudes: Sources, Applications, Paradigms* (Leiden, Brill-Nijhoff, 2007)
Gimbernat Ordeig, E, 'Sind die bisherigen dogmatischen Grunderfordernisse eines Allgemeinen Teils geeignet, dem heutigen Stand der Kriminalität, der Strafzumessung und des Sanktionensystems zu genügen?' in HJ Hirsch (ed), *Krise des Strafrechts und der Kriminalwisensschaften?* (Berlin, Duncker & Humblot, 2000) 151
Gluck, AR, 'The Federal Common Law of Statutory Interpretation: Erie for the Age of Statutes' (2013) 54 *William & Mary Law Review* 753
Goldwasser, V, *Stock Market Manipulation and Short Selling* (Melbourne, Centre for Corporate Law and Securities Regulation and CCH Australia, 1999)
Gounot, Essai d'application de l'analyse économique du droit à la réglementation boursière des operations d'initiés, *Revue de Science Criminelle et de Driot Pénal Comparé*, 2000, 335
Grabosky, P, 'Globalization and White-Collar Crime' in S Simpson and D Weisburd (eds), *The Criminology of White-Collar Crime* (New York, Springer, 2009) 131
Green, S, 'The Concept of White Collar Crime in Law and Legal Theory' (2004) 8 *Buffalo Criminal Law Review* 101
Gurney, WB, *The Trial of Charles Random De Berenger, Lord Cochrane and Others* (London, J Butterworth and Son, and Gale, Curtis and Fenner, 1814)
Gutzwiller, M, 'Das Internationalprivatrecht der durch die Friedensverträge eingesetzen Gemischten Schiedsgerichtshöfe' in 3 *Internationales Jahrbuch für Schiedsgerichtswesen in Zivil und Handelssachen* (Berlin, Carl Heymanns Verlag, 1931) 123
Halliday, TC and Shaffer, G, 'Transnational Legal Orders' in TC Halliday and G Shaffer (eds), *Transnational Legal Orders* (Cambridge, Cambridge University Press, 2015) 3
Handl, G, Zekoll, J and Zumbansen, P, *Beyond Territoriality: Transnational Legal Authority in an Age of Globalism* (Leiden, Martinus Nijhoff Publishers, 2012)
Hang, B, 'The SEC's Criminal Rulemaking in Rule 10b5-2: Incarceration Should be Made of Sterner Stuff' (2002) 41 *Washburn Law Journal* 629
Harasimowicz, R, 'Nothing New, Man – The Second Circuit's Clarification of Insider Trading Liability in United States v. Newman Comes at a Critical Juncture in the Evolution of Insider Trading' (2016) 57 *Boston College Law Review* 765
Hart, HM and Wechsler, H, *The Federal Courts and the Federal System*, 6th edn (New York, The Foundation Press, 2009) 609
He, D, 'Beyond Securities Fraud: The Territorial Reach of US Laws after *Morrison v. N.A.B.*' (2013) 1 *Columbia Business Law Review* 148
Heinemann, B, Jr and Heimann, F, 'The Long War against Corruption' *Foreign Affairs* (May/June 2006)
Helleiner, E, 'Regulating the Regulators: The Emergence and Limits of the Transnational Financial Legal Order' in TC Halliday and G Shaffer (eds), *Transnational Legal Orders* (Cambridge, Cambridge University Press, 2015) 238
Hellmann, U, *Wirtschaftsstrafrecht*, 5th edn (Stuttgart, Kohlhammer, 2018)
Herz-Roiphe, DE, 'Innocent Abroad?: Morrison, Vilar, and the Extraterritorial Application of the Exchange Act' (2014) 123 *Yale Law Journal* 1875
Hienzsch, A, *Das deutsche Insiderhandelsverbot in der Rechtswirklichkeit*, 1st edn (Baden Baden, Nomos, 2006)
Hirsch, HJ, 'Internationaliesierung des Strafrechts und Strafrechtswissenschaft' (2004) 116 *Zeitschrif für die gesamte Strafrechtswissenschsaft* 835

Hirst, M, *Jurisdiction and the Ambit of the Criminal Law* (Oxford, Oxford University Press, 2003)
Hock, B, 'Intimations of Global Anti-Bribery Regime and the Effectiveness of Extraterritorial Enforcement: From Free-Riders to Protectionism?' 9 *Tilberg Law and Economic Center, Discussion Paper No 2014-009* (13 February 2014) available at http://ssrn.com/abstract=2395156
Hohn, K, 'Marktmissbrauch' in C Momsen and T Grützner (eds), *Wirtschaftsstrafrecht* (Munich, CH Beck, 2013) 616
Hohnel, A, 'Wertpapierhandelsgesetz (WpHG)' in A Hohnel (ed) *Kapitalmarktstrafrecht* (Munich, CH Beck, 2013) 40
—— (ed), *Kapitalmarktstrafrecht* (Munich, CH Beck, 2013)
Hongju Koh, H, 'Opening Remarks: Transnational Legal Process Illuminated' in M Likosky (ed), *Transnational Legal Processes: Globalization and Power Disparities* (London, Butterworths Tolley, 2002) 327
Hume, D, *Commentaries on the Law of Scotland Respecting Crimes*, vol II (1797)
Hurtado Pozo, J, *Manual de Derecho Penal: Parte General* (Lima, Editora Jurídica Grijley, 2005)
——, 'Droit Pénal Économique: Questions de la Partie Générale' in J Hurtado Pozo and O Thormann (eds), *Droit Pénal Économique* (Zurich, Schultess, 2011) 92
Irving, R, 'French Insider Trading Law: A Survey' (1990) 22(1) *The University of Miami Inter-American Law Review* 41
Jara Diez, CG, *La Proteccion Penal Transnacional de los Mercados Financieros* (Madrid, Marcial Pons, 2014)
Jescheck, H-H and Weigend, T, *Lehrbuch des Strafrechts: Allgemeiner Teil* (Berlin, Duncker & Humblot, 1996)
Jeβberger, F, *Der Transnationalen Geltungsbereich des Deutschen Strafrechts* (Tübingen, Mohr Siebeck, 2011)
Jeβberger, F, 'Transnationales Srafrecht, Internationales Strafrecht, Transnationale Rechtsgeltung und Orientierung' in G-P Calliess (ed), *Transnationalen Recht: Stand und Perspektiven* (Tübingen, Mohr Siebeck, 2014) 528
Jessup, PC, *Transnational Law* (New Haven, CT, Yale University Press, 1956)
Johnson, KN, 'Regulating Innovation: High Frequency Trading in Dark Pools' (2017) 42:4 *The Journal of Corporation Law* 833
Jutzi, T, *Unternehmenspublizität: Grundlinien Eine Rechtlichen Dogmatik zur Offenlegung von Unternehmensbezogenen Informationen [Enterprise Transparency and Disclosure: Outline of a Legal Dogmatic about Enterprise-Related Information]* (Bern, Stämpfli Verlag, 2017)
Kaal, WA and Painter, RW, 'The Aftermath of Morrison v. National Australia Bank and Elliott Associates and Porsche' (2011) 8 *European Company & Financial Law Review* 77
Kaczmarek, SC and Newman, AL, 'The Long Arm of the Law: Extraterritoriality and the National Implementation of Foreign Bribery Legislation' (2011) 65(4) *International Organization* 745
Karmel, RS, 'IOSCO's Response to the Financial Crisis', *Brooklyn Law School Legal Studies No 268*, available at https://ssrn.com/abstract=2025115, 50
Kern, A, 'The Law of Insider Dealing: A Tale of Two Jurisdictions' (2013) 112 *Zeitschrift für vergleichende Rechtswissenschaft* 263
Kesper Biermann, S and Overath, P (eds), *Die Internationalisierung von Strafrechtswissenschaft und Kriminalpolitik (1870–1930)* (Berlin, Berliner Wissenschafts-Verlag, 2007)
Kirry, AF and Lee Wetzel, A, 'Evolution of French Constitutional Law and European Human Rights Law Related to the Non Bis in Idem Principle' (2015) 4 *European Human Rights Law Review* 384
Klein, B, 'Goodbye LIBOR, Hello SOFR', post in *Forbes New York Business Council Post* (19 April 2018)
Klöhn, L, Transnational Financial Markets Regulation – a Conference, 15 July 2010, available at http://ssrn.com/abstract=1640459
Knox, JH, 'A Presumption Against Extrajurisdictionality' (2010) 104 *American Journal of International Law* 351
——, 'The Unpredictable Presumption Against Extraterritoriality' (2011) 40 *Southwestern Law Review* 635

Kohler, M, 'The Façade of FCPA Enforcement' (2010) 41 *Georgetown Journal of International Law* 907

Kozel, RJ, 'The Scope of Precedent' (2014) 113 *Michigan Law Review* 179

Krever, T, 'Curbing Corruption: the Efficacy of the Foreign Corrupt Practices Act' (2007) 33 *North Carolina Journal of International Law and Commercial Regulation* 83

Laschi, R, *Le crime financier dans la sociologie criminelle l'histoire et le droit* (Paris, Masson et Cie. Éditeurs, 1901)

Leis, D, 'High Frequency Trading: Market Manipulation and Systemic Risk from an EU Perspective' (29 February 2012) available at htpps://ssrn.com/abstract=2108344

Leng-Chia Hung, 'Securities Markets – A Place to Get Rich Quick or a Quicksand Going Straight to Jail? The "Mens Rea" Required for Insider Trading Criminal Liability' (2010) 5 *National Taiwan University Law Review* 1

Lepage, A, Maistre de Chambon, P and Salomon, R, *Droit Pénal des Affaires* (Paris, LexisNexis, 2018)

Lermettre, JF, 'Quel Futur pour l'Industrie Boursière?: Analyse d'un Processus de Transformation' *Innovations* 2009/2 No 30, 157

Leuenberger, C, 'Die materielle kapitalmarktstrafrechtliche Regulierung des. Insiderhandels de lege lata und de lege ferenda' in *Schweizer Schriften zum Handels- und Wirtschaftsrecht*, vol 296 (Basel, Zürich, Dike Verlag, 2010)

Leval, PN, 'Judging Under the Constitution: Dicta about Dicta' (2005) 81 *New York University Law Review* 1249

Libarona, MC, 'Frias Caballero: su Cátedra sobre la Teoría del Delito' in *Homenaje Al Profesor Dr Jorge Frías Caballero* (Colegio de Abogados del Departamento Judicial La Plata, 1998)

Lin, TCW, 'The New Market Manipulation' (2017) 66 *Emory Law Journal* 1263

Lipari, L, *Gli Abusi di Mercato* (Rome, Aracne Editrice, 2017)

Londoño Martínez, F, 'Ilícito de Manipulación Bursátil: Fenómeno y lesividad. Aspectos de Política Sancionatoria' (2013) 8 *Politica Criminal*, available at http://ssrn.com/abstract=2531802

Lorez, K and Dobrauz-Saldapenna, G, 'Die revidierte Schweizer Insiderhandels und Marktmissbrauchsregulierung' (2014) 86 *Zeitschrift für Wirtschafts- und Finanzmarktrecht* 38

Lowell Brown, H, 'Extraterritorial Jurisdiction under the 1998 Amendments to the Foreign Corrupt Practices Act: Does the Government's Reach Now Exceed its Grasp?' (2000) 26 *North Carolina Journal of International Law & Commercial Regulation* 239

Lowenfels, LD and Bromberg, AR, 'Securities Market Manipulation: an Examination and Analysis of Dominating and Control, Frontrunning and Parking' (1991) 55 *Albany Law Review* 293

Malabat, V, 'Les Procédés de l'Internationalisation du Droit Pénal', *Revue Droit Penal* (LexisNexis) (September 2006) 23

Mann, MD and Lustgarten, LA, *Internationalization of Insider Trading Enforcement – A Guide to Regulation and Cooperation* (New Orleans, LA, American Bar Association–National Institute on White Collar Crime, 1990)

—— and ——, 'Internationalization of Insider Trading Enforcement: A Guide to Regulation and Cooperation', *Practising Law Institute*, Pli Order No B4-7024 (1993) 2

Manne, H, *Insider Trading and The Stock Market* (New York, The Free Press, 1966)

Markham, JW, *Law Enforcement And The History Of Financial Market Manipulation* (Armonk, NY, ME Sharpe, Inc, 2014)

Massé, M, 'Des Figures Asymétriques de l'Internationalisation du Droit Pénal' *Revue de Science Criminelle et de Droit Pénal Comparé* (October/December 2006) 755

May, P and Weber, M, 'Insider Dealing Legislation and Switzerland' (1989) 7(8) *International Banking Law* 153

Merton, RK, *Social Theory and Social Structure* (New York, The Free Press, 1968)

Mezger, E, *Strafrecht: Ein Lehrbuch*, 3rd edn (Berlin, Verlag von Duncker & Humblot, 1949)

Miedico, M, 'La Disciplina Penalistica degli Abusi di Mercati' in A Alessandri (ed), *Reati in Materia Economica* (Turin, Giappichelli Editore, 2017) 319

Miller, JM, 'Mens Rea Quagmire: The Conscience or Consciousness of the Criminal Law?' (2001) 29 *Western State University Law Review* 21

Mills, D and Weisberg, R, 'Corrupting the Harm Requirement in White Collar Crime' (2008) 60 *Stanford Law Review* 1345

Mir Puig, S, *Introduccion a las bases del Derecho Penal*, 2nd edn (Montevideo, Uruguay, Editorial B de I, 2003)

Multer, MK, 'Open-Market Manipulation under SEC Rule 10b-5 and its Analogues: Inappropriate Distinctions, Judicial Disagreement and Case Study: Ferc's Anti-Manipulation Rule' (2011) 39(2) *Securities Regulation Law Journal* 97

Muñoz Conde, F, '"Rethinking" the Universal Structure of Criminal Law' (2004) 39 *Tulsa Law Review* 941

Naucke, W, 'An Insider's Perspective on the Significance of the German Criminal Theory's General System for Analyzing Criminal Acts' (1984) 3 *Brigham Young University Law Review* 305

Nieto Martin, A, 'Americanisation or Europeanisation of Corporate Crime' in M Delmas-Marty, M Pieth and U Sieber (eds), *Les Chemins de l'Harmonisation Pénale/Harmonizing Criminal Law* (Paris, Société de législation comparée, 2008) 327

——, '*Regulatory Capitalism* y Cumplimiento Normativo' in A Zapatero and A Nieto Martin (eds), *El Derecho Penal Económico en la Era Compliance* (Valencia, Tirant Lo Blanch, 2013) 11

Painter, R et al, 'When Courts and Congress Don't Say What They Mean: Initial Reactions to Morrison v. National Australia Bank and to the Extraterritorial Jurisdiction Provisions of the Dodd-Frank Act' (2011) 20 *Minnesota Journal of International Law* 1

Panagia, S, *La Tutela dei Mercati Finanziari: La Fatispeccie Penale a Rischio di Default* (Turin, G Giappichelli, 2011)

Papadopulos, T, 'International Organization of Securities Commissions (IOSCO)' in R Wolfrum (ed), *Max Planck Encyclopedia of Public International Law* (New York, Oxford University Press, 2015)

Park, SK, 'Guarding the Guardians: The Case for Regulating State Owned Financial Entities in Global Finance' (2014) 16 *University of Pennsylvania Journal of Business Law* 739

Parrish, AL, 'Morrison, The Effects Test, and the Presumption Against Extraterritoriality: A Reply to Professor Dodge' (2011) 105 *American Society of International Law Proceedings* 399

Pieth, M, 'The Agents of Change' in M Delmas-Marty, M Pieth and U Sieber (eds), *Les Chemins de l'Harmonisation Pénale/Harmonizing Criminal Law* (Paris, Société de législation comparée, 2008) 369

——, *Wirtschaftsstrafrecht* (Basel, Helbing Lichtenhahn, 2016)

Plantamura, V, 'L'*Insider Trading* e la Manipolazione del Mercato' in A Manna (ed), *Corso di Diritto Penale dell'Impresa* (Milan, CEDAM, 2010) pt VI, ch V

Podgor, ES and Filler, DM, 'International Criminal Jurisdiction in the Twenty-First Century: Rediscovering *United States v Bowman*' (2007) 44 *San Diego Law Review* 585

——, Clark, RS and Dervan, LN, *International Criminal Law* (Durham, NC, Carolina Academic Press, 2016)

Putniņš, TJ, 'Market Manipulation: A Survey' *Journal of Economic Surveys* (8 April 2011) available at https://ssrn.com/abstract=1805642

Rabel, E, *The Conflict of Laws: A Comparative Study* (Chicago, IL, Callaghan & Company, 1945)

Radi, Y, 'Du Dilemme du Prisonnier au Jeu de l'Intégration: l'Internationalisation de l'Incrimination Pénale de Corruption Active Transnationale' in D Dormoy (ed), *La corruption et le droit international* (Brussels, Bruylant, 2010) 169

Ramphal, NR, 'The Role of Public and Private Litigation in the Enforcement of Securities Laws in the United States' in *Rand Dissertation Series* (Santa Monica, CA, Rand Corporation, 2007)

Raustiala, K, 'The Architecture of International Cooperation: Transgovernmental Networks and the Future of International Law' (2002) 43 *Virginia Journal of International Law* 1

Reuveni, E, 'Extraterritoriality as Standing: A Standing Theory of the Extraterritorial Application of the Securities Laws' (2010) 43 *University of California, Davis Law Review* 1071

Rider, BAK, 'The Control of Insider Trading – Smoke and Mirrors!' (2000–2001) 19 *Dickinson Journal of International Law* 1

—— and French, HL, *The Regulation of Insider Trading* (Dobbs Ferry, NY, Oceana Publications, 1979)

Roberts, A, *Churchill: Walking With Destiny* (New York, Penguin Random House, 2018)
Robertson, R, *Globalization: Social Theory and Global Culture* (Thousand Oaks, CA, Sage Publications, 1992)
Roegele, P, *Deutscher Strafrechtsimperialismus:ein Beitrag zu den Völkerrechtlichen Grenzen Extraterritorialer Strafgewahltausdehnung* (Hamburg, Verlag Dr Kovač, 2014)
Rotman, E, 'La Criminalidad Financiera en el Siglo XIX' *Revista de Derecho Penal y Criminolgia* (April–June 1969) 228
——, *Los Fraudes al Comercio y a la Industria* (Buenos Aires, Abeledo-Perrot, 1974)
——, 'Natur und Umfang der Wirtschaftsstraftaten in ihrer Abhängigkeit von einigen Grundzügen des heutigen Wirtschaftslebens' *Kriminalistik* (May 1977) 213
——, 'The Globalization of Criminal Violence' (2000) 10(1) *Cornell Journal of Law and Public Policy* 2
——, 'Extraterritorial Criminal Enforcement of Securities Fraud Regulations after United States v. Vilar' (2015) 70 *University of Miami Law Review* 53
Roxin, C, *Strafrecht, Allgemeiner Teil*, vol 1 (Munich, Verlag CH Beck, 2006)
Ryngaert, C, *Jurisdiction in International Law* (New York, Oxford University Press, 2008)
Sachs, JD, 'Globalization and the Rule of Law', *Yale Law School Occasional Papers*, Second Series, Number 4, 1998
Schmid, N, *Schweiserisches Insiderstrafrecht* (Bern, Stämpfli, 1988)
Schröder, C, 'Straf-und Buβgeldtatbestände im BörsG und WpHG' in H Achenbach and A Ransie (eds), *Handbuch der Wirtschaftsstrafrecht* (Heilderberg, CF Müller Verlag, 2012) 1169
——, *Handbuch Kapitalmarktstrafrecht*, 3rd edn (Cologne, Carl Heyman's Verlag, 2015)
Schünemann, B, 'Das Strafrecht im Zeichen der Globaliesierung' in *Goltdammer's Archive für Strafrecht*, 5/2003, 299
Sciumbata, G, *I Reati Societari* (Milan, Giuffre, 2008)
Seigel, ML, 'Bringing Coherence to Mens Rea Analysis for Securities-related Offenses' 2006 *Wisconsin Law Review* (2006) 1563
Sethe, R, *Anlegerschutz im Recht der Vermögensverwaltung* (Cologne, Verlag Dr Otto Schmidt, 2005)
——, '§ 8 Insiderrecht' in H-D Assmann and R Schütze (eds), *Handbuch des Kapitalanlagerechts* (Munich, CH Beck, 2012) 453
Shaffer, G, 'Transnational Legal Process and State Change' (2012) 37 *Law & Social Inquiry* 229
Sieber, U, 'Grenzen des Strafrechts' (2007) 119 *Zeitschrift für das gesamte Strafrechtswissenschaft* 4
——, 'The Forces Behind the Harmonization of Criminal Law' in M Delmas-Marty, M Pieth and U Sieber (eds), *Les Chemins de l'Harmonisation Pénale/Harmonizing Criminal Law* (Paris, Société de législation comparée, 2008) 386
——, 'Rechtliche Ordnug in einer Globalen Welt' (2010) 41 *Rechtstheore* 159
Siegel, JR, 'The Polymorphic Principle and the Judicial Role in Statutory Interpretation' (2005) 84 *Texas Law Review* 339
Silane, CA, 'Electronic Data Theft: A Legal Loophole for Illegally Obtained Information – A Comparative Analysis of US and EU Insider Trading Law' in 5 *Seton Hall Circuit Review* 333
Soler, S, *Las Palabras De La Ley* (Mexico City, Fondo de Cultura Económica, 1969)
Stelnick, R, *Mainframe: Madoff-size Money, Monstrous Misapplication* (2 November 2011) available at www.decodeqdscience.org/mainframe-madoff-size-money-monstrous-misapplication-logon/4918
Stevenson, DD and Wagoner, NJ, 'FCPA Sanctions: Too Big to Debar?' (2011) 80 *Fordham Law Review* 775
Story, J, *Commentaries on the Conflict of Laws: Foreign and Domestic, in regards to Contracts, Rights, and Remedies* (Boston, MA, Hilliard, Gray & Co, 1834)
Strader, JK, '(Re)conceptualizing Insider Trading: United States v. Newman and the Intent to Defraud' (2015) 80 *Brooklyn Law Review* 1410
Steinberg, MI and Flanagan, K 'Transnational Dealings – Morrison Continues to Make Waves' (2012) 46 *International Lawyer* 829
Suominen, A, *The Principle of Mutual Recognition in Cooperation in Criminal Matters: A Study of the Principle in Four Framework Decisions in the Implementation Legislation in the Nordic Member States* (Cambridge, Intersentia, 2011)

Sutherland, E, 'White-Collar Criminality' (1940) 5 *American Sociological Review* 1

——, *White Collar Crime* (New York, Holt, Reinhardt & Winston, 1949)

——, *White-Collar Crime: The Uncut Version* (New Haven, CT, Yale University Press, 1983)

Tiedemann, K (ed), *Multinationalen Unternehmen und Strafrecht: Beiträge zum Problem der Kriminalität ins grenzübershreitenden Geschäftsverkehr* (Cologne, Berlin, Bonn and Munich, Carl Heymanns Verlag, 1979)

——, *Wirtschaftsstrafrecht* (Special Part), 3rd edn (Munich, Verlag Franz Vahlen, 2011)

——, *Wirtschaftsstrafrecht. Einführung und Allgemeiner Teil mit wichtisten Rechtstexten*, 4th edn (Munich, Verlag Franz Vahlen, 2014)

——, *Wirtschaftsstrafrecht*, 5th edn (Munich, Verlag Franz Vahlen, 2017)

—— and Engelhart, M, *Wirtschaftsstrafrecht* (Munich, Franz Vahlen, 2017)

Tietje, C, 'Transnationalisierung der Wirtschaftsstrafrechts' in G-P Callies (ed), *Transnatinales Recht* (Heidelberg, Mohr Siebeck, 2014)

Tripodi, AF, *Informazione Privilegiati e Statuto Penale del Mercato Finanziario* (Padua, Casa Editrice Dott. Antonio Milani, 2012)

Twining, W, *Globalisation and Legal Theory* (London, Edinburgh and Dublin, Butterworth, 2000)

——, *General Jurisprudence: Understanding Law from a Global Perspective* (Cambridge, Cambridge University Press, 2009)

US Securities and Exchange Commission, *The Investor's Advocate: How the SEC Protects Investors, Maintains Market Integrity, and Facilitates Capital Formation*, available at www.sec.gov/about/whatwedo.shtml

van Ballegooij, W, *The Nature of Mutual Recognition in European Law* (Cambridge, Intersentia, 2015)

Velazquez, F, *Derecho Penal, Parte General*, 4th edn (Medellin, Colombia, Comilibros, 2009)

Ventoruzzo, M, 'Comparing Insider Trading in the United States and In the European Union: History and Recent Developments', *Max Plank Institute for International, European, and Regulatory Procedural Law, MPI Lux, Working Paper 5* (2014) 5

Véron, M, *Droit penal des affaires*, 10th edn (Paris, Dalloz, 2012)

Verstein, A, 'Benchmark Manipulation' (2015) 56 *Boston College Law Review* 215

Viellechner, L, *Transnationalisierung Des Rechts* (Weilerswist, Velbrück Wissenschaft, 2013)

Von Liszt, F, 'Zur Einführung: Rückblick und Zukunftspläne' in F Von Liszt (ed), *Das Strafrecht Der Staten Europas, Im Auftrag der Kriminalistischen Vereignung* (Berlin, Otto Liebmann, 1894) xxiv

Walker, G, *Internationales Privatrecht* (Vienna, Österreichische Staatsdrukerei, 1934)

Wallace, R and Martin-Ortega, O, *International Law* (London, Sweet & Maxwell, 2009) 265

Wang, WKS and Steinberg, MI, *Insider Trading* (New York, Oxford University Press, 2010)

Welzel, H, *El Nuevo Sistema de Derecho Penal: una Introducción a la Doctrina de la Accion Finalista* (Barcelona, Ediciones Ariel, 1964)

——, *Derecho Penal Aleman, Parte General*, 11th edn (Santiago, Editorial Jurídica de Chile, 1970)

Wittig, P, *Wirtchaftsstrafrect* (Munich, CH Beck, 2017)

Wohlers, W, '§ 14 Finanz-und Kapitalmarktstrafrecht' in G Ackermann and G Heine (eds), *Wirtschaftsstrafrecht in der Schweiz* (Bern, Stämpfli, 2013) 355

Yaeger, CA, 'Securities Fraud' (2014) 51 *American Criminal Law Review* 1720

Zaffaroni, ER, *Tratado de Derecho Penal, Parte General*, vol 3 (Buenos Aires, Ediar, 1981)

Zagaris, B, 'United States Treaties on Mutual Assistance in Criminal Matters' in M Cherif Bassiouni (ed), *International Criminal Law*, 3rd edn (Leiden, Brill, 2008) 385

Zerbes, I, 'Transnationales Korruptionsstrafrecht: Gestaltungsmacht privater Akteure hinter staatlichem Regelungsanspruch' in G-P Calliess (ed), *Transnationalen Recht: Stand und Perspektiven* (Tübingen, Mohr Siebeck, 2014) 541

Zöller, MA, 'Das Prinzip des Gegenzeitigen Annerkennung in der Europäischen Union' in A Sinn, Hsiao-Wen Wang, Jiuan-Yih Wu and M Zöller (eds), *Strafrecht ohne Grenzen: 3. Deutsch-Taiwanesisches Strafrechts Forum, Kaohsiung/Tainan/Taipeh* (2013) (Heidelberg, CF Müller, 2015) 15

INDEX

www.ingramcontent.com/pod-product-compliance
Ingram Content Group UK Ltd.
Pitfield, Milton Keynes, MK11 3LW, UK
UKHW020816290926
15470UKWH00003B/1186